HUMAN NATURE

THOMAS BELL moved to Nepal to cover the civil war there for the *Daily Telegraph*, *The Economist*, and other publications. He was the Southeast Asia correspondent for the *Daily Telegraph* before returning to Kathmandu, where he was a political officer for the United Nations during the peace process. His earlier book, *Kathmandu*, is an acclaimed history of Nepal's capital.

HUMAN NATURE
A WALKING HISTORY OF THE HIMALAYAN LANDSCAPE

THOMAS BELL

First published in the UK in 2025 by
Haus Publishing Ltd
4 Cinnamon Row, London SW11 3TW
www.hauspublishing.com

Copyright © Thomas Bell 2025

The moral right of the author has been asserted
A CIP catalogue for this book is available from the British Library

ISBN 978-1-914982-15-6
eISBN 978-1-914982-16-3

Please note that no part of this book may be used or reproduced in any manner for the purpose of training artificial intelligence technologies or systems

Typeset in Sabon by MacGuru Ltd
Printed in the UK by CPI Group (UK) Ltd, Croydon CR0 4YY

The authorised representative in the EEA is:
Haus Publishing
Casella Postale 32
50037 San Piero a Sieve (Fi)
Italy
gpsr@hauspublishing.com

For my parents, Martin and Veronica

'Nothing can escape what went before.'
—Charles Lyell

'… take people as they come … and the whole earth as a single house.'
—al-Hariri

Contents

Preface	ix
Part 1: Migration	1
Part 2: Agriculture	57
Part 3: Architecture	119
Part 4: Conservation	181
Acknowledgements	229
Notes	231
Select Bibliography	259

Preface

There is a fable of world history and the life of people in our environment that was written by Jean-Jacques Rousseau, a man who lived in Europe in the eighteenth century. According to him, humans are naturally lazy.[1] We resist cares of any sort unless they're absolutely necessary. In our natural state people had no use for onerous social ties. Men and women wandered alone in the forest, meeting only for as long as it took to procreate. The form of human teeth, the number of our nipples, and the fact we bear children singly or in pairs show that we were herbivores. There was rarely any occasion for violence, and if violence occurred there was no need for it to escalate. Natural people only breathed peace and freedom.

In Rousseau's story, civil society was founded by the first person who enclosed a piece of land and thought of saying, 'This is mine.' The others were simple enough to believe him. How much misery and horror the human race would have been spared if only someone had pulled up the stakes, filled the ditch, and cried, 'Beware of this imposter. The earth belongs to no one!' Equality disappeared in the instant one man assumed provisions enough for two. Prosperity was introduced, with it the abuse of riches, and all the misfortunes that have bedevilled our history. Metallurgy and agriculture produced civilisation, which ruined us. Vast forests were transformed into pleasant fields, and watered with the sweat of men. Slavery was germinated and flourished among the crops.

It soon became necessary not simply to be a person, but to have intelligence or beauty, skill or merit, or to feign them. In other words, it became necessary to seem other than one really was. Reality and appearance became two different things. The usurpations of the rich, the brigandage of the poor, and the unbridled passions of everyone stifled natural pity and made people greedy, ambitious, and bad. A perpetual conflict arose between the right of the strong and the right of the first occupant. The strong won and called it the law. Where people had once wandered the woods in happiness, communities now formed nations. People worked themselves to death filling chasms, razing mountains, breaking rocks, making rivers navigable, clearing land, carving out lakes and draining marshes, and covering the sea with ships. Savage man needed only to eat to be at ease with the whole of nature, but people in society don't have a moment's respite. The despised farmer is burdened with taxes, and leaves his fields to seek in the city the sustenance he should have brought there. The countryside is abandoned and the citizenry become beggars and thieves. Crime necessitates punishment, which doubles the loss. In this way, humans became wicked, although humankind is naturally good.

Rousseau was a misfit who struggled in his relationships with other people. It's easy to suppose that those painful experiences are reflected in his vision. His views were also partly based on the accounts of early European travellers to other continents, who described what he took to be more natural societies. Yet trade, travel, and conquest were bringing people closer together. Even in his days, different ways of living were becoming constantly more alike.[2] Expeditions to the East catalogued plants. Travellers made drawings of ruins and deciphered inscriptions. One does not open a book of voyages, Rousseau says, without finding descriptions of characters and customs, but one is altogether amazed to find that these authors have only learnt to see at the other end of the world what they could have seen without leaving their own street. He derided those philosophers who believe all people are the same, and claimed that in every place and age we're different. It is the capacity for change that enabled innocent humanity to become our own and nature's tyrant.

Obviously nobody agrees with Rousseau any more. Now we know that early humans had society and hierarchy, and violence, and that pulls the rug from under his theory. But he was a novelist as well as a philosopher, and like any good fable parts of his have the ring of truth. This book also sets out to be – among other things – a kind of history of people's life in the environment. It's not nearly as unequivocal as Rousseau's, because I don't have a grand theory, but I do have better information. It's about a particular place, the Himalaya, which is like anywhere else but also completely different. In modern times it's become ever more tightly bound to the rest of the world. This book includes several fables that were invented by Himalayan people to explain their history in their landscape. Those stories are partly like one another, and the opposite of Rousseau's. Even so, some of the things I've written are more like Rousseau than I first realised, and some of the developments in environmental thought that come towards the end are well known to follow him. Rousseau's fable entered reality and helped to change the way foreigners think about the Himalaya, and the way local people live here.

I came to Kathmandu as a young man and stayed until I am middle-aged. First I was a journalist, during and after the Maoist insurgency that ended in 2006. Then I started a family. And I did other work, including on human rights, and a spell as a political officer at the UN. I was always studying, often travelling around the country. My working life, and a good deal of my social world, was consumed by the political controversies of the time, which became maddening. Most of my companions eventually hauled themselves out of that cataract onto one shore or another.

I chose Himalayan nature as my next subject because I thought it would be relaxing. I'd already written a book about how – for nearly two thousand years – people created Kathmandu, and the city made them back. This book turns to the hills and mountains with a similar conception. It's a story about a famous landscape we hardly know. It's about how people create what we call nature, and nature makes us back. It's based on four walks I made in recent years across the central Himalayan region that became Nepal, an area that includes about a third of the Himalayan range.

From the Gangetic plain, which is just a couple of hundred metres above sea level, the land rises through a succession of steep ranges. The first low, young, and crumbling chain of hills is called the Chure. These days it's being carried off in trucks to mix concrete. Then there's the formidable Mahabharat ridge, two or three thousand metres high and very steep on the southern face, which encloses the rest of the system. North of the Mahabharat there's a maze of spurs and valleys called the Mid-Hills. The English word 'hill' understates these structures, but the true mountains are further north. Beyond them is the Tibetan plateau. In the central Himalaya three river systems gather in the tangle of valleys. They force their way through the Mahabharat ridge in three deep gorges. The great rivers Koshi, Gandaki and Karnali snake away towards the Ganga, wreaking occasional havoc across the plain.

This tract catches a piece of the wetter eastern Himalaya as well as the dryer western Himalaya. The distinct floras of those regions meet here. It also happens to be the section with most of the highest peaks in it, although I've avoided the sport of mountaineering. I'm not interested in that and there are plenty of other books about it. It's said that more than one hundred languages are spoken in this space. If the scores of related and unrelated ethnic and caste groups seem confusing at first that's a realistic effect.

So in its form this book partly resembles the travellers' accounts that Rousseau consumed in the eighteenth century, and which became ever more popular in the centuries of European imperialism. The earliest foreigners made scientific and political observations of the Himalaya. Later texts, as I'll describe, used travel stories to make ideological claims about Himalayan people, or to pursue fantasies of spirituality or adventure. In the national origin of its author, and the process of moving and describing, this book stands in that line. (As the geologist Charles Lyell said, nothing can escape what went before.) I've tried to make a different use of the form. To describe the scale and traditions of the landscape, I walked in it. Arranging it all between two covers was a conundrum. Every period in time, and every theme I recognised, exists in every place I went.

All the famous stages of history are going on today. There are still a few hunter-gatherers. There are plenty of farmers, of course, and a dwindling number of pastoralists who drive their animals up and down the mountains with the seasons. There has been trade in Himalayan commodities since before the British arrived 250 years ago, and much more since. Lately, there are national parks and forest rangers. Needless to say, the weather's changing. Two thousand years of history are telescoped into this land in an unusual way that's utterly absorbing.

On the first walk, which was in the spring, I thought about migrations – about all sorts of migrations, some of which are going on today – but especially about the migration of the first people into the hills. On the second walk, in the monsoon, I thought about settlement and agriculture, as well as the first appearance of Europeans here. During the autumn harvest I walked in a high mountain enclave and wrote about the taming of that landscape, and the European discovery of the wilderness they'd invented there. The fourth part, in the winter, is about conservation, the alien concept of national parks, and the lack of snow.

I begin by describing some of the atmospheres and environments of village life, to try to show what kind of places people live in and how they think about it, before trying to get under the surface. The first few days were a slog, during which I started getting to know Rajendra.

Note on pronunciation: Names and place names ending in e are pronounced with a sound like é.

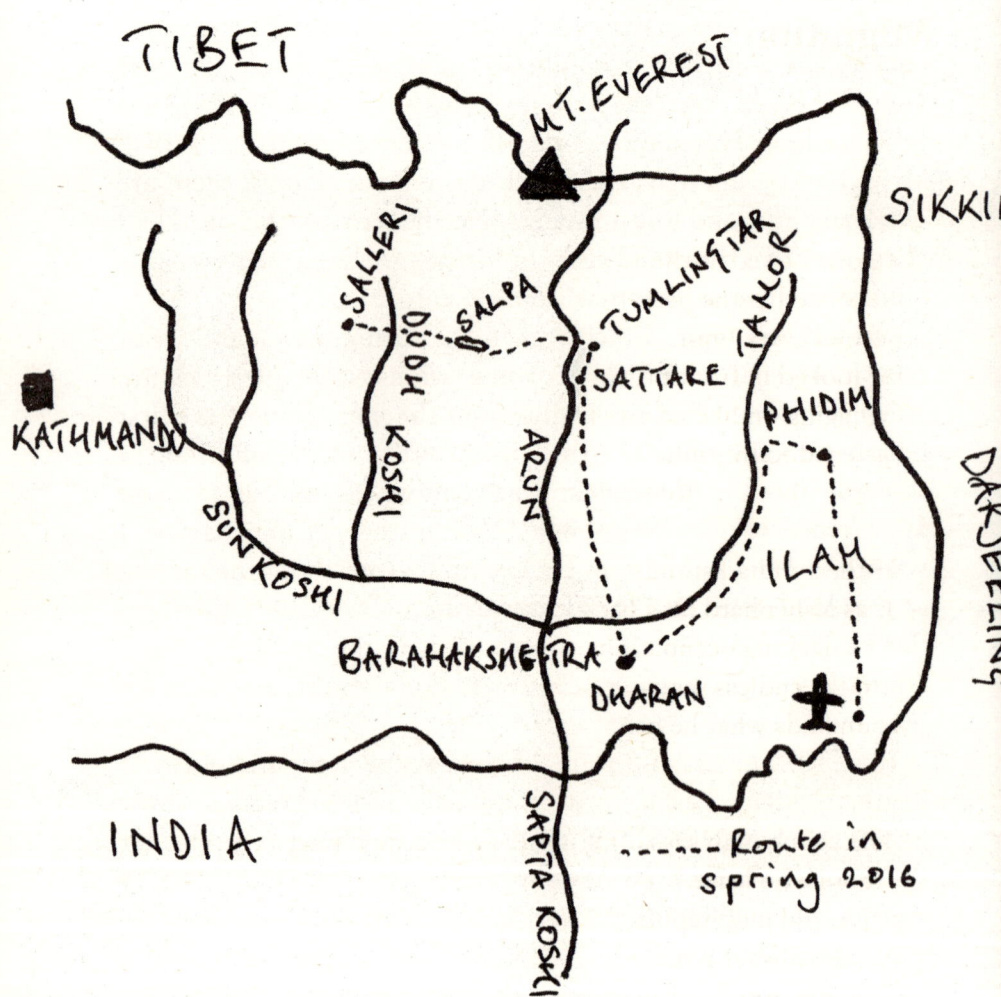

PART I

Migration

'Crow looked at the world, mountainously heaped.
He looked at the heavens, littering away
Beyond every limit.
He looked in front of his feet at the little stream
Chugging on like an auxiliary motor
Fastened to this infinite engine.'
                        Ted Hughes, 'Crow Hears Fate Knock at the Door'

'Hitherto I had stood
… as a shepherd on a promontory,
Who, lacking occupation, looks far forth
Into the endless sea, and rather makes
Than finds what he beholds.'
                                William Wordsworth, 'The Prelude'

'The young man says, "Hills are us, who stay behind. Rivers – those who leave."
    The old man replies, "Rivers forever hurry to somewhere, but also always remain here. Hills are fluid and ever changing, too."'
                                          Indra Bahadur Rai

On the plane from Kathmandu I could see the thunderheads building over the eastern hills after a month of drought. At the bus park, when I claimed my place in the front of the jeep, the soldier who'd already taken his said, 'This is going to be awkward.' He spent the first part of the journey asleep on my shoulder.

The road climbed through the clouds and tea gardens of Ilam. The neat little tea hedges were whorled around the round hills like the ridges on a fingerprint. The air was opaque with condensation, like every time I've been there. I was once told that this continually cloudy weather – 'the sun never shines, it's so depressing!' – accounts for the fact that Ilam has the highest suicide rate in the country. But a woman from here, whom I met in Kathmandu, said, 'No, it's because the kids' parents won't let them be with whom they want to be; they're lovesick, then their exams come, they come under even greater pressure, feeling their whole lives are at stake, and they drink poison or jump in a river.'

The music in the jeep was loud, and there wasn't much conversation until we began descending into Phidim in declining light. Beyond the steamed-up glass we saw a blur of rain, cloud, and forest, the lights of the town below, and white flashes of lightning. 'Mother!' squealed the young woman in the back, and the passengers began talking about deaths by lightning. In his home district they're quite common, Rajendra said. 'The victims are burnt black-black!' The jeep dropped people off at various places, lastly me and Rajendra at a hotel. He carried most of the bags and fishing rods upstairs.

That evening in the hotel restaurant I was joined by an engineer, who was living there while he worked on a hydropower project. It was stormy outside. We drank whisky and talked about fishing, which he was interested in, and about walking routes. After we'd been talking for a while, and it seemed I knew enough to get around, he asked why I needed a guide, referring to Rajendra, who he'd seen carrying the rods upstairs.

'I need someone to help me with my stuff,' I said.

I was planning to walk down the Tamor River, do some fishing, and make our way back through the hills to Kathmandu in two or three weeks. 'Start your walk from the village of Majhitar,' the engineer said. 'It's on your way, and the fishing will be good where a stream flows into the Tamor.'

※

In the morning a car from the engineer's project took me and Rajendra and dropped us a few kilometres away, which was as far as the road stretched then. The map I had was only ten years old, but very out of date, because in a short time the hills have filled with roads.[1] The footpath leading from Phidim towards the Tamor was in the process of becoming the Mid-Hill Highway, a major project that will coil over ridge after ridge across the whole country. We began tramping along the unfinished surface towards Majhitar.

Except for last night's squalls, the weather had been dry throughout the hills. Forest fires were in the news. Here, the villagers were ploughing in preparation for more rain, whereupon they'd plant maize. Where the immense red slopes were too steep to farm they were thinly forested with sal trees, which had shed their leaves to endure the arid spring. The braided streams of the Tamor came into view beneath us. After last night the water was a dirty, concrete grey. The road descended to Majhitar.

The name of this village means that members of the fishermen's caste – Majhi – are living on a flat piece of alluvial land called a tar. The first people we reached were rethatching their house ahead of the monsoon. Their nets were hanging in the rafters. Rajendra stopped to talk, and they fried some minnows for us. 'There are fish in this river as big as ourselves,' the Majhis said, 'but there's no chance of catching them in this black water.' They showed us the thick lines and 2-inch hooks they use, baited with minnows, to catch the big ones. 'Fish eat fish?' Rajendra asked.

For the rest of the day we crossed the slopes high above the black waters of the Tamor. We climbed steeply through a burnt forest, the path levelled out among fragrant pines, then we walked all afternoon in grinding sunshine and through leafless jungle, with little to drink. The brightness, heat and thirst, last night's whisky, the weight of my bag, and the awkward load of fishing rods swinging around my body made the world contract. By the end of the day I'd withdrawn into determination only to reach the village where we'd stay. When we got there the villagers asked us, for some reason, 'Are you from the land registry department?' They were also Majhis.

※

Archaeologists have speculated that fishing villages were the first permanent settlements, because even before agriculture they had a source of food in one place. It seems plausible that a similar principle is relevant here. This village, which only consisted of half a dozen stone huts, was built on a naturally formed terrace about 20 yards above the river. Each hut was a single windowless room, with a wall-less sleeping platform above it under a pitched thatch roof. Drunks were asleep on steps and benches at the end of the afternoon. We put our stuff down and were shown which house would take us. Rajendra and I asked them to prepare daal and rice for us, but they said they had no daal.

'Vegetables then?' They had no vegetables.

'Can I have a cup of tea?' There was no tea.

'Then give me a cigarette.' There were no cigarettes. They rolled the tobacco they grew in strips of fibre from their maize cobs.

While they were cooking our meal in their dark room I stretched out above, beneath the thatch. An old man climbed the ladder and crouched beside me. He farmed rice, maize, and millet. 'Sometimes it doesn't rain,' he said. 'My land's not enough. There's sorrow,' he explained gently. 'Sorrow, sorrow.' Of his children four were married and two still went to school, but only sometimes. 'In Nepal,' he said, 'the poor can't study.' For a while he wanted to talk about Britain and America. He'd heard about things like passports and visas, but he was unclear about them. Then he complained about Nepal's leaders. 'There's no development here,' he said, and indeed the only sign of development in this village was the footbridge we'd crossed the river by.

I could hear Rajendra chatting by the hearth below, trying to explain what caste he is: a Sunwar, which the Majhis thought was some kind of Rai. It was a description Rajendra was mostly willing to accept. He told them a charter myth, about how Limbus, Rais, and Sunwars are descended from three brothers, and therefore they're like brothers. But the Majhis, who were drunk, didn't seem to get the point. I was called downstairs to eat a plate of rice, and what felt like a bowl of fish heads and fins in the blackness, and to try to swim in the drunken chatter.

It's not clear where Majhis came from, or when they became Majhis. There's hardly anything written about them. That's despite fishing being such an interesting occupation. Were they the first hunter-gatherers to put down roots here? I've no idea. Besides being fishers, they used to be ferrymen. They built their settlements at places on the rivers where the current is relatively gentle, and took people across in boats they made from the hollowed trunk of a simal tree.[2] According to Corneille Jest, one of the few anthropologists to publish any data (writing in 1977), Majhis are independent of their neighbouring castes, and have their own system of values, their own social structure and religion.[3] Their principal festival, which was still practised back then – in some villages at least – was in the spring, when they worshipped the river and also their ferry. One can ask, reflected this anthropologist, how much longer these structures can be maintained, the most important factor being the disappearance of ferries, replaced by bridges. One can ask what will become of these small and isolated communities in the near future, emptied of their young blood due to labour migration, threatened by technology and things built for the masses. For the Majhis, he wrote, the old activities have lost meaning.

Folklore offers clues to people's origins, or at least to where things stood when the stories were created. That night, our host's own folklore was obscure.

'Majhis are not important people,' he said, as we ate fish in his black room. Millet beer was served from a kettle. 'The Limbus kept us' (referring to another ethnic group). 'They took our daughter across the River Tista. We had to bring her, and the son-in-law, back across and keep them. That's the old tradition. But now people have left that tradition. They go abroad to work. They raise cows and buffalos and chickens there. Then they become rich.'

'Are there Majhis still working?' Rajendra wanted to know.

'All along the river you can see them,' said the Majhi.

'Majhis are good people,' Rajendra said.

'When did you stop running ferries?' I asked.

It was eight to ten years since the ferries ended. Our host now recited all the Majhi villages, the old crossings, like a string of beads along the Tamor. 'There are only Majhis on this river,' he said. 'The places are Dhungaghat, above Ambakhor. Then comes Pinaseghat, then Nakauneghat, then Heunghat, and this place is called Simaraghat. Then is Nayaghat, further down is Lamhughat. You get to Haparaghat and then is Bhaiseghat. Then Gyastana. Further is Charuwa. Then we reach Mulghat. The river goes further.'

'Do Majhis worship the river?' I asked.

'We worship the river when we're about to launch a boat,' the Majhi said. 'Now we don't launch boats, so we don't worship.' He added a story which I couldn't understand, about how the

River Tamor is the Arun River's daughter. 'A stream called the Maikhola married the Tamor by mistake. He had meant to marry the Arun. Now he's angry.' He changed his mind. 'No! The Tamor had already married the Arun, so the Maikhola turned around and went back!'

I hadn't got the point. It was a clear night, and at eight I went outside to look at the sky. The twin stars of the zodiacal constellation that is called Mithun in South Asia were about to set beyond the huge black ridge in the west. They were followed by the waxing crescent moon in Karkat, the crab. Right overhead the planet Jupiter, like the brightest star in the sky, was in the lion Simha's groin. In the darkness by the riverbank the Majhis were moving about with their torches. I read that they believe, or used to believe, that carrying fishing nets on their shoulders would ward off evil spirits. This accounts for the fact that, unlike others, they're not afraid of riverbanks at night.[4] I laid down beneath the thatch again, in the lovely breeze the cool night sucked down the valley. While I tried to look at the sky my eyes closed. And though I didn't want to, I slept immediately.

Our route downstream from there followed a hillside path, which had become an unfinished road a few years earlier. Before a new map could be made to show it, the road was being washed away. The contractor had not dug a ditch to carry the rain running off the hill, so along its length debris was streaming, more quickly than in the common course of nature, down the slope towards the river. At one point a deep section had disappeared altogether in a summer torrent, and it seemed another monsoon or two might wash large parts away. A thin footpath had been rubbed by walkers into the loose surface, which sometimes separated and converged like the streams of the river below.

At around seven-thirty, when we'd been walking for an hour and a half, we stopped to rest at a place where the road glittered with thousands of dragonfly wings. Rajendra said he used this insect to bait fishhooks when he was a child.

The land was so dry we didn't drink water as we went. We emptied my bottle in a few gulps each only when we found a place to fill it. On our side of the valley the forest was newly burnt. On the other side, where no people lived, the trees were also leafless, but unsinged. At levels where the gradient was less they stood in front of one another from our perspective, so their twigs hatched grey swathes across the huge red hill.

Forest fires are hardly new, and in the past they were hardly accidental. The British botanist Joseph Hooker was a rare nineteenth-century European visitor to the Nepal hills. He received special permission from the maharaja to enter from Darjeeling and travel up the Tamor River. Hooker left an account describing an ancient pattern of life in the eastern Himalaya which is no longer to be seen. The Lepcha, he wrote, referring to a particular ethnic group – although his description would also have applied to others – never inhabits one spot for more than three successive years. His first operation, after selecting a site, is to burn the jungle; then he clears away the trees and cultivates between the stumps. At this season, he wrote, referring to the month of May 1848, firing the jungle is a frequent practice, and the effect by night is exceedingly fine. Heavy clouds canopy the mountains above, and, stretching across the valleys, shut out the firmament; the air is dead calm, as usual in these deep gorges, and the fires, invisible by day, are seen raging all around, appearing to an inexperienced eye in all but dangerous proximity. The voices of birds and insects being hushed, nothing is audible but the harsh roar of the rivers, and occasionally, rising far above it, that of the forest fires. At night we were literally surrounded by them; some smouldering, like the shale-heaps at a colliery, others fitfully bursting forth, whilst others again stalked along with a steadily increasing and enlarging flame, shooting out great tongues of fire, which spared nothing as they advanced with irresistible might. Their triumph, Hooker continued with relish, despite being an early advocate of Himalayan forest conservation, is in reaching a great bamboo clump, when the noise of the flames drowns that of the torrents, and as the great stem-joints burst from the expansion of confined air, the report is like a salvo from a park of artillery.[5]

As we walked, the Tamor gradually changed from grey to olive green. The heat of the day was pulling air up the valley, and the wind drove the water into little waves, turning it darker. When the footpath tracked close to the bank we scrambled over rocks to crouch down and drink like mules. Thunder rippled all around. The hills upstream disappeared in clouds and a gentle, pleasant rain began.

※

At the end of the afternoon we arrived at the village called Bhaisighat (buffalo river crossing), or Bhaisitar (buffalo flatland), where we would stay. There was a large area of dry fields lying between the houses of the village and a wide bend in the river. The fields were separated from the river, and any ready means of irrigation, by a sand and cobbled beach. It was a pretty, mixed settlement of Tamang and Majhi people. The two-storeyed cottages, which had balconies running right around them, were separated from one another by vegetable gardens, animal sheds and haystacks, bougainvillea, banana plants, and coconut palms. At the house where we would stay the daughter-in-law was smashing an unripe mango, which implied there might be chutney with our dinner.

Rajendra and I went down to the river with a fishing rod, and I waded out to a sand and cobbled bar. A Majhi was there, kneading a great ball of buffalo shit and maize flour which he trapped under stones in the shallows. Brown billows in the water would attract small fish that he'd catch in his cast net. He loved fishing, he said. It was all he ever did. He chatted humorously with Rajendra while they watched me fish for half an hour, casting into a channel, letting my lure wash around, pulling it up the edge of the fast water. The water was opaque. There was no practical reason for doing it, except to verify that nothing would be caught in these conditions. At the end of the spring, when the water turns dark, Majhis exchange hooks and lines for traps and nets.

That evening, at the house where we stayed, Rajendra and I sat on the dark veranda with the family and drank several glasses of raksi, which he called medicine for our aching bodies. Rajendra wanted information about jeep services, because he'd already had enough of this valley. He thought we should move on to the Arun. He also mentioned his fear of snakes. A green one had crossed him on the path that day. The old man of the house said there are only three snakes to be afraid of. Cobras, obviously. 'They come right into the garden here to eat the rats.' And there's another one which bites men where they pee, while they're fording rivers. Everyone found that funny. If he mentioned the third type I didn't write it down.

We saw the Majhis heading out across the fields with their

torches. 'They fish all night,' said our hosts, who weren't Majhis themselves.

At the end of the evening the old woman of the house turned sentimental, and she declared Rajendra and me to be her sons. She had one son, plus his pretty wife and their baby, living with her. And two daughters, who'd moved with their husbands to the town. She spoke of the no-good-love she felt for her absent grandchildren, which I took to mean anxiety. 'What if something happens to them in Dhankuta? Anything can happen to them!' she said. The sky had cleared a little, and from where I laid down that night on their balcony I could see the crescent moon through hazy clouds above their coconut tree.

A large portion of Nepali literature describes the hardship and futility, and especially the cruelty of village life, in which headmen and moneylenders gained their wealth by beggaring everybody else. This pessimistic, social-realist tradition was mostly written by men who emerged from village elites, so they would know. In a famous novel called *Basain*, which means something like *A Place to Live*, a man called Dhane decides to buy a buffalo.[6] He knows that dealing with the moneylender is like setting his own house alight, but he makes his mark on the paper. The buffalo's calf is soon possessed by a malevolent spirit from the forest, and it dies even as they prepare the exorcism. Next, the beast eats a neighbour's buckwheat, and Dhane is fined by the village council. Unable to repay the interest on his loan, the moneylender takes Dhane's pair of ploughing oxen, meaning his insufficient patch of land will be fallow. He needs to mortgage his house and land to borrow money to rent more fields, and the loan must extend to financing new oxen. The village headman offers to bail him out. But when it's planting time, on the night it's Dhane's turn to receive the flow from the irrigation channel, he discovers that the water has been diverted to the headman's field. Dhane curses the headman, so the headman releases his buffalo into Dhane's seedbed. Dhane strikes the animal, and it dies. He's ruined. His property is claimed by his creditors, which is what they were aiming at all along. His family must leave his ancestral village. They gather their three-year-old boy and their bundle of belongings. His grieving wife laments. Their old home is still wet with the sweat of Dhane's ancestors! She weeps over the sacred basil plant in the yard. She feeds the pigeons a final time, then nuzzles what used to be her goats, her dowry. And the tiny family departs to an unknown fate, like countless other impoverished hill families who created the Nepali diaspora in Sikkim, Darjeeling, Bhutan, Assam, and Burma.

When the botanist Joseph Hooker was in Darjeeling in the 1840s, he found the area was home to many Nepalis, mostly runaways from their own country, and afraid of being claimed, should they return to it, by the lords of the soil.[7] In the 1950s world of *Basain* the situation was not very different. Every conflict in the village, or transgression such as adultery, incurred fines and therefore debts. There were also debts to finance marriages and festivals, and gambling. Moneylenders were always willing to help. Families became tenants on their own land, while a small number of notables jumped on the least false step to increase their vast domains. Admittedly this is a stereotype, wrote Philippe Sagant, an anthropologist of eastern Nepal in the 1970s. A debt runs for three generations, parents sink to the depths of degradation, a lineage dies out, no one in the village cares – but the story is quite ordinary.[8]

Like other mountain regions, such as the Alps, the Himalaya has exported surplus manpower for centuries, soldiers being the most famous example.[9] The soldiers who left Nepal to find a living in the world were called Gurkhas by the British, but in Nepali they're called Lahures, because before they signed up for the British their predecessors fought for the Sikh king in Lahore.

On that first night in the Phidim hotel the engineer had surprised me by saying, 'My father worked for you.' He meant that his father was a British Gurkha. 'I'm here because of my father,' he continued. 'I'm here because of the British. They brought all their money home, then. All the money went straight to Nepal.

Before, in Nepal, a British soldier was something like a superstar. Now that Gurkhas have begun settling in Britain after their retirement, we don't even give a shit about them. But our fathers were like superstars in the villages. They used their money to buy land.' The families of Gurkhas had become educated, he explained. 'We are doctors, we are engineers, lots of us,' the engineer said. 'Because of the British.' And because he was drunk he grew emotional, and started to claim that even now he would fight for them. 'It's a history thing,' he said. 'It's a culture. I'd still fight for Britain. That's what my father said. You have to fight for your money.'

Not every returned migrant founded a prosperous household like the engineer's. Into the situation of poverty and outward migration described by Philippe Sagant, a Gurkha soldier returning to his village, with several thousand rupees of savings concealed on his person, was a threat, a money bomb which needed to be defused. He travelled home obsessed with the idea of being robbed, at the risk of getting drunk, losing it all at cards, being suckered in a trap involving a prostitute, or, the migrant's *bête noire*, falling ill away from home. If he managed to avoid all that and make it to his village, then the headman and the moneylender would start making plans to fleece him, by means which Sagant called picturesque and frankly illegal. His savings would evaporate like a puddle in the sun. He might as well never have migrated for work in the first place. So the men on top live at the expense of the poor, like a bull lives at the cost of fodder, without giving milk. One might conclude that it's only the sinister schemes of the wicked that prosper, while the innocent plans of the righteous hardly ever find fulfilment.[10] The country is impoverished and thwarted.

To look at it, Bhaisitar, or Bhaisighat, a place of buffalos, seemed a contented, pretty sort of poor village. I woke after dawn to find the daughter-in-law milling corn beside me. While we waited by the road for the daily jeep, Rajendra and I could see the farmers ploughing with their pairs of oxen, ready to plant maize when the weather turned. The handmade agricultural enclave made a tidy and intricate picture amid the scrub and rocky slopes. The fields were textured, as if by scraping a comb through paint. A pattern of dots was printed on, which were basket-loads of manure not yet ploughed in. It's an integrated system, in which the forest provides the fodder for the livestock, whose manure renews the fields' fertility.

As soon as the jeep arrived I was annoyed to be called a brown (haired) monkey by one of the passengers inside. He and the driver remained almost as rude for the whole long drive. We kept stopping to collect more people and tie cargo to the roof. At a hut under a lychee tree we paused briefly to buy lychees. The perfumed fruit was almost ripe, still sharp, and delicious. Its scaly remains soon littered the vehicle. The angry young man wanted my acknowledgement of everything he found wretched about the country. These villages, where the people drink river water; this pathetic jeep, held together by bits of wire; the awful road, which constantly threatened to rattle us against the sharp metal of the jeep's interior. We came to a place where a rivulet had carved a canyon in the track, and stopped for forty minutes while the driver and passengers rolled rocks and boulders into it so we could pass. 'Isn't it all great,' the young man said. 'Isn't it splendid? Have you ever seen such a place? How splendid, how *fucking* splendid!' This guy had been back in his village to collect the paperwork he needed to get a passport. He'd got a job assembling scaffolding on construction sites in Bahrain, for which he must have needed a loan from a moneylender. This whole valley was obsessed with migrating for work: the old farmer who spoke to me of sorrow, and his bafflement over passports and visas; and the Majhis by the fire, who thought people got rich abroad by raising goats and chickens there. All the young men or teenagers packed in the back of this jeep had plans, or dreams, of going abroad to work. They talked about whether they'd get visas. There even happened to be an overseas employment agent on board, who sold jobs in the Gulf for a living. He was a pleasant guy fiddling with two smartphones, who'd been home to see his sick mother in the village.

Several times we drove across broad, dry riverbeds, which were not so much like riverbeds as great sloping conveyors of gravel and boulders, like glaciers without ice. Fans and cones of rocky debris spilt on to them from cracks in the valley walls. So we came to Dharan, a town that had grown enormously since my last visit more than ten years earlier.

※

After we'd had some beer, Rajendra and I took a taxi to a place called Barahakshetra, which is a kind of pivot in this eastern journey. The scenery down there, though not very far away, was quite different from where we'd been. While we were pressed inside the jeep it had changed. Now the valleys were tropical gorges, ravaged by landslides. There were naked brown streaks through the evergreen jungle everywhere.

There are altogether seven major tributaries in the Koshi river system, converging through the eastern hills to form the Saptakoshi, which means Seven Rivers. The Tamor had joined with the Arun and Sunkoshi in confluences a few miles upstream. And here the united river forged through the final ridge in a giant chasm, then ploughed straight on into the plain. Although it was unlike a snake in every obvious way, it put me powerfully in mind of a giant python, a god-sized, world-changing monster. It was terrifying, chocolate-brown, seething with eddies, too implacable for waves, God knows how deep, between walls of rock 200 yards apart. In those walls, the force that made the mountains had thrust the strata vertically up.

The hills and mountains are still going up, just slightly faster than the rock is collapsing and dissolving. Rivers are the opposite of mountains; low where they are high, fast while they are slow, supple instead of brittle and stronger in the end. A procession of material is coming down on glaciers and in screes, rockfalls, and landslides, and as suspended sediments. The Arun River, as well as another of the seven which make the Saptakoshi, rises in Tibet and passes through the whole mountain chain, because it's antecedent to it. One day, in just a few thousand years, it's expected that the headwaters of the Arun will stray north on the Tibetan plateau to capture the Yarlung

Tsangpo, and divert that enormous river down here, changing everything.

For the time being at least, dwarfed by the horrific spectacle of the gorge and the monstrous river, there is a collection of white-domed ashrams and temples at Barahakshetra, as well as eateries and trinket stalls. The place is sacred to Vishnu. He was incarnated here as a boar who raises the earth on his tusks.[11]

✻

We travelled 120 kilometres up the Arun, reaching a small town called Tumlingtar in ten hours by bus. An old man at the Tumlingtar hotel said he used to do that journey in six days on foot, to bring salt home to his village. On one occasion, which he still remembered vividly, his party found bamboo fish traps by a ford and stole the fish. It was an incredible haul that would be impossible to find now. As they were in the act they became afraid that the trappers would return before they fled, so that night they camped some way off and celebrated with more fish than they could eat. The story is similar to something that became fixed in William Wordsworth's memory. As a child, while laying snares he discovered someone else's, and the bird that was the captive of another's toils became his prey. But when the deed was done he heard, among the solitary hills, low breathing coming after him.[12]

From Tumlingtar we walked a while to a settlement called Sattare, which was a row of three or four huts selling food by the trackside. From Sattare it was fifteen minutes down a steep wooded bank to the river.

The riverside where we emerged was a sand and stony beach that separated from the cliffs downstream to form a bar. The bar partly divided a large backwater from the main river. Half-burnt timbers from funeral pyres span trapped in the currents on the margin of the pool. On the opposite bank, maybe 50 yards away, there was a group of bamboo huts, and similar huts were scattered up the hill behind them. I saw a pair of kingfishers. But the Arun was no better than the Tamor; the water was brown, transparent at the edge only to the depth of a few inches. For the sake of it I had a go at fishing there, using a noisy lure in the dark water, and soon lost it on a hidden log.

We stayed at one of the Sattare eateries that night and watched the prime minister on TV, thinking small and acting big. There was a brief glimpse of the half-moon, then we went to sleep in a bamboo-walled space that was more a basket than a room exactly. I woke unexpectedly at four, and walked down to the river in the dark. It was hard to follow the faint track by torchlight, and I took care not to lose my way in the wood. In the night the water had risen at least 2 feet, and put a new channel through the bar, to turn the bottom half into an island and bring yesterday's backwater into the main stream. The charred logs had been released. They'd be miles away by now. More timbers were coming down at running pace.

At dawn I watched the people on the far bank emerge. They stared at the changed river for a while, in silence as it seemed through my binoculars. I watched the first smoke rise through the roofs of their huts, and from the other huts spread up the hill. A man began fishing by the bank with a cast net. Two teenagers hauled a dugout boat a hundred yards upstream, where they moored it again. I stayed there for a long time.

The fish I was interested in is called mahseer. They hatch upstream, and if they survive other fish, otters, and herons, then they swim down to the plain and grow until the age of two or three in the huge, deep rivers there. If a fisherman, dolphin, or crocodile in the plains doesn't eat it, then a grown mahseer returns to the mountain stream where it was born, evading nets, baited hooks, and giant catfish, swimming back into the Himalaya ahead of the monsoon. It can live for decades and grow up to 20, 30, 40 kilos and more. Still, not much is known about the mahseer, and now there are hardly any left. You have to go somewhere fairly inaccessible, like this, to find them. Sand extraction for concrete-making wrecks their spawning grounds, and hydroelectric dams thwart their migration. Several times on rivers near highways I've seen men trying to make a living at night, electro-fishing with truck batteries connected to electrodes on long bamboos.

I'd been on a fishing trip with a group of friends a year earlier in this season, over in the west, on the Karnali. The first day we camped on a beach below cliffs, at a bend in the river that seemed to have trapped every rubber sandal ever lost in any upstream settlement. That afternoon, all night, and the following morning it rained. For the rest of the week we were dry but the water never recovered, making our fishing almost hopeless. My friends tried live bait at night. They stitched a living minnow to a hook and hung it in the black, echoing water, where its scent and panicked movements might attract a giant predator. It was attached to nearly unbreakable tackle, and it could have been an invincible trap if the mahseer had been there and feeding, or not feeding on something else.

Towards the end of that trip there was some kind of hatch. The shallows broke out in living silver sparks, which leapt through the surface. I drew a fluttering silver spinner through the shoal. Then I thought that perhaps larger fish were feeding on the tiny ones, and it was on them in turn that the mahseer would feed. I attached something bigger, and when I drew it through the silver swarm disappeared instantly. That night in our camp we could hear the mahseer in the current, rolling over stones with their bony heads, foraging for crabs.

On this morning by the Arun, I saw that the river was dropping by about 2 inches every hour. I measured its temperature. I heard how the birds that were noisy at dawn were quiet two hours later. The boy from the hotel came down with buckets and cans to fill from the river, then he went off to climb the cliffs with my binoculars. When I got back to Sattare there was a row going on. A woman had found 1,000 rupees missing from her home, and she was accusing a man who had also disappeared of stealing it. I sat and read the news on my phone. Last month had been the hottest April on record, the twelfth consecutive hottest month globally, in a sequence that would last a few months more.

At the little airstrip in Tumlingtar, Rajendra and I consigned the fishing tackle and unused camping gear as freight to Kathmandu, then carried on walking up the Arun. There was evergreen tropical forest in the valley bottom, but sometimes the way led over sun-blasted sand at the riverside. Charred funeral timbers, bamboos, and plastic bottles on the beach showed the high-water mark. Approaching figures, shading themselves under black umbrellas, shimmered over the grey sand. The rain-affected river was also grey. I watched an elderly fisherman slowly working his way upstream. He caught a minnow and dropped it in the pouch at his waist. Drenched in sweat, I crouched down to drink from the river and fill my bottle with the alluvium-charged water.

We stopped at a hut, or shop, where the men were playing carrom and the women were sitting beside a display of bottled drinks in a basin of water. After boastfully introducing me, with a description of whatever he considered good, Rajendra's conversation turned to his usual topic: which community he belongs to. Sometimes we'd meet people who didn't know what a Sunwar is, and he'd get into explanations of how it's not the same as a Sunar. Sometimes he'd simply say it's a kind of Rai. This time he tried to make them guess. One of the young women, who'd been delighted to hear that my wife is Nepali and had been candidly staring at me ever since, guessed Rai straight away. Rajendra denied it, claiming to be a Magar, while the others ventured that he might be a Tamang, but the girl stuck hard to Rai. This kind of ostensibly contentless chat about people's communities filled all of our first meetings.

The same topic arose when we stopped at a mud house to buy lychees. The young woman was a Majhi, which she called the caste that plays in rivers. 'You seem to be from the caste which is called brown [haired],' she said to me, and teased Rajendra: 'Have you died your hair black, sir?'

'Oh yeah?' he said. 'Is it supposed to be brown?'

We sat on the back step while her husband went into the garden to throw sticks into their lychee tree. 'Everything goes up in spring,' said Rajendra. When the weather warms, animals and people migrate uphill.

'The fish also go up,' the woman said. 'We worship the river then.'

'You have to do rituals in the spring? What rituals?' I asked.

'There's lice in my hair,' she said, rummaging. 'It's biting! We call it kul puja. We worship the family gods, and worship the forest gods, so that they stay away.'

'And the river gods?' I asked.

'Once a year. Eighteen in total, taste one each,' she said, handing over the lychees that her man had brought.

*

The 1961 novella *Khaireni Ghat*, by Shankar Koirala, begins with the return of a migrant labourer to a village that's something like this one.[13] It took four days to walk there on a path that was narrow, stony, and dusty, but sometimes also slippery with dew. That path was somehow a frightening place, with no movement except the flow of the river below, where no one wanted to travel alone for fear of thieves and cutthroats. Bhaktabire, the protagonist, has been away for ten years, but the Majhi ferryman who takes him across to the village recognises him. 'Is it Bhaktabire? Where have you been lost?' he says.

Bhaktabire is the village headman's son, a headstrong troublemaker. He believes that the Majhis have simple, harmless minds. To establish his status he is going to put them under his thumb. He greets them as he enters the village.

'Are you well?' he asks.

They reply by saying things such as, 'Up to now the hour of my death hasn't come!'

They'll never understand my character, Bhaktabire thinks. Because although he can't read, he's seen the world, lived in Calcutta, and he knows about things like the dolphin in the zoo there. So he breezes past the villagers, and doesn't discover until he enters his house that his mother has given up on him. She encouraged his father to take a second wife, to provide an heir. So there's a baby, and Bhaktabire is disoriented to find that his new stepmother is very pretty.

The ferryman who took Bhaktabire across is called Singhabire. He hangs out all day at the river crossing with a bunch of other snaggle-toothed boozers, drinking home brew and comparing cigarette brands to local tobacco. In the evening Singhabire feels that his body is hot and his chest is about to burst open. After giving him some more beer, his wife fetches the shaman, who is named Mahebale.

After he's been served his beer, the shaman Mahebale begins to calculate the influence of Singhabire's planets. He says, 'Trouble from a restless spirit can be seen. There's a little menace from the water demon. Because the hunter-spirit has you in view, your chest burns too.'

The patient replies, 'Three times I ferried people across the river. The sun was as hot as a red chilli. I started to get sick when I came home. Is there any wine? Bring some. Oh, I'm in bad shape!'

The shaman Mahebale says, 'Please call on the gods. Go and find a crowing rooster. I'll get some things.' And he totters out.

This is the scene in Singhabire's hut. There's a kitchen fire in one corner, a goat in another, and Singhabire is laid out on the floor. His wife is preparing the place for the ritual, by coating the floor with fresh mud, when Mahebale returns in his ceremonial white tunic with a drum. A few villagers come to watch. They crouch on the ground. Mahebale arranges a lamp, patterns of rice flour, and a rupee coin on the floor in front of himself, then he begins to slowly beat his drum and chant. 'Himal, Himal [Mountain, Mountain], Wandering hunter in the woods, Hunter of the water …' and so on, invoking the goddesses of a couple of famous hills that even I've heard of. Incense and butter give smoke from the ritual fire. The shaman starts shaking and sweating. He's flushed. The watching villagers are whispering about which goddess has taken control of Singhabire.

Suddenly Singhabire rears up. His face is black and dripping with sweat. And he cries, 'This thing cannot be changed! Justice must be done! The mark of our sweat and blood is on these green leaves! The signature of our ten fingers is on this turf! Look in the river – there is our reflection. There the Majhi finds his royal seal, our ancestral property, these rocks and waves.'

'An evil spirit has got hold of him,' says Mahebale.

'It's an evil spirit,' another agrees.

'I'll need a coconut,' Mahebale says. 'Some cucumber seeds would also do. If there are any.'

In this way, the author establishes some of his characters and sketches the atmosphere and environment of village life. None of this stuff is going to be important in the plot which follows. It's just there to introduce Mahebale the shaman, and show what kind of place these people live in and how they think about it.

Mahebale is a Majhi, but his wife is a Dalit. In other words, she's casteless – formerly called an Untouchable. Mahebale doesn't think caste matters, but he knows that if the other villagers find out about his wife he won't be able to smoke and drink with them, so he pretends that she's a Magar. Yet he doesn't hesitate to reveal his secret to the headman's son, Bhaktabire, who has lived abroad, where (the shaman mistakenly assumes) he read books and gained enlightened attitudes. To Mahebale's horror, Bhaktabire immediately gives a pious little speech, claiming that like the waters of the Sunkoshi the blood of his heart flows for the sake of his Majhi villagers. Then he expels the progressive shaman from the village.

Bhaktabire, the headman's son, appears to be an archetypal shit. But really he's a vehicle for the socially concerned author to explore the conflicts arising from social change, and as the story goes on the conflicts occur within Bhaktabire, not because of him. In 1961, the issues confusing the returned migrant labourer were apparently women and sexuality (so far he's only developed a crush on his father's young wife), caste and intercaste marriage, and – to be introduced any moment now – the seeming rise of criminality and disorder. I like the story, because these themes, in a setting of drunken bawdiness, shamanism, rural poverty, and exploitation, correspond remarkably to what I encountered on my journey to the east in 2016.

Next, Bhaktabire goes hunting at night, encounters some bandits, and returns with them to their village. What he finds there astonishes and concerns him; even though hatred for Untouchables was all pervasive and found everywhere, among these neighbours it didn't seem to have developed. Even to speak of such a village was to raise fears of becoming an outcaste oneself. As Bhaktabire sleeps, the narrative cuts to the bandit who has brought him there, who talks lovingly to his wife. 'You are not just my Nima,' he says. 'You are my night, my hills, my jungles, my caves. In the dark you are my hiding place.' When Nima starts to weep, for fear of what will become of him, the bandit tries to calm her by saying that he's robbed comparatively few people. 'You don't see how the small houses in thousands of villages are being eaten by the big houses, like small fish being swallowed by larger ones?' he asks. Yet, despite his social conscience and self-deprecation, this man is getting somewhere in the world of bandits. A political party has been courting his services, he admits.

The bandit happens to resemble a type that's been described in partly similar, often mountainous places all over the world, such as north-east Brazil, Spain, Corsica and the Sardinian highlands, the Alps, Albania, and the Caucasus.[14] Poor and remote peasant societies, the theory goes, on the margins of authority, often with surplus labour, and mountain pastoralists in particular with their rugged and mobile life beyond the villages, are liable to produce socially sympathetic or somehow attractive bandits. Amid the general oppression and passivity of the poor a few free spirits stage a personal rebellion, and are cast as a noble robber or *le brigand au grand coeur*. According to this theory, bandits end up facing a dilemma. On the one hand they desire a complete escape from authority, which looks a bit like justice, but is liable to be short-lived if they take it too far. On the other hand, there's the necessity of accepting opportunities under politicians who are even bigger rascals than themselves. But although a fear of robbers is sometimes mentioned in the Nepal hills, and aside from in this novella, the traditions of social banditry rarely occur, as far as I know.[15] Politically protected mafia-like activity is another matter.

In the morning, in the novella, the bandit has gone, and Bhaktabire is once again at a loss in the presence of a beautiful woman: Nima, the bandit's wife. Or perhaps they all look beautiful to Bhaktabire. He tears himself away when she demands that he come dancing at a village fair, and he heads back home. The painful battle between men and women, just like caste turmoil, will never cease, he reasons.

Bhaktabire becomes a soft touch. 'You aren't like the headman,' he's told by pleasantly surprised villagers, and he agrees. 'I don't know why I can't cheat you. I can't order you around.' He sits, melancholy, under a tamarind tree. His ancestors, who were all headmen of this village, had hot tempers and were respected. Where has his spiritual refinement come from? Along with other government officials, his ancestors exploited the people who worked in the fields. Bhaktabire sees that these simple, ignorant farmers still don't understand that they've been oppressed, by being made to carry the headman's loads, obliged to plough his fields, and then forced into debt to him. He even impulsively gives some money away when he sees an injured stranger in need of medicine, although he knows that this is a ridiculous thing to do.

The book ends in a frantic scene at a festival. Young women and toughs from the surrounding villages are there. Traders have gathered, selling cloth and fruit and bangles. The poor village cobbler, whose four daughters are blooming like flowers, finds them surrounded and harassed by Brahmin boys.

'They never leave them alone,' the cobbler says. 'My daughters only have bad luck.'

The miller's daughter calls to Bhaktabire from a tavern, and fills him with beer. A notorious hoodlum is said to be on his way, and people wonder from which village he will carry a girl away this time. And suddenly here's the hoodlum, in the tavern, exchanging violent boasts with Bhaktabire and the others.

'I see that young widow, whose husband died last year, has come here too,' he leers.

'This village will beat up that village!'

'No, we'll do it to you!'

'Who can stop us?'

'Remember what happened to that blacksmith last year?'

'Last year, twenty-five young women were carried away across the Koshi.'

'I wasn't here last year,' Bhaktabire admits.

'This year,' say the drinkers, 'it hasn't been so much fun.'

The miller's daughter is a little frightened to hear this talk, and she waits for some sudden happening. Her dark cheeks have become red, like the two buttocks of a pig roasted in the fire. The ring in her nose is shaking. 'Shall I fill your bowls with raksi?' she asks. Bhaktabire notices the hoodlum noticing the way she moves, but he himself has just become aware of the brightly shining daughter of a Tamang villager. She's catching his eye. The night proceeds to dancing and the clashing of sticks at the temple. The sky is full of stars. Fruit-sellers' baskets are overturned. There are cries for help from the bangle and vermilion sellers, who are losing their wares. In Bhaktabire's drunken sight the dancing women multiply and coincide in the dark. And there's the radiant Tamang girl with the tight blouse, smiling at him. He takes her hand. He squeezes her wrist. She finds herself tumbled under a hedge with him. Her mother screams, 'WHO'S TAKEN MY YOUNGEST DAUGHTER!' No one gives her any reply. In the morning the miller's daughter says, 'Bhaktabire made the festival a success.'

Almost every element of this story cropped up in one way or another in the last part of our eastern journey, almost sixty years later.

※

We walked through a Brahmin village. Then — we smelt their musky shit before we saw them — we passed a caravan of mules heading into the mountains. For the first time on the way we passed a shaman, carrying a drum, a bushel of iron tridents, and other magical instruments.

Later in the afternoon a screaming wind sent branches and twigs crashing onto the tin roof of the restaurant where we sat.

The plastic leaves of the table decorations went flying around the room. At five or six o'clock there was thunder and lightning and hard, steady rain. On the Tamor, also, we'd seen the clouds building further up the valley in the late afternoon and heard thunder in the evening. And although we'd had little rain where we'd been, we'd seen the river rise at night and fall throughout the day. Where we'd been, the people were still ploughing. But up here, where the weather was happening, the maize was already standing thigh-high in the fields.

We'd pitched up in a peculiar construction. It was built onto the steep valley side, in a forest above the river. The restaurant where we sat, which we'd entered at ground level, was built of woven bamboo and tin. There were wire screens for windows. This superstructure was supported by concrete and stone masonry. A staircase descended from behind the counter to the bedrooms, which faced the windy forest and the thundering river, and seemed to be suspended like bees' nests over the valley. The front of each cell was made of wire nets to create a fantastic, airy sleeping space. There were shocking-pink mosquito nets in the rooms, and fresh candy-striped paint in the restaurant. A young couple ran the place. Their new business was thriving.

For a while I was engaged in tiresome conversation by two drunks. The wife of one came to take him home, but – although she had the sympathy of our hosts – no one had the power to refuse him more drinks. A middle-aged mute woman belonged to the household. Her black hair was a wild clump. Her expressions were alternately benign and possessed. She shuffled in and out, looking more or less tormented. A trio of young women was accompanying one another on a journey. There were pairs of young men travelling by motorbike. Outside, a carpenter from the plains was still making new benches for the customers who filled every seat as the night went on.

The drunk's wife sulked in a corner. When it was ready, the meal was served to everyone pretty much at once. The couple served drinks, fried fish, made snacks. They worked hard and were friendly to everyone.

A woman said to us, 'Are you going uphill?'

'Yes, we're going to Salpa,' Rajendra said. 'We'll sing "Saya doley saya" and dance.'

According to this woman, it was three more days until the festival would begin. 'Four,' according to Rajendra.

'It's on the full moon,' she pointed out, which we already knew; we'd been keeping an eye on it.

'Have you ever been?' I asked.

'There are a lot of leeches on the way,' she said. 'I still have the scars from when I went a year or two ago.'

We asked about the itinerary and accommodation, and received information which in good and bad ways would prove completely inaccurate.

'Will there be fights?' Rajendra wanted to know, and the woman answered that the local people sing a song, 'Saye saye saye la! If you're not from round here, drop by sometime!' which sounded pretty relaxed.

'They beat drums and sing "Saye doley saye"?' Rajendra asked.

'Yes, yes. They walk around jumping,' she said.

The hosts manoeuvred the drunk guy out, put his food in a plastic bag and handed it to his wife. He pulled the woollen hat off her head and threw it on the ground. They left furious, each thinking the other had won. A group burst in; they'd travelled from Kathmandu in a thirty-six-hour bus journey, culminating in a long, dark hike. They were a ('high' caste) Chhetri family – brothers, wives, and kids in high spirits – coming to their ancestral village to worship their ancestral god once in three years, on this full moon. The wives took the calendar off the wall and studied it. The kids ran around. The men had some knowledge of Rajendra's district. He was pleased to be recognised immediately as a Sunwar, and they began exchanging names: 'Do you know so and so?'

'The one who married a Tamang?'

'Yes!'

Another group arrived at the same moment, also wearing metropolitan clothes. They turned out to be a Rai folk–pop outfit, come to promote a movie at a festival. According to the Nepali calendar, which starts with the month of Baisakh, beginning in mid-April, this would be the first full moon of the year.

Before I set out on this journey I met a field biologist in Kathmandu named Kamal Rai, himself from eastern Nepal, who explained the phenomena, or season, or festival, which is called Ubhauli. 'For the Baisakh full moon all living things go up,' he said. 'Even fish, they need to go up, because they have to breed. Animals, I mean deer, they have to go up, because they feel hot, and the snow has already melted, grass is coming. In trees, sap rises. Danfe pheasants start croaking and in some areas they build their nests. And our ancestors realised that the movement of animals and plants, and the changing weather, is the time that's good for seeding.

'You know the goose?' he asked. He was referring to the bar-headed goose, which is the highest-flying of all birds. On their spring migration they climb the valleys and cross the Himalaya in a single night. They've been recorded at 7,000 metres and more, not so far below the cruising altitude of a jet liner. 'When they migrate north,' Kamal said, 'they honk like "karang kurung karang kurung". So the ancestors understood that this is the time for seeding, because these birds are asking, "Kankro pharsi? Cucumber and pumpkin?" So they start. Even in the night they plant their cucumber and pumpkin.[16] When they see the firefly flying at night on their farm, they feel the temperature is rising. They feel the conditions. The soil is good enough. The farm birds are singing around the farm. They watch it. It means it's a good time for seeding, so they go to Salpa to ask for good weather.'

Ornithologists sometimes suppose that bird migrations trace the route along which a species spread, back to the place of its origin. And while short-lived species use mysterious senses to find their way, longer-lived birds such as geese and cranes learn the route from their parents. In other words, the geese's migration route is a tradition among themselves.

This was Rajendra's description of the spring festival of seasonal migration. 'Ubhauli means everything goes uphill, cow, buffalo, and sheep. This time is Ubhauli.' And a woman whose house we stayed in one night simply said, 'Ubhauli means the weather.' It has its corollary in the autumn, when another full moon marks Udhauli, the time to bring the animals down the hill again. 'That's how it is,' agreed Rajendra. 'That's what our ancestors used to say while they were lighting incense for Ubhauli-Udhauli. They'd announce, "Now the livestock will move downhill", or they'd take the cattle uphill, beating a drum, tyang tyang tyang.'

Rai people, of whom there are about twenty subgroups in eastern Nepal, speaking mutually incomprehensible but related languages, have a grammatical facility which linguists believe may be unique in the world: an up/down locative case. In other words, any phrase in which someone is coming or going, or carrying something, or whatever, also expresses whether they are moving up or down hill. After all, there's almost nowhere around here that's flat. This shows something interesting about the way an environment influences people, with the opposite implication to Arctic people having many words for snow. Hundreds of languages are spoken in mountainous places, but only Rais have developed this grammatical dimension. It's not inevitable how it plays out.

Meanwhile, oddly enough, although the Rais (and to some extent their neighbours) have these festivals of seasonal migration up and down the hills, the words Ubhauli and Udhauli are Nepali – a relatively new linguistic arrival to the area, unrelated to Rai languages. Kamal the field biologist said his ancestors heard the geese honking 'kankro pharsi', 'cucumber pumpkin', but those are Nepali words, and his ancestors must have spoken Rai. What's going on, or how the processes of deep history and the environment have worked, isn't obvious.

The salient direction of travel throughout these hills is up and down, through bands of habitat. The subtropical valleys were malarial until a mosquito eradication programme in the 1950s. Clouds form at about 1,000 metres, and often the hills are lost in them. That's about the same altitude at which the rivers become unnavigable. Atmospheric moisture sustains the plants (such as ferns and orchids and trailing mosses) that grow from the trunks and branches of the trees. Geographers and botanists call this jungle the cloud forest. The amount of water in the air increases through the different altitudes of the forest, until a point around the treeline roughly 4,000 metres up, where it declines. Then there are alpine meadows with aromatic shrubs. As you walk across the country you must climb repeatedly up and down, to cross ridges separating valleys separating ridges in an alternating sequence of subtropical valley, field and forest, alpine pasture and crag.

Most species of plant and animal are confined to a stripe across the hill about 1,000 metres deep, so there's enormous biodiversity. There's also movement between the bands. The nineteenth-century British political official and zoologist Brian Hodgson deduced that the migration of Himalayan woodcocks up and down this system allows them always to remain in the same season.[17] Many people range across storeys on an almost daily basis to meet the needs of a single village, but most communities are traditionally concentrated within a particular altitudinal range to which their economy is adapted. So Majhis live below 1,000 metres, and pastoralists live high up.

The first outsider to travel extensively in the Nepalese Himalaya was a Swiss geologist named Toni Hagen, who walked almost every valley in the country beginning in the 1950s, in a journey which took him fourteen years.

Being a geologist, he drew cross-sectional diagrams of the mountains to show the strata of gneiss and granite, and other diagrams which don't look very different to show how ethnic groups live in altitudinal bands.

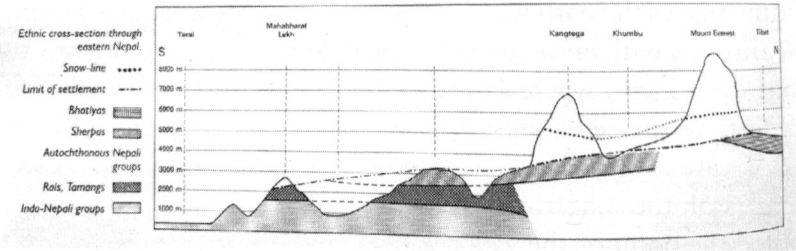

Toni Hagen's ethnic cross-section through eastern Nepal (courtesy of Katrin Hagen)

In the morning, the wet stones by the river showed that the water had been up and down two feet in the night. We set off over the shoulder of a hill, cutting a corner to join a tributary valley. Soon, but briefly, we had a view of snowy mountains to the north, not far away. The pretty cottages were half-timber, mud, and stone, and they had young maize standing in their fields. We were accompanied by a ten-year-old boy on his way to school who ran ahead and behind and alongside us for an hour and a half. As we went, I collected sprigs of leaves, from trees mostly, and stuffed them in the top of my bag: oaks, ferns, some laurel-like things, bougainvillea escaped from someone's cottage garden, rani bhaloyo, the lacquer tree. According to my field guide, which I consulted in the evening, the species indicated that we were on the threshold of the subtropical and temperate zones. This one's good for fodder, the book said, and this one's used for poisoning fish. Cicadas in the forest made their escalating, shrieking clatter. The brain-fever birds cried.[18] At the shop where we stopped for lunch the proprietor was busy with his ledger and chits, taking stock of a delivery that was being unloaded from a tractor trailer. He had cartons of biscuits, noodles, salt, cooking oil, rubber sandals, cigarettes, matches, exercise books, pencils, and whisky.

In the afternoon we kept company with other people who were walking up to Salpa. They were in family groups, or groups of people from the same village. A boy beat a snake to death, saying it bites. We were in a dense jungle of many greens. In some places the path was covered with bamboo litter, sometimes it glittered with mica. There were patches of terraced cultivation, but only a few, wherever they could be claimed from the steep forest. We passed a mule train, and after getting ahead of it we took care to stay ahead, because it's tiresome to be stuck behind mules on these narrow trails. A cascade of rocks and boulders filled the point of the valley's V. A geologist told me in an email that you often find the freshest granites from the mountaintops among these huge river stones. A strange phrase. A strange fact,

I thought. A stream plunged over and beneath the boulders, creating astonishingly clear pools a swimmer would take a couple of strokes to cross. Within the pools, each pebble seemed more clearly and brightly visible than if there had been no water over it, as if they were covered with clarifying bright, wet light.

Late in the afternoon, in clearings in the forest, we saw clouds of twenty or forty lilac butterflies, each the size of a small coin, flying around each other in a column that didn't move, like dancing flowers on a bush that had disappeared. For 10 yards the path climbed a craggy course that was part stream, part waterfall. The valley steepened and tightened, and seemed to coil around upon itself, so that I lost my sense of direction. After nine hours of walking we reached the village of Salpaphedi (base of Salpa), at the bottom of the headwall. Here, where the land obviously caught the rain before the season developed elsewhere, the maize was standing two feet higher than where we'd been that morning.

The village shop, which was also an inn, was receiving a delivery from a mule train when we checked in. Three women – young, getting on, and ancient – ran the place, and they were heaving and stacking and counting the sacks and boxes of rice and salt, cooking oil and biscuits, noodles and rubber sandals, exercise books and cigarettes, and all of that, which the muleteers were unloading at their door. All the time more groups, often surrounding a shaman, came in and stopped then carried on. There was a guy whose knapsack was bristling with iron tridents, and also (like mine, but for a different reason) with sprigs of leaves and herbs he'd selected from the forest. For a while the benches where I sat were packed with kids speaking Kulung Rai, which was the first language other than Nepali, and occasionally English, that we'd heard so far.

After it quietened down they poured us raksi and I sat making notes. The young woman was cutting potatoes with a khukuri, and the conversation took in the previous year's earthquake.

Rajendra showed off about what he'd seen in places further west which were more affected. The young woman's blunt observation was that we had too many people anyway. She was a bold, humorous type, whose manner seemed to say that she could see how stupid we were, and sooner or later she might spell it out.

Rajendra said he needed to get married. He'd decided to bring a Rai girl home from the festival. 'What kind of dance do you do at weddings?' he asked.

'Here we do modern dance,' she said.

'When you're married off,' he said, 'and you visit your parents' home, how do you do the ceremony?'

'Me?'

'Yes.'

'I'll put tika on my parents' foreheads.'

'That you do anyway,' said Rajendra.

'What's he writing?' she asked.

'About you,' Rajendra told her.

And she retorted, to my surprise, by using two English words. 'About our *family history*?'

What else would she come up with? Aren't you going to ask me about our *kinship structure?*

I asked her, 'What is your *family history?'*

'Oh. Just staying here. Working. Like this,' she said.

Rajendra pursued the family history. 'How far did you have to go to get salt in your days?' he asked her mother.

When she was fifteen, the mother carried six paathis of ghee for twelve days to Dharan and returned with seven paathis and nine manas of salt.[19] 'It was a lot of walking. My back hurt,' she said.

Rajendra, who is a charming guest, said humbly, 'In those days that's what they did. It's just stories for us now.'

'My father told me not to go,' the older woman continued. 'He said I wouldn't be able to do it, but a lot of my friends were going so I went.' She recalled what they ate on the journey, and how they broke up the big slabs of salt to fit more in their loads. 'You don't have to do that these days,' she said.

Rajendra told her, 'Yes. Women like you are strong. People today don't have strength like yours.'

She approved and furthered his sentiment by saying that everyone today eats plastic ghee and oil, by which she meant it comes in plastic packets like those the muleteers had just delivered. 'Now we eat rice that has been in factories and filled with chemicals,' she said.

I don't think Rajendra was only flattering her. He actually thought something had been lost. He said, 'This is an age of selfies, and we'll all die soon. We'll be dead by the time we get to your age.'

'No, you won't,' said the woman.

'My own grandfather lived up to a hundred,' said Rajendra. 'It's a good thing, to have lived up to a hundred. We had to take care of him during his last month. We went to all the shamans, but he died anyway. My grandfather used to say, "I'm about to be a hundred. I don't think you people will live this long." When I asked him why, he'd say it's because we don't know how to eat. He died talking, like we're talking now. We're not even sure if we'll live to fifty. How old are you, aunty?'

'I'm fifty-three,' the woman said. 'I was born in 2019 [1962–63

AD].[20] How old does that make me? I must be fifty-three now.'

'My father also carried salt in his day,' Rajendra said. 'When my father tells me of his struggles, I just shrug it off and say that I'd have been a bigger man if he'd sent me to school. When my father tells me how much he struggled, carrying loads so we could eat, that's what I say to him. Had he sent me to school, I would have come up. If you really think about it,' he reflected, 'life was hard before because of the geography. It's easier now.'

'Now someone will bring salt to your house. They just bring it to your door,' the old woman said. 'So, these days, no one's going to carry such a load.'

At least until the 1970s there was a notional division called the salt line running through the hills, dividing those who traded to the north for salt from those who walked south to collect theirs. Rai mythology includes a story of the first salt in these valleys.[21] In the days when people still wore animal skins, a hero called Mapa Raja went hunting and left his bag of ground meal – his lunch – at the cave where he was staying. When he returned he found his food had been replaced with rocks. After this happened repeatedly he decided to hide in a tree and shoot whoever was doing it, but as he drew his arrow back the twitching feather on his headdress betrayed him. The people who were exchanging his grain for lumps of salt called him down, introduced themselves, and showed him how to use the stuff to make meat taste delicious. They were Sherpas, that is, members of the community whose home borders the Rai area to the north, in the high mountains on the Tibetan frontier.

Needless to say, the specific details of the story probably shouldn't be taken literally. Kings hiding in trees with bows and arrows are a recurring device in Rai mythology. The people who are now known as Sherpas entered the area now known as Nepal about 500 years ago, so if salt here is older than that, which it must be, then the term by which the northern salt-bearers are described must have been updated in the tradition. Moreover, there may be something buried in the Himalaya that links the idea of salt to hunting and archery for some reason. A Tibetan myth also has a king's father discovering salt while hunting.[22]

But the story puts the origin of a fact of life into the traditional record, like Rousseau's fable describes the origin of inequality. The exchange of salt for grain was fundamental to economic life throughout the Himalaya.

※

Rai mythology gives an account of the Rai peoples which, read in a certain way, probably contains traces of an authentic record. The mythology also maps the stories onto real places in the landscape. So the stories are a social history, and a religious tradition, and a cultural vision of the terrain. They make the environment into a mirror of the moral world. They're an ecological ideology. They memorialise the victory of culture over wildness.

The stories begin when the world was only snake-infested water, on which a film formed like the skin on milk, which became the earth.[23] A stem grew from the earth, and some kind of worm or insect germinated in a knot in the stem. This creature was called Namprengma. She couldn't find a husband so she opened her legs to the wind and became pregnant with Miyapma. When Miyapma was grown up she also called out to the wind, but Namprengma was still around to prevent her from making a horrible religious error. 'What are you doing? The wind is your father!' Miyapma looked up and she saw Venus, but Venus didn't answer. She sent a bird to Venus, but by the time it arrived in heaven Jupiter had taken that handsome planet's place on the ecliptic, so he received Miyapma's message by mistake. Jupiter is leprous, with a goitre, and self-conscious about his looks, but he reluctantly accepted Miyapma's proposition. When he reached the earth she was appalled. Summoning her courage, she rejected the repulsive god. Jupiter was gravely offended and he inflicted a drought upon the earth, leaving fluid in just one place: some semen on a leaf.

Eventually, the very thirsty Miyapma drank the liquid.

She began to feel unusual. She was pregnant. In due course she gave birth to the different species: the thorny jungle creeper, tiger, bear, monkey, deer, wild boar, and the first man, Mini. So humankind was descended from the wrong god. 'How happy and long-lived we humans could have been if only Venus had come down,' said one of the informants who gave this story to an anthropologist.[24] 'What a splendid race humanity would have been!'

Evil was introduced to the world when Tiger ate Miyapma, his own mother.

Mini had two daughters, who were hornbills, and a son named Khakcilik. The sisters flew away to be the hornbill species of the upper and lower jungle, and Khakcilik spent his days fishing and living in a cave. One day he trapped a bird and discarded the seeds from its entrails, not knowing what they were. To his astonishment they grew. It was the beginning of agriculture. On another day he went fishing, but every time he cast his net it came back without fish. Instead he caught the same pebble on every cast, and threw it back each time. Eventually, Khakcilik took the pebble home and forgot about it. In the days that followed someone kept tidying his cave while he was out, and also cooked his food. The pebble had turned into a woman. Khakcilik laid in wait and grabbed her, and although she was angry with him, and covered with bruises from being thrown in the river, she became his wife. Her name was Wayelungma.

The institution of marriage was inaugurated by Wayelungma and Khakcilik, and they received the first wedding gifts from the hornbills. They had a son, and became the first happy family. Then they built the first house, but just as they were placing the central post in its hole the baby slipped from its sling on Wayelungma's back and was crushed to death in the foundation. A human sacrifice at the beginning of civilisation has equivalents in other mythologies, such as the killing of Remus at the founding of Rome. A similar idea appears in Ted Hughes's poem 'Fidelity':

I laid them
Under the threshold of our unlikely future
As those who wanted protection for a new home
Used to bury, Under the threshold,
A sinless child.

The couple somehow managed to carry on with their lives. They opened a patch in the jungle to plant their crops. In other words, they invented swidden agriculture, in which fire was used to clear some land to cultivate, until its fertility was exhausted in about three years – at which point the people moved on. Wayelungma and Khakcilik accomplished the Neolithic revolution together.

When this mode of living began here is anyone's guess. Most scholars seem happy to assume it's been a couple of thousand years at least, but the evidence is limited.[25] A study of pollen preserved in lakebed sediments at a site southeast of Mount Manaslu, in central Nepal, found that between 8,000 and 6,000 years ago people began managing vegetation with fire, but it's not known who they were, or even that they were involved in agriculture.[26] Whenever it started, swidden agriculture was probably the principal method of cultivation in the eastern hills until a couple of centuries ago, practised alongside foraging, hunting, and pastoralism. Swidden needs a lot of space, because after a patch of land has been used it will not be ready to cultivate again for many years. The system was still going strong when Joseph Hooker visited in the 1840s. It was practised, to some extent at least, until the twentieth century, when it was made illegal. Even today one sometimes comes into a newly made forest clearing around a hut of bamboo mats.

In the tradition, then, agriculture had been going on for a while by the time of Wayelungma and Khakcilik's grandson, who was named Khar. Nevertheless, he was the first man to do fertility rites in honour of the god of the fields. His son, Tunilu, was the first person to die. Human beings didn't know how to die until a lizard taught the trick to Tunilu.[27] Just like a snake can slough off its skin, a person can shed its body. This discovery created the need for funerary rites, to drive the souls of the dead out of the village to the land of the ancestors.

So far everything was taking place somewhere near Barahakshetra, where the Koshi enters the plains. (Rai mythology is unaware of the ocean – beyond Barahakshetra the waters are supposed to flow into the ground.) Tunilu's son led his people north, up the river and into the hills, where they still live. Various innovations came later, such as the salt trade already mentioned. The local geography was sanctified and socialised, as I'll describe shortly. The story ends by naming the members of successive generations, up to those who are currently still living.

※

Many of the indigenous people of the hills have a comparable origin story, which begins with a mythic past and describes how the facts of the environment and social life came to be. At some stage there's a migration to the place where the modern community is concentrated. The significant and powerful places of the landscape are chartered, and finally the generations are listed up (or down?) to the present day. There's an obvious comparison to the Hebrew Bible, in which a charter myth is compressed into a few generations, from the creation of the world to the settlement of the land, and framed as a family drama. Instead of Tinulu's son, Abraham and Moses lead the migrants into the land they revere. The tradition establishes the identity of a people and their relationship to a place.

In the central Himalaya these stories usually describe a migration from the north, where the linguistic and genetic evidence shows the ancestors of today's largest indigenous groups – Limbus, Rais, Tamangs, Gurungs, and Magars – once came from. In all of these traditions, when someone dies a shaman performs a ritual in which they accompany the soul on a verbal journey, or recitation of places, from the hearth of the home where the ritual is performed back along the route of the ancient migration, to the land of the ancestors. Shamans make similar journeys when a person falls ill and their soul needs to be recovered from a malevolent spirit.

The soul-searching songs of the Northern Magar, in western Nepal, are geographically exact, listing villages, river crossings, rest places, and landmarks that the shaman mentally passes by.[28] Also in western Nepal, the Gurung song or legend, which is called the Pye, describes an upland route hardly travelled now, through the ruined village of Khola. The route joins the modern

Annapurna Circuit trekking route for a while, reaching the inner Himalayan desert of Mustang, then goes onwards – back in time – into Tibet. Shamans aren't known to have bodily travelled this way in recent centuries, until an initiative in the 1990s when they invited archaeologists from Cambridge University to join them. That research broadly validated the Pye as evidence of an ancient migration.[29] The project reflects how politically salient these traditions have become in recent decades, as indigenous groups attempt to assert their political rights by arguing that they were here first.[30]

Tamangs, who are concentrated in central Nepal, also have a similar tradition. When the Tamang shaman, who is called a bonbo, makes his imaginary ascent via the holy lakes at Gosainkund en route to Tibet, Tamangs use the same verb to describe his journey as they use to describe a soaring bird of prey. While his spirit flies across the mountains to the land of the ancestors, his body remains by the hearthstones of his client's house.

It's noteworthy that although Rai languages are also Tibeto-Burman, and their ultimate origin is clearly to the north, some Rai shamans escort the souls of the dead along a mythical ancestral route that leads south, down the river to where it enters the plains at Barahakshetra. This has led some scholars to speculate that their ancient ancestors may have left Tibet further to the east and passed through parts of modern India before re-entering the hills. The shamanic journeys are taken as valuable evidence of the ancient migrations because there's no other verbal record of these peoples before modern times except their languages themselves. But the traditions can't reveal when the migrations took place.

Just as the Neolithic revolution was not accomplished in a single step, real migrations are usually a protracted process, not a single group movement. When a comparison with other evidence is possible, it shows how complicated the reality is. A study of river names has revealed a linguistic stratigraphy created by successive residents, who sometimes added their own word meaning 'water' or 'river' to an existing river name.[31] So, for instance, the Daron-di Khola's name means Daron River

River and Yan-guwa Khola is Yan River River in the languages of successive peoples. (The last layer, khola, is Nepali.) This data suggests that over a long period linguistic groups have drifted from west to east. Other linguistic studies claim that in about the fourth century AD the populations that are now called Gurung and Tamang were still a single group.[32] In fact, one of the pitfalls of this issue is to assume that today's ethnic groups have always been meaningful categories. For much of the past in these hills the idea of clans might better describe how people were organised, and ethnic identities were sometimes firmed up only recently by people such as British Gurkha officers, anthropologists, and Nepali bureaucrats, who gave members of some communities their last names only after the 1950s.

Many of the people we saw trekking up to Salpa had smartphones. In the morning, at the Phedi Hotel, Rajendra found that his charger and battery pack were missing. Some kids who'd also stayed the night had already gone.

At about eight-thirty we began to climb the immense sixty- or seventy-degree slope that disappeared into the cloud above us. The path was a perpetual staircase of roughly laid stones. Every step was a step upwards. It was like spending the day climbing Manhattan towers by the fire escape. Among those going up, usually some way behind, was a handsome man with one leg missing below the knee. He travelled by hopping from stone to stone, using a bamboo cane for balance, playing folk music on his phone. He reminded me of all the one-armed Maoists I used to see during the civil war. What happened to those guys? You don't see them around anymore.

Our loose group reached the cloud level and looked down on what we'd looked up at the day before. The trees were holly and alder, and other plants were growing on them: ferns and orchids.

There was a Sherpa village here, with bamboo houses and a tin-roofed monastery. There was folk music on a radio, and there were prayer flags in the breeze. Beside the houses were small fields of wheat, where women were clipping the seed heads from the stalks and dropping them in their baskets. Here, and at every home where we asked for water along the way, Rajendra invited the unmarried daughters to join him on the trail, and claimed that this district has the prettiest women, so maintaining good spirits and making people laugh.

We were pleasantly enveloped in cool cloud. All the plants had small leaves now. The oaks were of a smaller-leafed variety than in the valley, with moss and lichen nearly covering their trunks. There were small-leafed thorny bushes and small-leafed rhododendron, but the forest was denuded by grazing. Only the plants that cattle don't eat were thriving. We climbed along and up the ridge into a higher storey of the cloud forest, where the holly, oak, and larger rhododendrons were fully clothed in other plants. I saw shrubs I recognised from my grandmother's austere Northumbrian garden, which were presumably selected for Britain by a nineteenth-century plant hunter, such as Joseph Hooker, for their adaption to wet and sometimes cold places. Some of the people who were going up had a bamboo cylinder strapped to their backpacks, which contained milk, and they carried sprigs of leaves, and pigeons in baskets, and tridents and bells. A group came out of the cloud ahead of us, beating a drum and a tin plate. A shaman had feathers in his headdress, which he said came from five birds. One was a peacock, obviously. Some looked like the white-banded flight feathers of an eagle. Others like the lustrous, dark tail feathers of a cock.

We emerged from the forest into upland pasture, with clouds above and below, and a view of how much further we had to climb. The single building there was a smoky shop where we bought noodle soup. Rajendra complained about the theft of his charger and power bank. 'I was going to dance and take selfies at the festival,' he said. 'Have three boys and a girl come this way?'

'They won't get good dharma at the festival, such sinners,' said the woman of the place.

After eating we walked through juniper, which people were collecting to burn as incense. Then we entered a rhododendron forest, where the different species had different structures. Some multiplied branches from the base to make a bush, or they had a great trunk you couldn't get your arms around rising into a classical tree. There were swathes of towering, slender, slightly twisting trunks. Small branches sprang from the top to hold a canopy over a tract of naked, crazy poles. Then we came to the mighty Himalayan firs, spreading handsome branches like cedars. Finally, there was just grass and crags, before we reached the cloud-wrapped chorten on the pass. Cow bells pealed in the mist below. We'd climbed about two and a half vertical kilometres in six hours, I reckoned. There were other people also resting at the top whom we'd met the day before. Rajendra asked if they'd seen the four thieves. 'People like that won't get good dharma,' an old woman said.

※

In the shamanic religions of the central Himalaya, which are sometimes called animist, any natural feature, at least potentially, has a spirit in it, with its own intentions and the capacity to take action in the world. In particular, the forest is home to a host of frightening powers. They vary between groups, but similar creatures or spirits are common to many – such as the banjhankri, which simply means forest shaman. Among the Kulung Rai her name is Laladum, and she's a naked, dishevelled ten- or twelve- year-old with backward-pointing feet, who lives in the wildest, most inaccessible parts of the jungle. She has a rhyming, singsong voice, and she's very dangerous. It's she who calls human shamans to their vocation, and only they can deal with her.[33]

In the forests near where Tamangs live there's a creature called Nyalmo, whose breasts are so big they can trip her, so you can escape from Nyalmo by running downhill.[34] (When I was in the Canadian Rockies, I was told that this is also a way you can try to escape from a bear.)

Another reckoning has six or seven banjhankris in the Himalayan forest, plus seven banko burheni (old women of the forest). They are Lahti Burheni, who causes deafness, muteness and blindness, and lives in hot and cold places; her accomplice Kali Burheni, who lives in mountain forests; Seti Burheni, who pulls on people's nerves; Chamki Burheni, who pulls on people's eyelids and hair, and who walks in flat areas, sandy places, and bamboo thickets; and Khut Khatti Burheni, who leaves footprints like a hen's. People who follow her tracks go crazy and die. Thanne Burheni has dirty clothes and causes headaches, coughing, and flu. Finally, Phurlun Burheni bothers people while they are eating by causing sneezing and yawning, which doesn't sound that bad – except her attacks are always followed by the other six.[35]

Besides this lot, and others, the forest is crowded with the ghosts of those who died as suckling babies, by violence, in accidents, or in childbirth. In the larger scheme of things, the forest is apart from the human world of ordinary living people, of the village and the fields. It's wild, it's dangerous, it's antisocial. It's primordial. The village came from the forest when culture and agriculture grew out of the hostile wildness. But the forest is still a place you have to go for firewood and fodder, and to collect other useful things. It's also the place for hunting. So a hunter might appeal to 'the lady of the forest' or 'the lady of game animals' for protection before he sets out.[36]

※

Before I set off on this walk I met up with a friend called Dinesh in Kathmandu. He's a filmmaker who's been recording shamans at work for years. Dinesh described the current state of the profession, and how people (who are usually men or boys) discover their shamanic vocation. 'It's like a mental thing,' he said. 'You become weird, I suppose. The spirit enters you. You start shaking and all that stuff.' (This is called a psychological crisis in the literature, which is endured by many shamans in their youth.) 'The knowledgeable shamans are all dying out,' he said. 'There used to be a guy in Dholaka. His name was Dhabake. That's a nickname. Dhabake Thami. I met his younger brother, who was also very old, and he was also a good shaman, "but," he said, "I'm nothing like my brother was." He said, "My brother had one finger. One finger on each hand." That's because they have this spirit which they conjure with. It's called Bir Masan, and apparently you can make it do things for you. And this guy used to – the term is play – he used to play with the spirit. But the thing is, it demands something of you. It demands blood. Or it demands your child. Or your wife. So to appease it, he used to cut off a finger and give it that. What do you call that? Do you call it mentally unstable?

'This was many years ago,' he continued. 'I'm not sure. Maybe he just had a couple of fingers missing. He kept chopping his fingers off, anyway. There were some fantastic old shamans! They're all dead now. And some of the stuff I saw them doing was quite amazing, you know. It's hard to describe, but you get the feeling, this awe, that maybe there's something to it.

'All over, from west Nepal to Sikkim,' he continued, 'there's a jhankri called Banjhankri. He's this high,' he said, gesturing a dwarfish height, 'and he just abducts you. If you're a person who can be a shaman, you get abducted by him. And you're taken to wherever. And you're given this training. You're tortured a bit.' (He used an airy tone, as if describing what you have to go through to get a driver's licence.) 'His wife, who is a witch, tries to kill you …' (as if he was saying, 'and then they make you wait all morning …'). 'Something like that. And after that, you're returned to wherever you were taken from. There are quite a few of these abduction cases, you know. It's hard. People won't believe it …'

I said, 'And that's how you become a shaman?'

'That's one way. The other way of course is to take a guru. Some are born into it. Some learn it.'

'So why's it going out of fashion?'

He might have answered by observing that the social relevance of the forest and the landscape is changing. Like for the Majhi, perhaps, the old activities are losing their meaning. He went at it like this. 'One thing is that it's ridiculed. Shamans have a very bad name, in a way. You hear cases of people being accused of being witches and made to eat shit and all that stuff. Things like that have given these old shamans a bad name. And it becomes embarrassing for the kids. I mean, they're all hanging around in school. Before, a shaman was a respected member of the village. Not anymore. It just seems a bit of a ridiculous thing to do, apparently, these days. So not many young people are taking it up, even though they have the capacity.

'They say that some people become shamans naturally, and you can't put it off. If you try to put it off, it's not good for you. There are cases I know of kids who undertake rituals to get rid of it [their shamanic vocation]. Another thing is that, these days, people trust medicine more. They go to shamans mainly for things that are mental. Also for bodily ailments, but especially when someone's acting weird. When people think "some spirit has got to this guy". Or if someone is suffering from something for a long time. Then they think, "a spirit's got this guy".'

I read in an anthropology book, explaining the shaman's role as a psychopomp and exorcist, that death shakes a person's mind and profoundly transforms his or her outlook and character.[37] According to another writer, properly integrated ancestors are a force for good. But a good portion of mankind's woes are attributable to the spirits of the dead.[38] They weigh like a nightmare on the brains of the living. So the shaman confronts the just-died with their condition, then escorts them reluctantly from the village to the land of the ancestors. And when things go wrong, he searches for the culprit. He invokes the support of as many nearby divinities – or, in other words, places – as possible, then he sets off to return the soul of the suffering person to the world of health.

Salpa Pokhari is a holy lake that's not particularly big. It's just a dimple on the ridge, with some shrines on the shore and a new stone wall around it. But when it's in the mist, and perhaps at other times, it has an enchanted feeling. With no sky or anything else reflected in it, the lake looked like a gap in the world. Devotees were making offerings, and groups of people were dancing around shamans. The shamans were coming and going, beating a drum with a barking deer's antler, for instance.

This landform is the first real rampart of the Everest country. The famous mountain is not very far away to the north. Coniferous trees were profiled on the misty crags like in a Chinese painting. The ridgetop itself was a massive boulder heap. There were rocks the size of houses, which looked as if they'd fallen there from somewhere, although there was no mountain above for miles around.

The theology of Salpa involves a mythic king and queen, who are deemed to be present in the water in the form of serpents. People make offerings to the raja and the rani in the lake for the success of their crops, and also for personal problems such as conceiving children or overcoming other hardships. I heard different versions of the story, which I wasn't able to fully understand.[39]

After telling it people would say things like, 'I'm not sure if that's quite right, but it's what I heard.' Or, more confidently: 'That's what the history says. The stories and the ancestors say so.'

There was a committee responsible for organising the festival. I met some of its members drinking tea under a shelter of branches and leaves, avoiding the rain.

'What's the meaning? The king, the queen, tell me everything,' I said.

'I don't know if my story corresponds with the committee's here,' the first man volunteered. 'As far as I've heard …'

'We realised that there is some truth in the stories of the old people,' another committee member said, 'when we tried to build a wall three times, and each time the stones fell in the lake. Either god or ghost, whatever is there, it does exist.'

Another man said that whenever anyone comes here in a helicopter there is a hailstorm and everything is destroyed. But once the helicopter leaves the sun comes out again.

Rajendra, who was still upset about his phone charger and power bank, said, 'Today's the festival, and most people are here out of belief. But there are some rotten apples. I'm sorry, it's not a nice thing to say, but I have to say it. That's why the gods do this on this day.' He was referring to the drab weather.

'You're absolutely right,' someone said. 'The entire world is changing.'

'I think maybe there's some truth in the stories,' someone reflected.

'Not maybe. There is truth. We have our belief,' Rajendra insisted.

Notwithstanding the changed times, and – as most people agreed – the smaller crowd, this fair now takes place more often than before. People are gathering at Salpa on most of the full moons of the year. 'Before, we used to come here for two days. Now the festival is about to go on for five,' said a committee member. 'It's been very difficult for us to manage.'

'We have to make Sir dance.'

'I don't know how to dance,' I said.

'You can just do what the others are doing.'

✳

It was a wet day. I spent hours talking with a man who spoke English, who'd spent many years as a worker in the Middle East.

A girl in his village had disappeared for a week, kidnapped by the banjhankri. Since coming back, she's had a remarkable eloquence and the ability to read and write. Her father is a migrant labourer in Malaysia, only her mother is at home, and the girl also stayed at home to feed the animals, so she had little chance of learning. This man was sceptical but curious about the banjhankri, and he went on to compare the phenomenon, by association at least in the stream of his conversation, to incidents of hysteria in factories and schools, which he said sometimes occur around the world.

'Tonight,' he remarked, 'there'll be some fights at this festival.'

All day more groups arrived, dancing around a shaman, singing 'Saya raja saye saye, Saye rani saye saye'. We sat on the dry hay drinking tea in one shelter after another. And as Rajendra retold the story of why he couldn't take any selfies, he became increasingly convinced that it was not the other guests but the hospitable women of the inn themselves who had stolen his power bank and charger.

He interrogated some shamans for me. 'Is he the main shaman, or are you?' he asked. 'What is this puja about? How is it done? Let's talk about the past. What gods spent the night here? What do we get by worshipping them? He's a journalist, I'm here to ask questions. Doing this pilgrimage makes your wishes come true, is it true or not?'

And the shamans said the kinds of things a scrupulous holy man should say. 'It's your belief. It comes from the heart. We have to work for what we want ourselves, and only then will it happen.'

'How many feathers are there in your headgear?'

'These are porcupine quills,' said the shaman. 'This is our old tradition. We also wear rooster feathers, peacock feathers, and pheasant. This is a bunch of orchids. We call this todom or tonkamma or sirip. These are called wossa.'

'What are those around your neck?' asked Rajendra.

'This is a rudraksha mala worn by Shiva,' the shaman said, indicating a garland of the sacred seeds. 'This is a snake's kaara,' indicating a 4-foot bandolier of vertebrae.

'Did you kill the snake?' asked Rajendra.

'Of course I had to kill the snake,' said the shaman.

'If the snake weren't dead it would have bitten me,' said a woman, who was presumably his wife.

I didn't stick around for the fights in the evening. It was cold and wet. A twenty-minute walk along the ridge was the place where we were staying. I sat by the fire in the kitchen and drank raksi with the people there. I looked out and saw the full moon in a clear patch of sky, above it the repulsive planet Jupiter. I went to bed. The room where we'd been shown to sleep had been empty the night before. Now it had people laid out in every space, and in the corner a scenic group of shamans was chanting around flickering lamps. I laid down. The chanting ended. By stages the room slept. At some point in the night someone pulled my blanket off, explaining that there weren't enough, and since I had a thin sleeping bag and was wearing all my clothes, I didn't mind. But I was annoyed when a kid woke me with a torch in my face and asked to share my sleeping bag.

By six-thirty in the morning we were ready to go, and went to pay a polite visit to the monk from the committee whose home was the only other building on the ridge. We found him in his smoky bamboo kitchen, feeding cooked rice from his mouth to pigeon chicks. He picked each ugly, scrawny thing from a basket, stuck its beak between his lips, then dropped it on the floor. He insisted on giving us raksi before our walk. Against my urging, his wife melted some ghee in a tin jug on the fire. She burnt some Nescafé in the bubbling fat. Then, egged on by Rajendra, to my annoyance, she filled it up with a bottleful of moonshine. The old monk had worked for four years as a cleaner and filing assistant at a hospital in Saudi. Every time I sipped the cocktail he topped it up solicitously. 'We feel bad about your power bank, but we'll look out for it,' he told Rajendra.

So we set off a bit before eight, down a laboriously made staircase of stone chunks, through the moss-strewn forest beside a crystal stream. It ran over boulders and through gravelly pools. Rajendra was pissed out of his head, stumbling about, shouting, singing, and talking nonsense to everyone. All the Kulung kids heading down were running past us on the steep sections. I was glad to keep pace with them as the path levelled out and leave Rajendra far behind. I was pleasantly drunk and the day was beautiful.

At dawn the view had cleared. The clouds were arrayed in high stripes and layers, so the ocean of hills to the south could all be seen, and to the north a snowy ridge was revealed. We were descending in that direction into a huge, forested valley where patches had been cleared for terraced fields. As the valley deepened immensely the path stayed high, so I had a view of the opening landscape and an easy walk. It was a different-feeling world from the other side of Salpa. There were Sherpa villages, with monasteries. After some time there were great amphitheatres of terraces below us, and then the first Kulung village. Our surroundings became a seemingly long-settled, carefully handmade landscape. In fact its current appearance, of terracing and permanent agriculture, might be just a couple of hundred years old. Dry stone walls retained the terrace banks. Water was provided beside the path by mossy conduit stones. A shaman's small procession, with drum, emerged from the forest above us and wound around the edge of the potato, maize, and cardamom fields.

Eventually, we descended into a hideous chasm, which I hadn't realised lay even further beneath the valley. The Hongu River charged blue and white at the bottom, in a gorge of maple trees that were draped with moss and orchids, drenched in the river's spray. It was a micro-climate, a cloud forest sustained by the foaming water. When we climbed out we fell in step with a student. Rajendra, as usual, asked him his caste. 'Are you a Brahmin?'

'No,' said the boy. 'A Dalit.'

That shut Rajendra up, because there's no good way to make light of it. Then we reached Cheskam, which was the first village founded by the ancestors in the Kulung Rai mythology. As night fell we could hear a shaman drumming in one of the houses.

That evening we witnessed the fight the festival didn't provide. The house opposite where we were staying had a shop on the ground floor, where men were sitting on a bench clinking bottles of beer. One was shoving and slapping another, once even standing up to punch him in the face, although he didn't get a good connection. Two children were watching from outside. All the time more beer was opened and clinked. The target sat there, not raising a hand, weeping and pleading his case. They were an uncle and his nephew. The issue was money, and although the dispute was mostly in Kulung I could understand the uncle when he said 'mother fucker' in Nepali.

My own money was nearly finished, so it was time to go as quickly as we could. The last long walk was down the Hongu Valley. Sometimes the path was routed for maximum efficiency across the fields by making use of boulders too large to be removed, forming a burnished strand across the rocks. Where it tracked the field boundaries the path was paved with flat slabs, and also edged with slabs arranged upright. Everywhere we were accompanied by the sight or sound of clear water burbling in the irrigation channels. Whole hillsides were carved in a neat and tidy monumental system of terraces. The terraces were supported by choice trees. The trees had been sculpted into weird shapes by fodder-cutting. It was a lovely sunny day.

We climbed or crossed fresh landslides, and at last we descended to the Dudhkoshi, which drains the southern side of Everest. The Dudhkoshi's name means Milk River, because it is white with mica from the Everest granite. There was a long, swaying bridge high above the water, then a 1,000-metre slog straight up the face of the next hill. On the way up we met four Hindu sadhus dozing in the shade. They were travelling from another festival to Salpa, where they planned to light a hundred thousand lamps, after which they'd carry on. They weren't friendly so we didn't stop. When I stepped onto the ridge after an hour and a half, every stitch on me was drenched with sweat and blood was thumping in my ears.

The idea was that we'd get some kind of vehicle on from there, but the news was that the road was broken. Overhead there was steady helicopter traffic to and from Mount Everest, where it was the climbing season.

We arranged a lift on an open tractor. We were getting shaken around all over the place, perched on the wheel arch, holding on tight above the dreadful big back tire. It grew misty, then it started to rain. Then it got dark. 'What the hell am I doing,' I thought, 'I've got kids.' In the forest we encountered three men running alongside and driving up behind us on a motorbike. 'Go, go, go!' yelled Rajendra, and the driver took off up the hill, making me think I'd be shaken under. We rushed along the awful track, on the edge of the steep slope, around bends, weaving to block our pursuers, the one working headlight hopelessly misdirected. But how could we outrace a motorbike? And why would getting robbed be worse than dying in a tractor crash? Wouldn't the kind of people who rob the kind of people who travel by tractor at night be quite easily satisfied? They only wanted to get past. Eventually they managed to, and, swearing at us, disappeared into the night.

In these circumstances it was a relief after three hours, as the drizzle turned to rain again, to reach a darkened bazaar. There was light beneath a door, so we hammered on it. The door was opened by a woman who made me think of the song 'Shelter from the Storm'. We were admitted to a welcoming, smoke-blackened room to drink raksi by the fire. The eastern journey ended there. The next day, by jeep, we were back in Kathmandu.

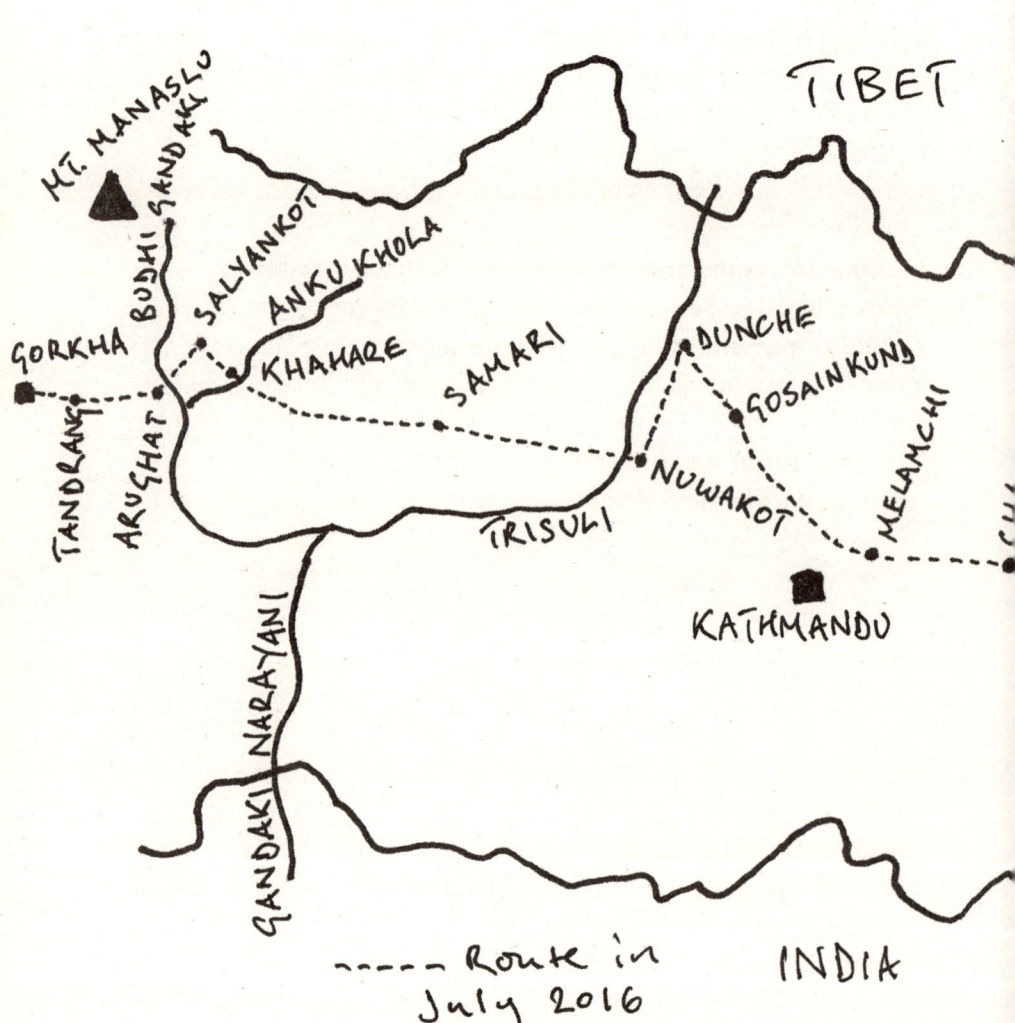

PART 2

Agriculture

'Tribes are, in the first instance, an administrative fiction of the state; tribes begin where states end. The antonym for 'tribe' is 'peasant': that is, a state subject.'

James Scott

'[It is a] truism that in any society, systems of land tenure develop within the framework of its political philosophy ... The concept of property rights in the land, divorced from the requirements of personal use, emerges only through sovereign powers of government and is based on law and documentary evidence.'

Mahesh Chandra Regmi

Two months later, in the monsoon, I took a bus from Kathmandu to a small town called Chautara. The place had been ruined by the earthquake, which ran through the fault right under it the previous year. Most of the debris had been cleared from the bazaar, but the old stone shops were tin sheds now. Some of the neighbouring fields were still occupied by tented aid projects, which had arrays of solar panels outside, and all the surviving hotels were full of people working on the aftermath.

This time I was accompanied by a friend called Girish, who's a journalist in Kathmandu. Even on the short walk into town, Girish and I ran into two people we'd known in their previous jobs, before they became involved in the recovery. One of them, Sachin, offered to gather the local reporters to put us in the picture. So while we waited for a solution to the problem of where to stay, we had tea with Sachin and the journalists. And although the earthquake was more than a year old by then, they talked first about the violence of the original disaster.

Sachin had been hired by the health ministry to monitor the organisations responding to the earthquake, and his education was as a medical anthropologist. The journalists represented national daily papers. 'People don't know, many people. They don't know where to go for medical attention,' Sachin said. 'People were rescued three days, four days, five days later.' And the horror of the information he wanted to share was amplified by his manner of speaking, from under hooded eyes, hardly moving any part of his body except his lips. 'They were taken and amputated. Steel rods were inserted. It's a small district,' he said. 'People were rescued after six days. For six days people remained with bleeding hands, blood dripping from their veins.'

Later he took us to a rehabilitation centre run by an international organisation, which he praised. 'When you look at some specific cases, yes, they have been careless,' he said, 'but overall they've done a good job.' There were still a dozen patients left, learning to walk again, and one person whose arm was severed by a falling rock that hit him on the elbow. 'Right on the elbow!' the two young women working there exclaimed, as if in wonder at the chance that nipped his arm off so well.

'The other interesting thing is this,' Sachin said. 'You're researching landscape. If this is a hill' – he formed it with his hands – 'and the hill is curved, then the houses inside the curve have not been destroyed so much. It's quite surprising. In a lot of places I've seen that. In Ghumthang, Thulo Dhading, even Pantang. Then Boldu has been damaged, but Manthang is all right. Some villages, whole villages, have collapsed, and in some nothing has happened.' On they talked, Sachin and the three reporters, debating Sachin's observation. 'Did you go to Yangla?'

'No.'

'That whole village, they can't even complete the excavation with the money handed down by the government.'

'It was a beautiful Tamang village.' *Was*, they emphasised. *Used to be*. All gone now. The conversation took in the loss of traditional architecture. 'Before,' they said, 'you could tell a village by its face. Now all that's obliterated, and it won't be coming back.' They meant you could tell the caste or ethnicity of the people by the style of their houses. But in the future looking at a village would tell you nothing about the traditions of its people.

The next morning Girish and I began our walk. In the spring I tried to give an impression of some indigenous groups' environmental traditions. In the rain I'll try to show how the same land made a state. Our route would take us along old thoroughfares to the royal fortress at Gorkha. It also happened to be the earthquake's route, back along the fault to the epicentre.

It was an easy track on the first day, following the shapes of the hills, which were broad and gentle by Nepali standards. A blanket of cloud lay above all but the highest ridge-points. It didn't rain on us, but sometimes the view disappeared as it rained nearby. Depending on whether a field was irrigated by a stream or rain-fed, the rice was ripening on the terraces, or it was still just seedlings in the mud, or it was being transplanted as we passed. And women were also planting millet between the standing maize.

Every village we passed had been transformed into a tin shanty. Bougainvillea that once beautified cottages grew outside buildings that had disappeared. The stones the old homes were made from had been neatly stacked beside the tin shacks. The tin sheets, which were distributed to survivors after the disaster, were now doing service in a second monsoon. There was no rebuilding going on, but we saw people wearing T-shirts with the United Nations Development Programme logo and the English slogan 'Building Back Better', and we saw posters showing approved rebuilding techniques. We stopped to talk to people and Girish recorded their accounts on his phone – of the loss of their daughters, or how the promised reconstruction grants weren't enough.

In an earthquake the ground is revealed for what it really is, which is mobile and unstable, and that destroys people's basic belief that the earth itself is a guarantee of continuity. A couple of months after our walk researchers found that 36 per cent of people in this district were suffering from psychological trauma, which was manifested for example by sometimes being startled while sleeping.[1] Even those whose home was not destroyed had been too afraid to move back inside for months, or even a year after the disaster.

There were houses without facades and facades without houses. The earth had cracked open. Water sources had dried up. Fields were rendered useless, and whole hillsides unsafe. Farming suffered. 'We are eating stones and earth,' someone told us. But after a hiatus the bureaucracy had reasserted itself. In one village we passed a crowd of people who were preparing their land papers to apply for the rebuilding grants which were finally being rolled out.

At the end of the day we descended into a town called Melamchi Bazaar on the bank of the Melamchi River, which was thundering under the bridge in spate, and checked into a hotel. It had rained heavily in the previous few days. In Kathmandu a school had collapsed, killing two children. On the television in the restaurant of our hotel, a landslide in Gorkha had just killed three people. The woman in the hotel said the area where we were going was badly affected, too. Girish and I exchanged screwed-up faces. Neither of us had much appetite for risk.

There was a major engineering project at Melamchi that had been going on for decades, to divert part of the river by a tunnel through a hill and relieve Kathmandu's chronic drinking-water shortage.[2] The following morning we took a short bus ride to one of the tunnelling sites, at the end of the access road the engineers had made, in the direction we were heading.

The passengers greeted one another cheerfully using familial terms. 'Hey, sister-in-law, where have you been?' The folk songs which jangled from the bus's speakers were about travel.

'Cross the Bhuje pass. Come, let's go see Nuwakot!' the singer sang. Or:

As a driver, I drive my bus.
And my love awaits,
Her tear-filled eyes resting on the road
Under the Laukri tree.

We soon reached the tunnelling works and climbed out among piles of debris, huge machines, and fascinating holes in the mountain. It was then that I realised I'd left my camera on the

hotel bed. I could make arrangements to get it back, but for the rest of the journey I'd have to use this other thing I'd brought, which is more or less a toy with a plastic lens. It was loaded with the same type of film, but of a different size and shape. It's an equally objective machine, in a less accurate, more inflexible way, and the pictures it takes don't look very similar to the ones from the camera I'd left behind.

We stepped into a tin-shack kitchen and found a small, cheerful crowd speaking Tamang. We ate our lunch, then set off up a narrow valley that was reminiscent of the way to Salpaphedi. After a while we each settled into our own walking pace.

It was a steep dirt road, which was surely never passable to any vehicle except the digger that made it. It led through a forest with orchids and ferns growing from the trees, and clearings of terraced fields. Rivulets of rainwater gushed from the sides over cascades of platey gravel. There were landslides too, one with boulders as big as cars. At one place the hillside both above and below the track was freshly collapsed, and a slender path was pressed onto the loose debris. I emerged onto a low pass at the cloud base and sat down to wait for Girish. It was cool in damp clothes, but not unpleasant. I watched the cloud generating in front of me, appearing to blow upwards even as it kept remaking itself in the same place. Beyond was the ocean of valleys and hills, terraced, green, and abundant looking, the sun breaking through gorgeously in places, fading to blue in the distance.

※

There was a village on the pass in which every house had fallen down and only one had been rebuilt. It was a small hotel, which paid for itself, and smelt of paint, because the owner was preparing for the pilgrims who'd come this way in six weeks' time.

The way onwards, in the morning, was again by a useless, severely eroded road. I wondered whether these half-finished projects, which so often help the hills collapse, represent the faltering advance of social improvement, or are they mostly an accounting trick to extract resources through a fiction of tendering and construction?

The ridge that Girish and I climbed for the next couple of days is a major watershed. On the right, the Koshi River system drains all of eastern Nepal. On the left, the Gandaki system drains the centre. On that day the ridge also divided Nepal's mobile telephone duopoly. On the eastern side you could get Ncell, to the west NTC, but in most places there was no signal. There were lovely rivulets of clear water running over the ground, and cow bells in the mist. At the place where we had lunch, the couple who lived there had been foraging in the forest for mushrooms, which we ate.

We met more men gathering mushrooms in the afternoon. They showed us that when you break the fungi open inky stains appear on the yellow flesh, meaning they're the type you can eat, not the type that kills you. We rounded a corner with the mushroomers, and they stepped into an army post, where they charged me for my national park permit. We walked on into the cloud forest.

A deer hurried across the path in front of me. A gentle and persistent rain began. In a glade that was presumably created for grazing, or anyway made by people for some reason, the path was so overgrown with yellow flowers it was hard to pick out. And now it was pissing down. The rain felt like hail. It was more uncomfortable to walk in than to stand drenched beneath a tree. Girish found me there, and when he stopped he noticed that his boots were crawling with leeches. I looked around and saw the leeches converging across the rotting leaves. We hurried on. In half an hour we came to a welcoming inn in the forest, where a fire was burning, and I went straight to our room and took off all my clothes, searched myself, and put salt on the leeches.

According to our hostess, leeches only drink bad blood. 'We get so many all the time, but it does us no harm,' she said. The rain hammered down outside, lightened, and hammered down again.

A photo-calendar published by a political party was hanging on the wall. 'They come round here when there's an election,' the woman said, referring to politicians. 'The rest of the time, even if we want to bow to their feet we can't find them.'

As we sat there by the stove a pulse ran through the wooden house, which seemed to travel from north to south. It was another crust adjustment after the great earthquake. Outside, it rained and rained.

※

At dawn I climbed crags to a signposted viewing place. Handsome and picturesque conifers stood over the rocks, or clung to them. The mountain plunged beneath me to the south. Kathmandu was down there under a blanket of cloud. I phoned home, where my son had just gone to school, but my daughter still wasn't old enough and I described to her what I was seeing. The saw-toothed ridge of Gosainkund, which we can often see from our roof, was right above me. All the way to the east the main Himalayan range stood up almost unbelievably high, in spectacular silhouette below the pale sky, above banks and strands of cloud. The kids had wanted me to collect certain very specific gifts for them on this trip: 'an interesting stick' and 'a stone that looks like a fairy'. I promised again that I'd definitely find them.

The route up to Gosainkund by this ridge does not permit shortcuts or diversions but it still manages to be several routes. It's the way taken by Tamang shamans on their verbal journeys to the ancestral home in Tibet. It's a pilgrimage that Tamang villagers take every year, to the fair at the Gosainkund lakes on the full moon in the month of Shravan, which is usually in August. It's a pilgrimage that caste Hindus take each year, to the same place on the same day, for *their* festival celebrating Shiva. It's a trekking route taken by tourists like me and Girish. It's one of the ways that shepherds and herdsmen drive their animals from the winter valleys to the summer highlands, trying to keep the beasts ahead of the spreading leeches.

There are stones on the way that are said to have been marked by Padmasambhava, who's also known as Guru Rinpoche. He was an eighth-century Buddhist master from Swat, in modern Pakistan,

who introduced Buddhism to Tibet. He's supposed to have come this way, which is an ancient route through the mountains from India to Tibet via Kathmandu. The marks show, for instance, where Guru Rinpoche beheaded and ate the man-eating demons he encountered. The demons' remains writhe on as the leeches.[3]

We met a man named Pemba Dorje Sherpa, who was sitting on a rock by the path not far from his shelter. He was heading up the mountain with his thirty yak–cow cross-bred cattle. I asked him about a small shrine of stones I'd seen a little way down the track.

'That's the place of Guru Rinpoche,' he said.

'Oh really?'

'He gave blessings there, so that the population of the village would increase.'

It had been a few days since Pemba Dorje left his village. He would be one week in this camp before moving on, then he'd go further into the highlands on a journey that would last two or three months. Girish ran through the questions. Nine of Pemba Dorje's cattle were giving milk, which was enough to fill a copper vessel every day. He and his father made the milk into ghee, which they sold to the Tamangs, who ate it. He wasn't married yet. He'd been to Kathmandu five times, and he liked the *buildings* there (using the English word). His grandmother had a house on the edge of the city.

'Then why are you people staying over here, instead of going to Kathmandu?' Girish wanted to know.

'What to do?' replied Pemba Dorje. 'One has to work to earn money. All this hard work is for the money.'

Girish said, 'You might find work even in Kathmandu, if you work hard.'

'I didn't feel like going. I didn't find a job,' said Pemba Dorje. So here he was in the mountains, where there's not many people, just cows. Which he milked. He made ghee, earned money, cut firewood, cleaned the dung. Just that.

'Doesn't it make you feel bad?' asked Girish.

'No, it doesn't,' Pemba Dorje claimed. 'Father says, "this is our place". In the village I plough the fields, carry the loads, go to the places, attend the rituals,' he said.

'Do you ever go to the festival at Gosainkund?' I asked.

'One time I went,' Pemba Dorje answered. 'The shamans dance, the Brahmins and the Chhetris go there, the Sherpas and the Tamang people go …'

All that's well known, so I asked about something different. 'Do you hunt?'

'We do sometimes, when we feel the mood,' he said. 'If we feel like doing it, we do. We can find deer, boar.'

'With a gun?'

'Yeah.' He described a country-made muzzle-loader. 'We hide it, and whenever we feel like hunting we take it out. These days they catch people. There are CCTV cameras installed here.' Or anyway – there are CCTV cameras on the other side of the national park. Not in the mountains, where he goes.

We were approaching the area we'd been warned might be dangerous, where we should take advice on the state of the trail. 'There are big stones placed in absurd ways,' someone had told us.

'The path's the path,' Pemba Dorje said, realistically. 'Sometimes it's good. Sometimes it's not.'

✳

At the bleak homestead where we stopped for lunch the proprietor claimed there were a lot of landslides ahead. 'The local people are very strong,' he said. 'But you've lived in a city and you're a foreigner. You must be knowing it's the monsoon. If you slip and fall then you'll be dead.' Not only that, but all the places we could stay between here and Gosainkund were closed, so if things went bad there'd be no refuge. There was a solution, though. We could stay the night with him, and take his man as a guide in the morning. In that case there'd be absolutely nothing to worry about. As the rain lashed the kitchen after lunch this situation cast a pall across our frame of mind. The only good part was that he might just be trying to rip us off. That idea was strengthened by the high price he wanted for his guide. Late that night we went to bed in good spirits, after a boozy conversation about politics.

The weather was clear when we set off after six in the morning. The only clouds were below us. We had a view of the pass, and most of the long route to it. Our guide, the hotelier's man, had equipped himself with a litre of home brew, which he finished long before we reached the place of danger. Where we crossed a small stream he said that at this place, in this very month, even mentioning the date, a doctor from Kathmandu was swept away after a rainstorm. He was found far below, hanging by his leg from a tree, with the top of his head and all its contents gone. The locals were paid Rs 2 lakh to bring his body down to Helambu.

The landslide area wasn't actually very dicey at all. By the end of the morning we were at the tree line at the bottom of the pass, where our guide turned back. The clouds had closed and it was steadily raining when we started up through juniper scrub and stony meadows that were strewn with yellow primulas. Girish is a slow walker, and as the afternoon trudged on I began to entertain dramatic thoughts of what we should do if we were still on this hill when night fell. We had no equipment, hardly even any warm clothes. There were some herdsmen's shelters, which were sometimes visible from the path when the mist opened. For a while we sheltered in a ruined shed, where we took our wet shirts off and dried ourselves to feel warmer. When the rain eased we carried on, walking between boulders and aromatic dwarf rhododendron through thick, wet clouds. It was raining steadily again when, to my surprise, we reached the steepling heaps of stones that mark the top, and tramped on.

The first lake we came to, which is called Suryakund (Sun Lake), was eerie. The far shore was invisible in the cloud. Yet somehow the lake was reflecting, on the surface and even in its depths, a radiant, bottomless pale blue from the blank, white sky.

I was up here once before more than ten years earlier, in a blizzard, and it was otherworldly that time too. The sky, land, and air were all white, but the lakes were jet black like sheets of vinyl. It had seemed a completely colourless world, with holes in it.

The second lake, which we came to now, below us on the other side, was a richer blue than Suryakund. Then we reached Gosainkund itself, bigger and darker still, with prayer flags and other holy stuff where the water runs in at the southeast end. There was no one else around. We came to the ashrams, which were deserted. Then we came to the hotels, which were all locked up. We tried all the doors. We cupped our hands to squint in through the windows. The hotels were closed, which was something we hadn't expected.

✳

On one level – the deepest – Gosainkund is similar to other lakes in the mountains which are pilgrimage destinations and sites of shamanic ritual. Tamangs come here in a similar way as Rais go to Salpa, with the difference that their religion includes elements of Tibetan Buddhism that the Rai tradition doesn't. For them the Buddhist master Guru Rinpoche is present here, in addition to a shamanic pantheon.[4]

There's also a deep Hindu layer at Gosainkund. This tradition relates to a famous event when the gods churned an ocean of milk, which produced a poison that the great god Shiva drank to save the world. The poison turned his throat blue and, in central Nepal at least, it's believed that Gosainkund is the place where he struck a mountain with his trident and released water to quench his burning thirst. A Hindu pilgrimage to Gosainkund is first recorded in 1447, when a king from the Kathmandu Valley made an elaborate journey here.[5] This was a period when Kathmandu flourished as a prosperous cultural centre, based on trade with Tibet. It's significant that Gosainkund lies on the ridge above an important trade route. In fact, its modern name

Detail from 'Pilgrimage to Gosainkund', a 14-foot-long painting in the Philadelphia Museum of Art. Gosainkund lake is at the top right.

refers to a religious order, the Gosains, who were both holy men and merchants.[6]

There's a wonderful nineteenth-century painting, probably copied from an earlier original, which records the journey of a group of seven pilgrims, both women and men, from the Kathmandu Valley to Gosainkund.[7] It seems that the pilgrims may have commissioned the work when they got safely home. The scene, which is over 4 metres long, is partly a landscape panorama, with white mountains along the horizon. It's partly a narrative of their journey, even showing two of the women catching a third when she tripped. And it's also partly a map, with seventy-seven places marked and labelled. On the left (to the south) are the cities of the valley, with palaces and temples quite accurately drawn inside their walls. In the cities the houses are tiled, but in the countryside there are circular thatched huts. Serpentine rivers and paths coil across the canvas, passing by distinct species of flowers and trees. Among the other lordly pilgrims, porters, and merchants crowding the route, the seven subjects climb the steep paths like ladders, and then descend them like flights of stairs in the narrative method of a cartoon strip. There are naked Hindu babas sitting on tiger skins, and a Tibetan yogin in a cave guarded by a fierce dog. At Gosainkund there are throngs of devotees. The likeness of the recumbent god Shiva is visible beneath the water, and three springs gush into the lake where the prongs of his trident struck the rock.

This painting shows how Gosainkund was integrated, as a Hindu pilgrimage site, within the sacred landscape that the courtly Kathmandu Valley discovered around itself in its heyday.[8] Gosainkund is made into an outpost of that nearby urban culture, which I wrote about in another book. Water from here is said to flow by a long tunnel to a spring inside the valley, at a temple called Kumbheshwar. Hindus and Tamang shamans celebrate there on the same full moon that the festival happens up here, as a more convenient alternative for those who can't manage the journey. This idea – of water travelling long distances through an underground channel from a holy place in the landscape to another holy site, a temple – occurs at several places in Hindu South Asia, as a means for the one place to share the other's power.[9]

In Kathmandu I occasionally used to go to talk to a former foreign minister, a man who had a photograph in his sitting room of himself addressing the UN in New York. He told me once that this hydraulic tunnel from Gosainkund to Kumbheshwar (presumably a bit like the drinking water project from Melamchi) showed how advanced ancient Nepali engineering was. That was a very anachronistic point of view, because obviously the idea used to be that the connection between Gosainkund and the city is innate, not a human contrivance.

On the August full moon of 1973, a geographer named Harka Gurung came here with a friend. He joined the pilgrims bathing in the water, which was as cold as it looked. He was basking in the sun afterwards, watching boys scoop coins from the shallows, when a novel idea flashed through his mind.[10] If a keen numismatist, he wrote, could devise a better tool, or somehow dredge the lake, an archaeology of ancient coins might be recovered from Gosainkund. Kings came here to bathe after their coronations, so centuries of monetary offerings must lie on the bottom. When the sky is clear a massive pale slab can be seen in the blue depths (probably a piece of mica-gneiss, Dr Gurung supposed). It is identified as a self-made image of Shiva by Hindus, and as the bodhisattva Avalokiteswara by Buddhists.[11]

We didn't pause at Gosainkund any longer than it took to realise there was nothing there for us, and walked on to Lauribina, which thank God isn't far.[12] When we gratefully entered the warm lodge we found a group of foreign tourists in one corner, and on the other side of the room a young baba, or sadhu, a Hindu mendicant, a kind of wandering monk. He was regaling a pair of eager environmental science students from Kathmandu while packing his chillum.

A sadhu is someone who has renounced everything and devoted his, or occasionally her, life to a perpetual pilgrimage, or sometimes to an intense and solitary religious practice in a single place such as a forest, or a cave on a wild mountain. The primal and ultimate sadhu is Shiva himself, who with total unconcern for his social image, naked except for animal skins, with wild hair and a cobra around his neck, set himself up on top of Mount Kailash to practice extreme austerities. His wife Parvati is the daughter of the mountains. Her father, Himavat, is the landscape itself, so the Himalaya have a great attraction for sadhus.[13]

It's said that many of them choose this life to escape an unhappy home, and their reputation is often as rogues and charlatans. They're a wandering community of nutty, antisocial people.[14] My wife once got a cheer, as a teenager, when she scolded a pair for smoking weed and had them thrown off a city bus. But occasionally a true saint will be found among them.

When Girish and I were in dry clothes we sat down with the sadhu, who told us about his journeys in a dull, stoned voice. At the time of the earthquake, when he happened to be in central Nepal, he saw a whole hill collapse. 'It just fell into a river,' he said.

'I keep on moving and the move decides where I go. If I've been that way before, I know the road. If I want to travel a new road, if the weather's favourable, then I go that way.' For sadhus, like all Hindus, and all pilgrims of any religion, places are objects of worship. But a sadhu's whole life is an offering to geography.

Girish asked, 'How do you manage your expenses?' 'Some people give me things, like here,' he said. 'They gave me marijuana.' His clothes were thin, his sandal was broken, and he'd been up at the lakes for three days. It was cold, he acknowledged, but it only becomes colder if you think about it. 'This is good for me to sleep,' he said, indicating his chillum. 'From here I'll go down to Trisuli, then Pokhara, then I'll know where to go from there.' He'd go on taking lifts, in one truck after another. True wandering should be without any regard for one's destination, but that's almost impossible to achieve.

The young baba was up before me in the morning, sitting in the sun, picking the seeds out of his grass. He told me about his itinerary of annual festivals while I spread my wet stuff out to dry. The weather seemed to have changed. The valley of the Trisuli River (which must be older than the mountains because it goes right through them) was below us to the left. Branching off it, curling around to the right as we looked north, lay the moon-shaped valley of Langtang.

There's an idea in Tibetan Buddhism that Guru Rinpoche concealed certain valleys on the southern slopes of the Himalaya, called bayul, or hidden valleys, which would be used as refuges for good people in a future disaster. In the late seventeenth century, Langtang was identified as one of those bayuls.[15] I've sometimes wondered how literally to understand the suggestion that in mountains like these the presence of a whole valley might actually be unknown.

It was obvious from up here that for as long as people have been going to Gosainkund anyone could see where the Langtang Valley is.[16] Neither is it safe from disasters. About 30,000 years ago one of the most destructive known incidents in the history of the world occurred in Langtang, when an 8,000-metre peak collapsed in an unimaginable convulsion, which displaced 10 cubic kilometres of rock and released so much energy that stones turned to glass.[17] That event had a minor sequel in 2015, when the earthquake shook ice loose from high in the cirque of mountains that remains from the first cataclysm. The ice swept down a hanging valley, gathering rock from glacial moraines. It lost contact with the ground as it hit the valley lip like a ski-jump, and crashed onto the community below with half the force of the bomb that destroyed Hiroshima.[18] A woman called Bhunti, whose place I'd stayed at a few years earlier, was getting married that day in Langtang. The shockwave in front of the avalanche was enough to obliterate the village, which was then instantly buried under many metres of debris that now covers forever the upper Langtang Valley.

I'd thought about going up there again this time. But a Langtang man I telephoned warned that the trails were still scoured by landslides, and the worst thing about them, he said, is that you can hear them coming through the forest but you can't see them, so you don't know which way to jump. That beautiful morning in Lauribina none of this was visible, and I noticed instead the curly wisps of cloud that clung to the mountains, which seemed to me exactly like the curly wisps of cloud that are shown in Tibetan paintings. I didn't know at the time that that style of painting clouds is imitated from Chinese art, not from the Himalayan sky.

※

All day we walked down through the forest to reach Dhunche, a small town in the Trisuli Valley. This valley has been a trade route since at least the first millennium AD, but its motorable road was first built in the 1980s. Since the earthquake wiped the alternative route off its hill, this had been the only road linking Nepal to China.

The following morning we wanted to catch a bus south, but the discouraging news was that a landslide slightly to the north had trapped all the vehicles on the other side. It was afternoon before the traffic got through. After we got started we stopped again right away for a lengthy search by soldiers looking for smuggled wildlife. And we soon ran into another jam. A few hundred yards ahead, down a slope of deeply rutted mud, two yellow machines were removing a rock-fall. There was another queue of trucks and buses on the other side. The passengers were all standing around or squatting at the edge of the plunging hillside. There were women with babies tied around them, old people, trendy tough guys, and a drunk who briefly entertained people. Everyone was commenting and joking, taking photos and smoking. While we waited we were enveloped in cloud.

After an hour or two the vehicles from the other side started coming through, slithering like fish in the mud, engines screaming to get a grip, wheels spinning, because these trucks were unloaded. The young men climbed onto the cargo beds to put more weight on the axles. Then the jeeps started coming, emerging from the mist at a distance of 50 metres, with boys bouncing on the running boards to get some traction. Our bus started its engine and we climbed back in. The aisle was heaped with luggage and packed with people. We careened onwards alarmingly, because the driver was making up lost time. The grey, rocky slope plunged hundreds of feet into the cloud beyond the barred windows and the Trisuli River roared somewhere below.

We left the alpine zone and descended into a vast panorama of the mid-hills. The land spread out before us looked like a rolling garden, which is what it is: all cultivated, and soft and gentle feeling compared to where we'd been. The cloud, which was above us now, made beautiful light effects where the sun reached through. In other parts we saw rain showers playing. Then the bus filled with smoke from underneath. Everyone climbed out and we were delayed for another half an hour.

Girish and I were grateful to be dropped off not long after at a place called Nuwakot. I thought about how these conditions are mistaken for natural poverty, but really it's how people are forced to travel when the administration is corrupt. People endure it and it's called resilience, but really they're prisoners. We watched the bus drive madly on, without headlights, in the thickening darkness. It would reach Kathmandu after midnight, if it didn't meet another fate on the way.[19]

In this fat land there were nice hotels, with pleasant beer gardens. We checked in and sat down in one. Insects and frogs clattered in the warm night. According to Girish, the passengers don't complain about bad driving because – although they know it's dangerous – they don't know that it's against their rights. 'You know when you said the driver's a maniac?' he said. Then he began telling a story about local politics up around Dhunche, which used to be controlled by a powerful contractor who made a lot of money from public works. Maybe he'd built that lousy road. 'The local people would always swear never to vote for him again. But at election time the candidate paid for feasts and drinks. After three or four days of revelry, the villagers would wake up after the election and ask how they'd let him win again.

'We are talking about the drivers now,' Girish said, 'but it isn't the mistake of the driver. It's the mistake of the committee that runs the bus service, and if you try to find out who is the owner of the system, he must be someone from either the Congress Party or the UML. Or the Maoists. The root cause is in politics.'

※

At this point it's worth briefly summarising what can be said so far about the history of the central Himalaya, or what specialists surmise from the clues that survive. At, say, the beginning of the second millennium AD, the region was largely forested, and sparsely inhabited by clans of people who spoke a variety of Tibeto-Burman languages.[20] No one knows when their ancestors entered the region in the migrations remembered by the mythologies. People's lives were based on variable combinations of hunting, fishing, and foraging; a shifting swidden cultivation of vegetables and grains such as barley, buckwheat, and millet; as well as pastoralism, driving their animals up and down the slopes with the seasons. The descendants of these groups, who call themselves indigenous today, include quite large communities such as Limbus, Rais, and Tamangs in the areas where I'd been walking, and Gurungs and Magars who are concentrated further west. There are also many smaller groups, such as Rajendra's Sunwars. There must have been – and still is – great variety between and even within them, but the groups had several things in common. They typically had communal landowning systems and relatively egalitarian social structures. They had little or no writing. What kind of political organisation there was isn't well understood, but it seems that those who were in charge were more like chiefs than kings, although they're called kings in the folklore because there were no capitals and no administrative records. They had shamanic religious cultures, which I've tried to describe. In the midst of all this there was a courtly and mercantile culture in the Kathmandu Valley, on the trade route between India and Tibet, but it had more in common with the distant places it traded with than the hills that surrounded it and it's not a big part of this story.

During the middle centuries of the second millennium life in the hills took a different turn. Politics, the economy, and society were transformed by a new relationship of people to the landscape.

※

The valley here at Nuwakot was malarial and dangerous to live in for part of the year, until the mid-twentieth-century mosquito eradication programme using the insecticide DDT, funded by the United States. The oldest places are halfway up the hill, where the mosquitos didn't reach. In the morning Girish and I walked up there to see the eighteenth-century palace. It's a rectangular brick tower with elaborately carved windows and a pagoda-like arrangement of tiered roofs. It had survived the earthquake with large cracks. The street of old houses leading from the gate was ruined.

This site long guarded the ancient trade route between Tibet and Kathmandu. It was captured in 1744 by a backcountry prince whose name was Prithvi Narayan Shah. Girish and I found that the palace is still occupied by a contingent of the army Prithvi Narayan led, which is now called the Nepal Army. We examined the site from all angles. Then we walked down the ruined street outside, where hens and ducks were rooting in the muck. There was a woman sitting on the step of her wrecked home. Inevitably we first talked about the earthquake, and she spoke beautifully.

'I nearly fainted,' she said. 'The land started to tear open. I was thrown from my place, and I could hear loud crashing from below. So many people died. An earthquake does not come all at once. It keeps coming again and again, like the wind. Like waves. Had it been an up and down movement it would not have been so bad. But when it's like winnowing then it's dangerous. This used to be such a nice place earlier. Now everything is haywire. Everything collapsed. Everything's under the rubble. The world is going to end. We do not have people like we used to have before. People don't even speak properly. Now, no one cares. No one.' And she began to lament the fate of the latest flood victims, elsewhere in the country, who were in the news at the time. 'I feel so bad when I see that. Look at their pain,' she said.

'These are all natural disasters,' said Girish. 'It's always like that. It was the same before.'

But she blamed these pitiful conditions on the decline of government authority. 'Before, a headman would run the village so well, with just a word. Now no one gives an ear to *what* the government says. Power should always be with one, and then it will be strengthened. But everyone looks to grab power, everyone looks for how to earn for themselves, and no one thinks of what the people are going through. The world is like this. Nepal has so much money donated by other countries, but *we* didn't get it. Eventually everyone has to die, so let everyone feel happiness. Let their pains be lifted. But here, if one goes up, another pulls him down. So Nepal has failed to develop.'

Girish, who complimented her on how eloquently she spoke, noticed that she had an aristocratic way of conjugating her verbs, so he asked if there were any families from the royal Thakuri caste around here. 'There are a couple,' she said, and in fact she was from one of them. Not only that, but by what seemed a remarkable chance, or perhaps it's not so unusual in these parts, I thought, she was directly descended, twelve or thirteen generations later, from Prithvi Narayan Shah himself, by his third queen. Where she lived now was her late husband's place. But when she was a child in her father's house – this was more than fifty-five years earlier – Prithvi Narayan's heir King Mahendra Shah had paid a visit to her district. She remembered the crowds, and lines and lines of horses. 'The king himself was on a horse. There were garlands. It was so beautiful,' she said. 'Everyone was waiting for the king at their door with garlands.' Her father was the village headman and the king gave him 1,000 rupees that day. Her father also received, if I understood her right, a regular allowance of 100 rupees, which was later increased to 500, in recognition of his remote royal status.

If those days were grand only by comparison to her fellow villagers' days, these days were less grand still. She hadn't married well. 'Women married here are not happy,' she said. 'The men eat and talk and drink. The culture is very devilish. People here don't follow godly virtues, and in such places women are never happy.' Her house, which previously had three storeys, now had one. Her children were dispersed. One daughter had eloped, and now lives with her husband in the south. 'I think she's happy,' she said, 'but I try not to ask too much.' Another daughter had married a man who went to work in Korea thirteen years ago and never came back. A son was working in Abu Dhabi. Another son lived in Kathmandu.

'He owns his house?' Girish asked.

'It's rented,' she said. 'Why lie?'

'What caste are you?' she asked Girish.

'Sanyasi,' he said. Girish is descended from people who once renounced their caste to become sadhus, and then renounced being sadhus and became a caste of householders again.

'Sanyasis branched away from Thakuris,' the woman said, and she recalled the story that explains it.

We said our goodbyes and made our way. She was the first person we met whose family history relates them, and where they live now, directly to the events of Prithvi Narayan Shah's time. In her children's generation her family is being scattered by modernity. But her conversation made a point that would be reiterated in various ways in the country we walked through next; that many people's lives are still rooted, quite directly, say twelve or thirteen generations deep, in what happened here in the mid-eighteenth century. Girish and I set off along Prithvi Narayan's route, albeit walking backwards, as it were, to where he started.

Prithvi Narayan Shah was a military and political genius, from a micro-kingdom in the hills called Gorkha. Before his death in 1775 he conquered the Kathmandu Valley, making it his new capital, and under his successors the Gorkhali empire briefly extended throughout the Himalaya from Sikkim to the Punjab. Prithvi Narayan's success is normally attributed to his unique talent, which is said to have been guided by his patriotic vision. According to this notion he was a unifier, who brought together a country that was somehow waiting to exist. There's also a more systematic story, often told, which says that by rewarding his soldiers with parcels of land as they conquered it he created a land–military complex in which every victory fuelled further growth.

But the ultimate explanation is much deeper and longer, and that's the story of farming – and especially of rice. Rice growers had been spreading eastward from what's now far-western Nepal, creating dozens of tiny kingdoms for a few centuries before Prithvi Narayan emerged and consolidated them. (Rice was farmed in the Kathmandu Valley since ancient times, but there is no evidence that it was transmitted from there into the surrounding hills.[21]) In comparison to pastoralism, foraging, and swidden, growing irrigated rice made greater political and military organisation possible and necessary. When he built his empire in the hills, Prithvi Narayan completed a process of several centuries' expansion of wet rice agriculture.

❄

From about the twelfth to the fourteenth century there was a kingdom in the Karnali River basin, in what's now western Nepal, stretching from the base of the hills up onto the Tibetan plateau, which was ruled by a dynasty called Malla.[22] Not a great deal is known about this kingdom; in fact, its existence was largely forgotten before being rediscovered in the mid-twentieth century. The Malla belonged to a Hindu ethnic group called Khas, which seems to have been gradually moving eastward through the Himalaya (perhaps from Kashmir) for several centuries.

The Malla kingdom's origins may be obscure, but from the three centuries it lasted about 150 stone inscriptions survive, some of which are regarded as the oldest documents in the Nepali language. The inscriptions describe the construction of reservoirs and temples, corvée (forced) labour obligations, royal land grants to Brahmin priests, and tax exemptions covering – as the stone pillars say – all of the thirty-six taxes.[23] The taxes related to agriculture, slavery, adultery, and so on. The taxation was so heavy it is sometimes suggested that the Karnali River was named after it (kar means tax in Nepali). That's surely a folk etymology but the suggestion is telling. The remains of pipe irrigation systems in the Karnali region have been carbon-dated to the middle of the Malla period.[24] Whatever mysteries remain, it's clear from this evidence that the Malla kingdom was a highly taxed economy which included the use of forced labour, that the rulers patronised the priestly Brahmin caste, and that they grew irrigated rice on the alluvial flat lands of the valleys. Today, and presumably in the past, those fields also produced winter crops of wheat or barley.

Around the same time (from the eleventh to the thirteenth

century), there was a migration into western Nepal from the south, of caste Hindus fleeing the Muslim conquest of the plains of India. These people included priestly Brahmins, and others who claimed princely Rajput caste status who are known as Thakuris, which is the royal caste. Like the Mallas, the high-caste refugees were rice cultivators. The main documentary source for these migrations are the vamshavalis, or genealogical chronicles, that these families still maintain. They include Brahmin families with names such as Bhatta, Bhandari, Adhikari, Gyawali, Aryal, Pokharel, and so on, who are found throughout Nepal today, and Thakuri families with names such as Chand, Shah, and Singh.[25] The chronicles typically record the migrants' prestigious foreign origins and their establishment in a new location.[26] Often the Brahmins brought their god Shiva with them, who at a certain place would simply refuse to move any further, so there they'd stop. Or they'd discover him somewhere in the form of a stone, and decide to stay there. For the Thakuris, the lineage deity they brought was always a form of the goddess.

Some of these migrants found a place in the Malla kingdom. In some instances the chronicles describe how they settled in virgin wilderness (jangal, that is, jungle) and turned it auspicious (mangal) by their cultivating presence.[27] This idea is absolutely standard for agricultural settlers, such as in America, where the puritan Cotton Mather described the colonists bringing cultivation, civilisation, and godliness to the howling wilderness of the Massachusetts forest. In some places, the chronicles (and the survival of indigenous Magar place names) indicate that the new settlers displaced previous residents. In either case, to this day the settlement pattern often has the rice-growing caste Hindus on the irrigable, alluvial soils of the valley bottoms and table lands. Magars, or other indigenous groups, often live closer to the forests, pastures, and unirrigable farmland further up the hills. Over many centuries, a complicated mosaic of settlement by different groups developed.

There's an intriguing clue to this process in the varying designs of wooden ploughs (usually with iron tips) that are still used by rice farmers today. The distribution of these designs

seems to show how the technology was carried across the hills by the advance of the Hindu farmers centuries ago.[28] Amazingly, in some places the variation still corresponds to political boundaries that have long since disappeared – except in the techniques of conservative craftsmen who have never moved again, nor changed the way they make their tools. The distribution of plough designs maps different phases in the process of agricultural colonisation across the Himalaya.

In the fourteenth and fifteenth centuries, as the Malla kingdom disintegrated, numerous micro-kingdoms began to appear in the western hills, which were ruled and partly populated by caste Hindus. Each tiny kingdom consisted of a capital (really just a village) on a ridge, at the centre of three or four valleys, including at least one alluvial tableland or tar, which allowed for extensive irrigated rice farming. Whereas hunter-gatherers or swidden farmers require large areas to support a small population, settled agriculture allows a far greater concentration of people. A king's wealth was estimated in the number of households on his land, which was generally a few thousand. His revenue was the grain surplus they produced. He used the surplus to make gifts of land to Hindu temples and priests, who sanctified his authority. Rice was so esteemed that it was the only crop suitable for religious offerings. A new way of living on the land, with fields and ploughs, produced a new moral world of kings and priests, which is normally referred to in Nepal as feudalism.[29] The agricultural surplus was extracted by means of taxation, corvée labour, debt bondage, serfdom, and slavery. Cereal grains, as the political scientist James Scott says, are the premier political crops.[30] Because whereas pastoralists or swidden farmers are very hard to tax (it's too easy for them to run away), grains on permanent fields ripen in clear sight, all at the same time. Rice-growing peasants have nowhere to go and must accept their serfdom. To manage all of this the states developed a written administration of laws and records.[31]

It's understandably assumed that it was people who domesticated plants and animals. Some writers have been clever by turning that reasoning around and saying that cereals domesticated people. A certain plant evolved a form, in contact with humans, that made people work for it, which other plants could not do. In Mesopotamia it was wheat. In Asia it was rice. The people gave up their carefree, leisure-rich lives as hunter-gatherers, which archaeology suggests were easier and healthier than the lives of peasants (or, for that matter, than the lives of industrial labourers). They settled in villages and dedicated themselves to propagating and protecting the plant that had made them its prisoners. Settled cereal cultivation produced a revolution in the relation of people to their environment. To maximise yields villagers began changing the landscape more radically than people had ever done before, through larger-scale forest clearances, irrigation, and the backbreaking work of terracing.

*

The tiny rice states of the central Himalaya slowly proliferated eastward from the Karnali basin, crossing the Kali Gandaki River at the end of the fifteenth century. The chronicles of high-caste families describe gradual eastward movement, pitching up in the service of one micro-state after another. By the eighteenth century there were said to be twenty-two principalities in the Karnali basin, and twenty-four in the Gandaki basin. One of those was Prithvi Narayan Shah's kingdom of Gorkha.[32] Rice farming, along with ploughing and terracing, seems to have reached what's now eastern Nepal, where I began these journeys, only after the region's conquest by Prithvi Narayan and his successors in the late eighteenth century.[33]

The earliest known laws of the region are the edicts of Ram Shah, who was a king of Gorkha (1609–33). Many of his laws dealt with grain, agriculture, land, and the environment.[34] All land belonged ultimately to the king. Two laws describe how real estate should be marked out, with pegs driven into the ground, whenever the king made donations to priests or temples. There are laws on weights and measures; the measurement of land (according to how much grain it produced); and interest on debts, which were contracted in either grain or money. There's a law for sharing water from irrigation channels. Another law grants any man who creates new fields from the jungle three years of tax-free cultivation.

Edict thirteen proclaims a royal order to preserve trees along the roads, because, it says, the wretched poor who work become tired, and indeed everyone who walks the way becomes hot and searches for some shade. There was a fine of Rs 5 for cutting down these trees.

According to edict fourteen, forests should be preserved at watering places too, because if there are no trees the water will dry up. Without forests the householder's work cannot be accomplished (because trees provide fodder for livestock, which provide manure). And if these forests are cut down there will be landslides, which will destroy the fields. Again, a fine of Rs 5 was imposed.

In short, the twenty-seven surviving edicts of Ram Shah

show a notable interest in environmental stewardship, and they describe a social and economic system based on hierarchy, official religion, and irrigated rice cultivation. With agriculture and settlement came kings and laws.[35] There are endless points of comparison. I mentioned the Bible in Part 1 so I'll say here that the Ten Commandments (inscribed on stone slabs) are clearly not the laws of a band emerging from the wilderness. Like Ram Shah's, they're the edicts of a farming people, with cattle and oxen and servants and property which seem to have got backdated later on. Such innovations are the disaster described by Rousseau as the beginning of civilisation. However, as we've seen, the struggle of societies to claim an area of culture from the wild can also take place in other ways, without settled farming. Henceforth, the cultural landscapes of the indigenous groups would coexist with the landscape of the farmers.

※

Girish and I walked through a lush green scene under a bright blue sky. People were ploughing and planting. It was hot. Towards the end of the afternoon there was a downpour and we sheltered in the home of a man who'd been a baggage handler in Dubai.

The rain stopped and we started again. The last time I'd been this way the path was a broad, cobbled track, befitting an important old thoroughfare. This time the last stretch had been carved up by excavators in the process of making the Mid-Hill Highway. The road was a canyon of mud beneath towering heaps of gravel, which seemed to stand tens of metres above us. The heavy rain resumed and there was water everywhere. This was a frightening place to walk, or even to run in parts, where the black banks were slithering down. But as we climbed, and looked back to where we'd been, we saw a beautiful terraced landscape carved out before us. Enough light was piercing the clouds to pick up the water standing in the rice fields. The ridge we'd climbed along a week earlier faded into the clouds in the east.

The final stretch of this track was littered with stones, which had fallen from the unstable cliffs above. I scampered on, keeping an eye on the rocks overhead. It was after dark when we reached the village of Samari, in a low pass or saddle on the ridge.

※

The earthquake had devastated Samari, but only one person died here. Luckily, most people had been outdoors nearby watching a village football match.

This is where Prithvi Narayan Shah lived while he prepared his attack on Nuwakot. The remains of the building where he's said to have stayed were among the many ruins. According to a parable, after his failed first assault on Nuwakot the young king went to the home of an old woman who sold rotis (flatbreads). He took one and tried to swallow the whole thing at once. 'No,' she told him. 'You're just like that Prithvi Narayan Shah! You have to start with the edges, then you can eat it all.' Thus came his strategy of encircling his objectives, and also the name of this village which means delicious bread in the Newari language. Admittedly the story does no credit to Prithvi Narayan's legendary acumen, but presumably it's not literally true. Perhaps it was even inspired by the village's name, rather than the other way around.[36]

The following day we met various people while we walked. We met two schoolgirls who were best friends, both called Sarita Tamang. We met a woman who was walking with her mother and carrying her two-month-old son. The baby was named Election Biswakarma. The woman said she didn't know what the word means, or why it meant so much to her husband. We passed a man with a suitcase on his back. A little further on we caught up with his brother, who was returning home on leave from the Indian army. The soldier was carrying his wife's handbag; his wife was carrying their baby.

We stopped at a tin-shed teashop, which replaced a structure destroyed by the earthquake. 'What will the government do for us?' the woman there asked. 'Nothing,' she answered herself. 'Sorrow. The karma of Nepali people is sorrow.'

We dropped in on a village meeting, where two young women, who were engineers from Kathmandu, were trying to deal with the large number of people whose families didn't meet the criteria for receiving the government's reconstruction assistance. 'In fact the procedures have not been clearly stated, and it doesn't help that those who give the instructions don't follow their own rules,' the engineers said, citing incomplete lists and appendix-this-and-that of the Reconstruction Authority's documents. 'The victims are being even more victimised, so please write about these things too,' they requested.

In the district where we began our journey the broken homes had been dismantled and neatly stacked, but here they were still half-standing. Some were vacant and rapidly decaying in the damp, but others were patched up with tin sheets and plastic, and people were living inside. I remembered these as handsome old villages, befitting the country's heartland, with carved timber piers and wooden grilles in the windows. Now the villages were half empty, so tea and food were not available. In Samari they'd warned us there were cutthroats and thieves on the way, which we didn't take seriously. But their warning that it would be hard to get refreshments, or a meal, was true.

Nevertheless, people were ploughing with teams of oxen, and transplanting rice. I was very much taken with something I'd read: that the irrigation system is a record of the farmers' families.[37] The primary canal represents the common ancestor and the channels springing from it are the family's branches, showing how the patrimony has been divided in each generation. The junctions in the channels are sometimes named for the families which take their turns with the water, opening and closing water-gates of stones and earth at those points. Across the alluvium of the valleys, irrigation spread like a genealogical table as families cleared land and divided it between their sons.

✸

From the appearance of a rice-growing culture in the Karnali basin, later spreading from west to east as an archipelago of small, cultivated enclaves, which were tiny kingdoms, and finally the consolidation of those kingdoms into a quite large state that's now called Nepal, the whole process took about 600 years, the consolidation being achieved in a few decades. Perhaps these conquests were experienced as a unification by some people, even at the time. Many of the little kingdoms that Prithvi Narayan absorbed were culturally near identical to his own. The obsession with genealogy, the needs of marriage, and the practice of people sometimes moving on had already formed a web of high-caste family connections throughout the region.

In the final years of his life Prithvi Narayan transferred his attention to incorporating the Koshi River basin in the east. Relatively few caste Hindus had settled there, but there were some in the service of the rulers in the area. Some of them clearly had a deeper loyalty to Prithvi Narayan's project than to their own employers, and they conspired to give him knowledge of the land, such as how to cross the rivers. One Brahmin family sent him a clod of earth, as a potent token that the place they lived would fall to Gorkha.[38]

Many members of indigenous groups – especially in the east – clearly experienced this as a conquest, not a unification. There was an attempted rebellion in 1793, timed to take advantage of a moment of weakness when the Gorkhalis were at war with China, and it was harshly suppressed. There were occasional, failed, indigenous uprisings during the nineteenth century too. Equivalent differences exist today, in people's attitudes to Prithvi Narayan Shah's legacy. Whether you think he was a conqueror or a unifier is quite likely to correspond to which eighteenth-century community you're descended from, and ultimately to whether that community traditionally relied on rice farming or another way of living.

✻

In the second half of the eighteenth century, two fast-growing empires were running up against one another in the central Himalaya. There was the Gorkhali empire, named for Prithvi Narayan Shah's original kingdom of Gorkha. And to the south there was a vast existential threat to it in the form of the British East India Company, which was establishing its control in the Gangetic plain (also by seizing control of agricultural taxation) at just the same time. The British thought Nepal was so rich it must be a land of gold mines. They saw that the country controlled the trade routes from India to Tibet and western China, where the Company hoped to find markets for British products. They found that the Gorkhali raja's regime was militant and expansionist. So they regarded the mountainous territory to their north with a military eye, and their early contacts were concerned with spying out the geography and natural resources of the land. The Gorkhalis sought to preserve the secrecy of their geography.

The imperial–political salience of the Himalayan landscape, and its natural history, was distilled in the year-long British diplomatic mission to Kathmandu of 1802–3. A member of that delegation was a Scottish surgeon and botanist named Francis Buchanan, who also acted as something like an intelligence officer, studying among many other things the country's natural defences.[39] Buchanan crossed the Terai forest (at the margin of the hills) and wrote that after April this tract becomes unhealthy, travellers are subject to fevers and disorders of the bowels, attributed by the natives – he said – to the Ayul, or poisonous air, which many of them imagine proceeds from the breath of large serpents. The existence of such serpents in any considerable number is very doubtful, Buchanan thought, and rational men assign a more natural cause: the rotting of leaves during the first rains, that by their putrefaction corrupt the air. Other contemporaries also attributed the virulent malaria of the Terai to a noxious miasma: the baleful exhalations of iron oxide seeping from deep ravines.

Buchanan was a natural historian at the forefront of his science. He noticed that the Himalayan trees are similar to those of Europe, a few years before Alexander von Humboldt published his essay on the geography of plants.[40] Peaches, pears, pines, oaks, willows, and alders were thickly scattered through the forest, while raspberries grew on every bank.[41] He described 800 Himalayan plant species. He noticed beautiful and curious things, such as mynah birds, which can imitate the human voice, were considered the property of the king, and along with parakeets they were captured and sold in India. In most years it snows in Kathmandu, he thought, which if it was true then has not been so for a long time.

Much of his research was dual use, both scientific and military–political. His information on agriculture and pastoralism, gathered from informants, is part of the basis on which we know how some indigenous groups lived in the past, with vast herds of sheep that were used to carry the salt they exchanged for grain. On the whole, half of the cultivation among the mountains may be said to consist of transplanted rice, Buchanan believed. The Nepali language, he wrote, was already making rapid progress in extinguishing the aboriginal dialects of the mountains. It was a process he would have been familiar with from Scotland. He noticed valuable plants and sources of timber, medicinal herbs and cash crops such as cardamom and ginger, and the dreadful root of aconite, which he simply called bikh, meaning poison. Large quantities of bikh were annually exported to India where, according to Buchanan, it was in universal use for poisoning arrows, and also – he suspected – for the worst purposes. The Gorkhalese pretend it is one of their principal securities against invasion, he wrote, and went on to discuss its possible use in poisoning the water supply of an invading army.

In the person of Buchanan and others, the imperial demand for military and commercial knowledge arrived in the Himalaya, mingled with the European fascination for natural history. The origin of the modern study of the ecology, ethnography, history, and geography of the Himalaya lies with men like him. Buchanan couldn't be a photographer, although he would have liked it. But it wasn't long before photography arrived too, and was put to use as a tool of the imperial project to record geographies, peoples, and cultures.

The first serious map work was done by Major Crawford, who was a member of the same mission. Efforts continued throughout the nineteenth and into the twentieth century. In 1809 the mountain Dhaulagiri was measured with a theodolite from the plains as standing at 26,862 feet.[42] This was the discovery that the Himalaya are higher than the Andes. In 1814, when war between the Gorkhalis and the Company finally broke out, Buchanan was consulted by the authorities in Calcutta on invasion routes and strategies.

One of the invading British was John Shipp. He came into this wicked world and untoward generation, as he put it at the beginning of his memoir, at Saxmundham in Suffolk in 1785.[43] Shipp was orphaned amid rural poverty, enlisted in the army at the age of nine, and reached India at eighteen. In 1816 he entered the wild and romantic territory of the Nepalese as an officer in General Ochterlony's army.

The men crossed the notorious forest at the margin of the plain in January. According to Shipp this jungle was the awe of man and the haunt of beasts, the terror of the East and the bulwark of Nepaul. And then they beheld the hills. The summits were crowned by milk-white clouds and fringed with glittering gold. Shipp added more similarly wrought description before noticing the manoeuvres of the enemy. The British had found the defenders' barricades deserted in the forest. Now suddenly they caught sight of them withdrawing a short way off. They seemed to coax and invite Shipp and his company to advance and view their picturesque country, but the invaders were wary. They sometimes came upon their own dead and mutilated spies beside the road. Secret knowledge of the terrain was the key to the defenders' strategy and the attackers needed to avoid, for example, being destroyed by boulders rolled down the cliffs, and eventually to gain a position from which they could bring their artillery to bear.

Shipp described entering nature's masterpiece in a style that makes one wonder, did children in the army receive good schooling? He writes of golden woods that would have defied the pencil of an artist; glittering hills that vied in brilliancy with the rising sun; and rippling rills of water that whispered 'come ye thirsty souls and drink of the crystal brook.' Of weeping willows and golden fish, and of the blushing rose and gaudy tulip. These descriptions are partly fanciful, and in fact the whole thing was presumably written from memory a decade after the event, because Shipp says elsewhere that he lost all his papers in a riverboat accident in the plains.

He continued his account melodramatically. Oh, that ever-human blood should defile these beauteous scenes! Or that the horrors of war should disturb the sweet harmony established by nature in the fertile valleys of this sweet and picturesque country! For in this paradise of beauty, he thought, there dwelt a cruel and barbarous people, proverbial in their bloody deeds, whose hearts were more callous than the flinty rocks that reared their majestic heads above the woody mountains. They were more savage in their nature than the hungry tiger that prowls their dreary glens; cruel as the vulture; cold-hearted as their snowy mountains; subtle and cunning as the fiend of the night.

Shipp's popular memoir seems to have been conceived mainly to exculpate himself from the disgrace of a court martial. He had been convicted of unofficerlike, ungentlemanly, and insubordinate behaviour in connection with a dispute over a racehorse. Yet he stands at the beginning of two linked traditions – of romanticising Himalayan scenery and Himalayan people. The landscape was sublime. And although he thought the Goorkah was a bastard Tartar, a race pre-eminently bloodthirsty and cruel, Shipp remarked on the kindness that existed between the wounded of both sides and recalled that upon signing the peace treaty our enemies became our friends.

After the war of 1814–16 these mountains became a source of soldiers, whom the British recruited from among certain indigenous groups but not caste Hindus. They called them Gurkhas (derived from Gorkhali, which referred to the national government). Shipp's Romantic, Gothic-inflected vision became a sentimental affair for the Victorians, who were possessed by ideas of good stock and chivalry. They developed a theory of blood, climate, and topography which made the Gurkhas into a martial race by nature, because they came from mountains.[44]

According to a Victorian general, extra-wild Goorkhalees were the most trustworthy sort.[45] Another military author believed that the Gurkhas hardened their character as solitary herdsmen, moving around the remotest Himalayan valleys, perched on the heights, seldom coming into conversation with other folk.[46] If we are to judge by the Gurkha soldier, he believed, mankind is happiest and most honest where civilising influences are least.[47] They preferred the spoils of war to the tedium of weaving blankets, tilling the fields, and minding their flocks. In some ways a Gurkha turned out to be similar to a Britisher.[48] He could hold his drink, like the gentleman he was, and his polygamous marriages showed he was a great man with the girls.[49] Being fellow highlanders (and – in English eyes – tribals) there was a mutual attraction between the Scottish soldier and Johnny Gurkha, another officer wrote.[50] One hundred and fifty years after Shipp's encounter, in the British military memory, 1814–16 had become a good, clean war in which each side seemed to have enjoyed the other's company.[51] The Gurkhas acquired a mystique that was later attached to other Himalayan people, such as Sherpas, as well.[52]

At the end of the war the British policymakers more or less followed Buchanan's advice, declining to annex Nepal (for fear of upsetting the Chinese, according to his reasoning). Instead they deprived the Gorkhalis of plains territories in the south and hill districts in the west under the treaty of 1816.[53] The conclusion of the Anglo-Nepal War was the first time Nepal's southern frontier was clearly mapped or delineated. The complex overlapping way in which lands were held in the plains had no use for the concept of a frontier until then. The Gorkhali government continued to see the secrecy of their landscape as their ultimate strategic asset. Now that they were compelled to accept a British resident and his staff they strictly limited their numbers and confined them to the Kathmandu Valley. To prevent future invasions, the government especially preserved the formidable southern forest.

An order was given to remove all settlements between the Mahabharat ridge and the Chure range – that is to say, within the southern margin of the hills – and to let the whole region grow wild. Tracks were deliberately rendered unusable by planting bamboo and thorny bushes.[54] Households living along the ridge were given special duties to enforce checkpoints and to stop criminals and refugees, local people or foreigners, beggars and mendicants from travelling that way. Arrest them and send them to Kathmandu if they resist, the orders said, and if they can't be overcome, shoot them with poisoned arrows![55] Similar provisions were maintained for many years. As late as 1920, *National Geographic* magazine, reporting on a rare foreign visit, declared that maintaining the roads in a bad condition seemed to be a national doctrine.[56]

Brian Hodgson, who was the Company's resident in Kathmandu from 1833–44, was another keen natural historian. He recorded scores of bird and mammal species. He also gathered intelligence from informants about the terrain, producing numerous itineraries which describe routes through the hills. He provided a glossary of thirty words of landscape vocabulary to make the instructions comprehensible. Written in his italic charactery, the list includes:

> *Lekh ... a high and dry mountain flat covered with jungles*
> *Danda ... the ridge of Hill*
> *Bhunjang ... a saddle or subsiding junction of two ridges*
> *Phedee ... the foot of the mountain*
> *Tar ... any low or slightly elevated table land destitute of water but cultivated in the rains*
> *Byasee ... A glen, or Vale, well watered & cultivated*
> *Khola ... a rivulet or Hill torrent or dry bed of one*
> *Maree ... a Valley cultivated but malarious*
> *Pakha ... Dry flat[t]ish slopes of mountainsides*
> *Bheer ... any difficult or inaccessible part of a mountain*
> *Dobata ... the junction of two roads*
> *Patee ... a small caravansary, or asylum for travellers*[57]

By 1852, the year that Everest was measured, seventy-nine of the highest Himalayan peaks had been surveyed from the plains. In the 1860s the British authorities began sending the explorer-spies known as pandits into the mountains, who counted their steps as they made long journeys disguised as pilgrims. As Clements Markham of the Royal Geographical Society wrote in 1877, all really efficient administrators of the first order are geographers by instinct.[58]

Back in 1837, the British deputy resident in Kathmandu, Archibald Campbell, produced a long report entitled 'Agriculture in Nepal'. It looked like a promising source for my interest in the development of farming, but it's almost entirely limited to the particular case of Kathmandu.[59] More remarkable is a confidential report prepared in the Intelligence Branch of the Quarter Master General's Department in 1884. 'Chapter VII (Resources and Supplies)' reads like a celebration of seasonal foods.[60] According to this, many European vegetables had been in produce for the past sixty years, and most of them were reared in great perfection. Of wild fruits there are many, and of cultivated fruits the valley produces strawberries, pears, quinces, plums, apricots, and a few grapes. The apples and pears of English stock thrive well. Oranges and lemons grow most luxuriously and are of very fine flavour. Maize, millet, and buckwheat are much grown in the hills, and in the small hot valleys almost all the fruits of the plains of India grow freely, so that in the season the bazaar is well supplied with mangoes, jack, pineapples, guavas, and so on. By April there are cucumbers and also peas, French beans, lettuce, cabbage and cauliflower, asparagus and artichokes. In July there are plums, apricots, apples, and quinces. In September, mustard, garlic, lettuces, capsicums, fresh ginger and turmeric, radishes, potatoes, and Jerusalem artichokes. In October, beet, figs, and pomegranates of immense size. And so on, much of it grown in the low-lying valley below Nuwakot where Girish and I had just been.[61]

※

Now Girish and I were walking on a ridge, with a view that was both huge and gentle. The lower Ankhu Valley was beneath us, warm, domesticated, and affluent seeming – as it goes. Our ridge plunged through forested slopes to the alluvial farmland. The river coursed clear blue at the bottom, but almost everything else was green. Dull green pasture, deep green forest, bright green fields. Green hills receding to faint blue in the distance. Blue sky above. Apparently, in a different season, we'd be able to see sharp white peaks not far to the north.

We descended by an ancient-seeming track that had worn a cutting between the field walls. In parts the path was integrated into the irrigation system, so clear water burbled around our boots before being diverted back into the paddies. I stopped to take a photograph of a new tin hut beneath an old tree, then sat down with the woman who was outside it. She gave me mangoes and a cucumber to eat.

'The earthquake has made people poorer,' she said. Her adult son cheerfully recounted examples of the wickedness and impunity that prevails. According to him, the Maoists killed *so* many people, and they're lousy hypocrites, which is true. King Gyanendra killed the rest of the royal family, which is false. His son Paras killed the popular singer Praveen Gurung, which is true. And the sainted politician Madan Bhandari was assassinated, although his highway jeep-plunge was surely an accident. I wrote his comments down, and repeat them now, because they show how confusing things become, and how implausible the truth can be, when crazy things happen only some of the time, conspiracy is the primary mode of politics, and leaders' claims are excessively misleading.

In the flat valley bottom we walked through an area of newly transplanted rice, where I'd walked five years earlier, in the autumn, with my dad. It had been just as charming at harvest time, when the fields were gold and people were reaping, as it was charming now when the young plants had just been planted in the mud. There were fine old farmhouses, and old temples under trees.

We crossed the Ankhu Khola by a bridge. Some men were chasing a pig that had gone in the river. Then we reached Khahare Bazaar. Despite the whole valley's appearance of old prosperity from the ridge, the bazaar was a ruin. Wood and tin shopfronts had been crudely erected in front of broken houses. And the settlement was due to be flooded anyway, as we were told, by the Budhi Gandaki hydropower project. Apparently Khahare Bazaar hadn't even been here twenty years ago, and soon it would be 10 metres below the surface of a reservoir. The people were only waiting (for ever, as it seemed) for the government to compensate them and move them on.

※

Girish has an interesting family history. His paternal grandfather's ancestors lived in a fold in the hills somewhere above Khahare, where they were in the service of a local aristocrat named Nirjung Shah. Meanwhile his paternal grandmother, who when we made our walk was about eighty-five years old, was born by the first of her father's five wives into a Brahmin family in Jajarkot, which is way off in the hills to the northwest. There were many children in her family, Girish said, 'and no good care'. His grandmother was the friend of a Jajarkot aristocrat's daughter, who was to be married to the aristocrat from over here: Nirjung Shah. The child bride asked to take her best friend with her. It was the way it went in those days. So, aged something under ten, Girish's grandmother was launched on a great journey across the hills, which she can no longer remember. Her friend's new husband, Nirjung, held an important administrative position in the plains. His various dependents accompanied him there, and in Nirjung's household a match was made between Girish's grandmother and his grandfather. His family remained in the south for two generations. The men got into politics: first communist, then royalist. His father became the mayor of an important town and was murdered by the Maoists. Girish himself moved to Kathmandu, but he still had a distant uncle at his ancestral home in the hills above Khahare.[62]

The following day, when we were climbing up to Girish's village, he asked me if I'd ever participated in deusi, which is a kind of festive singing in the autumn, when people go from house to house collecting coins or treats.[63]

I said I hadn't.

'It's changed its cultural meaning now,' Girish said, 'but it used to be so nice. It used to give such a nice feeling of life in the hills.

Red mud, deusi-re
Slippery path, deusi-re
Falling all about, deusi-re
We have come, deusi-re.'

The slippery red mud path climbed through sal forest. We stopped at a point where the hill caught the breeze. 'The air feels so good,' he said. 'People say susaunu. You can hear it now. It's a beautiful word for the sound of the wind or a river. It appears in so many folk songs. There's a book called *Salla Susaai Dinchha. The Pine Forest Whistles.*' Our path came out of the trees and levelled out. We rested on a stone platform beneath a tree, where a group of old men joined us. I asked them if there are any ghost stories in connection with the earthquake, but they said no. There were only horror stories.

'Over there, Jaynarayan's grandson and Bastola's granddaughter were killed. In Mulpani twelve people died in the same house, while they were watching television. At Salyantar it was so difficult to recover the corpses the army came to dig them out, but even they couldn't find them. They'd gone to fetch firewood when the landslide came.'

We could see a temple on the ridge opposite, which attracted me and I entertained thoughts of putting it on our route. They said it was a goddess temple called Salyankot. There's a festival there in the winter month of Mangsir. And they said that the hill the temple stands on, which is steep on one side, is called Rajmare, or King Killer, because it's the place where Prithvi Narayan Shah's men chased an indigenous king, or chief, known as a Ghale raja. He fled on his horse, fell down the steep slope, and died. Now whenever someone from around here is followed by a ghost they make a model of a horse from banana fibre, fashion a crown on its head to symbolise the royal rider, and they throw it down that hill.

I don't know whether there was such an indigenous king, or Ghale raja, in Salyankot in Prithvi Narayan's time, or whether the story is adapted to show that Prithvi Narayan made himself the master of all. Perhaps the Ghale raja is a memory from an earlier time and was transferred to Prithvi Narayan's days because that's when so much is said to have happened here.[64]

In another episode related by the old men, Prithvi Narayan's army was thirsty and drank water from a spring, but their thirst wasn't satisfied. 'We don't know how small the flow was, or the number of men waiting,' said the man who did most of the talking, whose name was Chandra Bahadur Dhakal. 'But the water wasn't enough. They decided to make a goat eat salt, so when it gets thirsty it will go in search of water. If we follow the goat it will lead us to the source. So they searched for a goat, made it eat salt, and it's believed that the goat went to that well over there, which is why it's called Bakhrepani.' Goatwater. 'It was a goat that found out that source. This is what we've heard around this place from the legend of Prithvi Narayan Shah. In Gorkha there is a different story. Nuwakot has its own story. Different places have different histories.'

Girish asked, 'What effect can you observe in this village from these tales?'

'This is our share of the unification story,' Chandra Bahadur said. 'We've heard that there used to be a lot of small kingdoms and he united them all. During the unification, it's believed that people felt peace for some time. Later,' he said, 'there were hard times and oppression. Then other changes came. And now, these days, things have taken their own route. There's no clean politics.'

'So,' Girish asked, 'are people happy over here or are they not?'

'There's neither happiness nor suffering,' Chandra Bahadur answered. 'When do people feel happy? When they don't have an empty stomach. Some time ago, when there was no road down there, people were miserable. Even at this hour of the day their hearth would not be lit. But now they're living in comfort. When the road came many businesses reached the village, so these days people can have a full stomach. In earlier days, even when they worked hard they slept on an empty stomach. To eat in the winter they had to plough the master's field for a kilo of rice. But during the summer they had to work without food. The food they had in the winter, they had to pay back through work in the summer. Remembering those days,' the old man said, 'to me, those who say they're still miserable are liars.'

Whereas Chandra Bahadur, who was aged fifty-eight, said he never went to school, 'now more or less everyone gets the chance to study, at least up to class eight or nine. Even Dalits, up to class five at least, and that's also an interesting thing,' he said. 'I tell all the kids to study until they're eighteen years old. You have the opportunity, so take it.'

The old men were carrying planks to mould a concrete water tank, paid for by an international charity.

'I always come forward for the social tasks,' Chandra Bahadur said.

'You haven't joined politics, have you?' asked Girish.

Chandra Bahadur is a 'high-caste' man, a Brahmin. There's another social group whose entry and dispersal through the hills is associated with agriculture and Hinduism. They are the artisans of very low status known as Dalits, formerly called Untouchables. Frequently there are communities of Dalits still living near the old forts where the rulers lived, because their ancestors served the micro-kingdoms' musical needs, such as singing ballads of the ruler's genealogy. Or they made clothes, shoes, and baskets. According to the principles of religious purity, only Dalits can work metal. They made the ploughs and swords on which the state depended. These two objects, which go together like love and marriage, were integral to the whole social, economic, and political system. There was no Hindu farming community, or state, without Dalits, and for their efforts the state and the community treated them with atrocious cruelty in return. These days the kings are gone, but the Dalits are still grotesquely oppressed.

We arrived at Girish's village and saw the slightly leaning, empty wooden frame of his ancestors' house. Beside it there was a stone cube erected by his father for their lineage god.

As Girish said, 'Even if you move, the lineage god cannot be moved.'

His uncle lived around the corner, in a traditional building recently shorn of its top two storeys. The epicentre was now only one major ridge away. The family gave us a huge, ghee-soaked meal to eat. And yoghurt mixed with cold water to drink. It's the most refreshing thing you can have when you've been walking in the sun. We sat back on their porch and looked out over the expansive alluvial tableland of Salyantar. Around it were the two valleys that would soon be a reservoir.[65]

'It will be a good place to make a resort,' I said. 'Water-skiing, fishing, barbeques.'

'That's what my brother said,' said Girish.

And what about building a large dam on a major seismic fault? Girish reckoned that with the backing this project has, that wouldn't stop them.

On our way down the hill we interviewed a shopkeeper named Lalit Bikram Shah, who is reputed as a local historian. He gave us tea and mangoes, and began his history close to the very beginning with a famous event involving the Hindu gods which happened here.

Girish interrupted him. 'We know the story of Hiranyakashipu.'[66]

'Let me tell it to you briefly,' Lalit Bikram said, and he did anyway.

'This is a mythical tale,' said Girish. 'But what the history of Nepal tells us …' And he pressed the old man about the time of the unification.

For Lalit Bikram, the mythical history prefigured and ordained what had happened just a dozen generations back. The mortal kings were associated with the places where the gods had their palaces. There were all sorts of links and correspondences, which he pointed out. Prithvi Narayan offered a necklace to the goddess of the river waters. We could see her temple just down there. The great king inaugurated the current festivals, which until recently were attended by the royal family, arriving by helicopter. Yet the festivals have fallen into decline since the lands that endowed them were nationalised in the 1960s.

'The worship takes place rarely, because the government

hasn't made provision. Unless some responsible person from here takes the lead,' said Lalit Bikram, 'the state won't know what our condition is.'

Prithvi Narayan Shah had endowed the temples, 'and,' Lalit Bikram said, 'it seems he also set up all the castes that are living here, with the division of work among them.'

'We're Sanyasis,' said Girish, 'and this is where our root is. But how did we get here?'

'The thing is,' the old man said, 'the Sanyasi, Damai, Kami, Sarki, Brahmin, these all came according to the need.[67] It seems there was a need for every kind of caste.'

'So did we come along with Prithvi Narayan Shah?' asked Girish.

'It seems like that,' Lalit Bikram Shah confirmed. 'He must have assigned them certain jobs.'

'To bear responsibility for the temples?' asked Girish.

'It must have happened so,' the old man replied. 'That's what I've found in my experience. The Sanyasis control certain temple lands.'

Girish asked, 'Is it because of your interest in history that you have such information regarding these matters?'

And the old shopkeeper answered, 'I want to make one thing clear to you. Although I am a Thakuri of the Shah dynasty, I am an uneducated man. I never got the chance to attend school. The history of the Thakuris is a very long one. Now I've reached sixty or sixty-three years of age. During my childhood, my family was the family that ruled this place. There seems to have been some problem with the system, with our ancestral property too, and it got lost in bygone years. Our family belonged to the feudal system, and I fought against that system. In the year 1990 we defeated it, but by that time I'd lost my youth. I've studied a little, but regarding spirituality I have deep faith. So I am interested in things related to the gods and goddesses, how they operate, and how the world operates. You may not believe it, about what is going on around the world, and what is going to happen in the future, but I have faith in my beliefs.'

'There used to be a person called Nirjung Shah,' said Girish.

'He was one of our forefathers. He used to be a clever fellow,' the old man said.

Girish didn't pursue the point. Instead the old man raised the matter of earthquake relief, because he was troubled that some local people's situation had not been properly registered by the authorities. After explaining whatever we understood about the reconstruction polices, we left.

We carried on down, past men ploughing and women planting on the tableland, to the place called Arughat, meaning the riverbank of peaches, which were not currently in season. It was a ruined town on the bank of the Budhi Gandaki River, which was roaring beneath the bridge in terrifying black spate.

A historian has written, with Europe and North America in mind, that the celebration of the landscape is the bedrock of nationalism.[68] When asked why he would volunteer to fight in the First World War, the British poet Edward Thomas, picking up a handful of soil, said, 'Literally, for this.'

It wouldn't be right to speak of nationalism in the Himalaya quite yet, but the Gorkhali empire had an ideology that held the germ of nationalism. It was militaristic, it was xenophobic, and it claimed divine authority for its existence.[69] It wasn't a clearly marked territory on a map, but rather a kind of world-unto-itself of purity and sacred order, with a godly caste system preserved by the law of a divinely ordained king. Like any empire, Gorkha ruled many peoples who had different customs, to whom different laws were applied according to their status.

Although the Gorkhalis ruled a slither of the plains known as the Terai, theirs was a hill country, distinct from the lowlands of India or the world of the high plateau in the north. Political sentiments were rooted in the land, by legendary and historical stories of what had happened in particular places, and by the presence of gods and goddesses in a network of hilltop-forts-cum-temples called kots. In the Gorkhali coronation ritual, right up to its final performance in 2001, the king's body was anointed with soil from different parts of the kingdom.[70]

*

Nepal's great economic historian, Mahesh Chandra Regmi, called it a truism that a country's land tenure system reflects its political philosophy. At first, according to him, land belonged to whoever cleared and cultivated it, or it was held by clans in communal systems. The development of government, documentation, law, and property rights made it possible to control land far beyond one's personal requirements. Under the land system of the micro-kingdoms, which was extended and entrenched by the Gorkhali empire, all land was ultimately the property of the sovereign, representing, as Regmi said, the unlimited prerogative of an absolute government.[71]

The system made sharecroppers of the peasant population. Taxes were extracted at a rate of 50 per cent or more of what the fields produced, in addition to numerous other obligations, so that people lived on the threshold of subsistence and destitution. A list of twenty-one taxes from 1830 runs from land revenues to a levy on shamans, to the provisioning of visiting dignitaries, and fines for sexual offences such as adultery.[72] There was a tax on Majhis' fishing rights, a tax on boats, a tax on the capture of falcons, and a tax on weavers and on poultry farmers.[73] There was hardly any resource or action in rural life that didn't require the peasant to pay a ransom. As an historian has written in another context, feudal rights extended their clutches over every force of nature, everything that grew, moved, or breathed.[74]

Most of all the taxes were on rice, which was prized above everything. When I went through published administrative documents from the nineteenth century, I found that rice yields and rice lands were frequently the only crop or type of farmland that was specified. The rest were simply categorised as 'other'. As a result, the other crops (and pastoralism) were less visible in the documents than they must have been in life, but the guiding obsession of the government was clear. The state was prosperous to the extent it could amass and exploit rice farmers.

Similar laws to Ram Shah's edicts remained in effect 200 years after his were made – for example, giving three-year tax breaks to those who cleared fresh fields from the forest. And the government took other steps to enlarge the area under cultivation. A royal order of 1810 instructs officials to procure settlers from India to reclaim and settle virgin lands in Morang district, in the Terai plains. Promote reclamation and settlement in such a manner that land-tax revenue does not decline, it says.[75] Another royal letter, of 1812, commands: Reclaim the land and promote settlement, and appropriate the produce. In case you do not comply you shall be a sinner, be reborn as a worm, and live in human excretion for 60,000 years.[76] As cultivation spread, forest cover declined dramatically.[77] So, like in Ram Shah's edicts, there was a tension between production and conservation, and there were sometimes expressions of concern that deforestation to increase the tax base was drying up water sources, damaging the rice lands on which the army depended.[78]

Another commodity on which the army depended was metal, for weapons and munitions. Mining and charcoal manufacture for metallurgy caused more deforestation, until guns supplied by the British reduced the need for that industry after 1895.

A final necessity was communication. At the beginning of the nineteenth century the route from Kathmandu to the Gorkhalis' most westerly possessions, in what's now Himachal Pradesh in India, was at least 800 kilometres long, crossing several major rivers. Majhis took care of the river crossings, and they were under orders to ensure that military supplies were transferred without a moment's delay. In between, there was a system of porter relays at two- or three-hour intervals, with eight pressed men at each station, on twenty-four-hour duty without pay. By 1807, to discourage these porters from escaping, they were offered a tax break, which was increased to a full tax waiver in 1809, plus guaranteed tenure of rice lands. It was a constant struggle to make the system run smoothly, because it relied mostly on coercion. In 1808 it was necessary to order soldiers not to beat the wives, sons, or daughters of the porters, or force them to carry soldiers' personal supplies.[79] Similar orders were necessary again in 1849.[80]

The Nepali state was so reliant on various forms of corvée, or forced labour, for agriculture, metal production, and porterage, that the historian Mahesh Chandra Regmi has called the whole country a vast labour camp.[81] It's been calculated that even in the 1950s, Tamangs in Nuwakot were pressed to do ninety days' unpaid work a year.[82] There were repeated warnings from Kathmandu to local officials not to oppress the peasantry beyond what they could endure, and anxiety about emigration. An order of 1850 to the Limbus in the east announces: We have received reports you are leaving your lands and going abroad, due to the pressure of money lenders, revenue collectors, and government officials. All those who have gone abroad should come back, pay rents and till the rice lands.[83] But the brutally extractive nature of the state, which was managed to squeeze every last scrap of value from the fields, left many with no choice but to migrate for a livelihood. The pressure grew worse as the expansion of agriculture left ever less viable land to reclaim from the forest. By 1891, over half the population of neighbouring Darjeeling, in British India, was of Nepali origin. A proclamation of 1931 tried to lure the migrants home with the offer of land in a newly cleared forest.[84]

The morning of our last day's journey was bright and very hot. The brightness bored into us like the heat, like the throbbing cicadas, and it made our light bags heavier. We were grateful when the sky clouded over.

At first our path was a slick red ribbon through high-standing maize. Rice was not the only crop that transformed the Himalaya in the second millennium. Maize was brought from the Americas to India by the Portuguese, and it seems to have arrived in the Himalaya in the seventeenth century. At first it provoked horror, as several chronicles record, when priests and astrologers warned

that the invasive plant would cause a famine.[85] There were rituals to send the maize away. But by the nineteenth century, according to brief references in British accounts, maize was widespread in upland areas on fields that could not be irrigated. It is the second most important crop today.

The potato was introduced by the British to Bhutan in the 1770s and had reached some highland valleys of Nepal by the mid-nineteenth century, including the Everest region, where it's credited with transforming religious life by enabling the foundation of several monasteries. Both of these American plants, on which the administrative documents are largely silent, greatly improved people's ability to feed themselves, especially from unirrigated and upland land where indigenous groups are more likely to live. They probably supported a large increase in the population.

Indigenous people's ways of living underwent a process of change, which spread from west to east. In the west, where rice has the longest history, many Magar regions adopted settled farming at an early date.[86] In central Nepal, Gurungs gradually abandoned pastoralism and moved down the slopes in a process that can be observed in foreign accounts from the nineteenth and twentieth centuries.[87] Sometimes those who bought fields had earned their money as British Gurkha soldiers. Rice agriculture, terracing, and ploughing reached the Limbus in the east the last.[88] Settled agriculture influenced the techniques of animal husbandry, because manure was needed to fertilise the fields. But within this clear trend there was also great variation, creating the complicated pattern that exists today.[89]

Not only were the people domesticated: the gods were too. The origin of Bhumi, the goddess of the fields, seems to be as one of the forest spirits. She started protecting farmers on the land that used to be her jungle.[90] The religion of the forest went into relative decline, but retained some salience of course. In the early nineteenth century the government employed shamans (who are forest specialists) to protect travellers in the Terai jungle from tigers. When they failed in their duty, the shamans were fined.[91]

There's a story called 'Vir Caritra' ('Adventures of the Hero'), which was composed in Kathmandu at the end of the nineteenth century to be performed for courtly ladies. An anthropologist, Marie Lecomte-Tilouine, has shown how this seemingly crazy saga is an analogy for the ruling class's way of seeing the country and its taming. The story contrasts three ways of ordering nature and the world according to the three systems that were available at the time: the indigenous spirits of the forest; the unnatural contraptions of colonial modernity; and the right and proper hierarchy of Hinduism.[92]

To simplify it greatly, the story goes like this. The hero, who is a Brahmin named Agnidatta, has begun a journey to make a new life as a sadhu at a certain holy river confluence. A series of seemingly arbitrary happenings leads him through an opening in the earth to enter the kingdom of Banjhankri, the forest spirit I mentioned in Part 1. Of course there are no coincidences. Agnidatta's weird journey was orchestrated by the spirits. Specifically, Banjhankri's queen, who's called Nidhini, brought him here. She's the indigenous ghost of women who've died in childbirth.

Everything in this other world inside the mountain is inverted. The residents eat the opposite of good food with the opposite of good manners. Their feet point backwards. And women are in control. As the author ironically remarks, they're even consulted on family matters, because – unlike men – they're sharp, enlightened, and know when to speak appropriately. What's more, the female spirits led by Nidhini have capacious sexual appetites, taking whoever pleases them before discarding him. Nidhini's men are all destroyed; either transformed into statues, or simply fattened up before she feeds them to her husband. In fact that's why Agnidatta has been brought here, to briefly experience the pleasures of love and life with Nidhini before being turned into another stone figure in her garden. Instead, he returns four of her statues to life. They turn out to be Hindu princes. Then he escapes.

All of this is taking place in a labyrinth of underground chambers and passageways, with staircases leading the hero ever further down. But although it sounds fantastical, Lecomte-Tilouine claims that this idea is still widespread in Nepal. For instance, she writes, children will warn newcomers of small holes in the rocks which lead to the immense palaces of ghosts.[93] The world is apparently strewn with such openings.

These days, when our world is so modern that even we can hardly believe it, the spirit world is old-fashioned seeming. At the end of the nineteenth century, when the court at Kathmandu knew it was behind the times, the spirit world was full of the latest devices. Everything in those caverns was artificial. The light was electric. The plants were paper. The pools were made of glass. And wars were fought with rifles, revolvers, bombs, and torpedoes. Agnidatta journeys to the world of the Sun Jhankri (gold shaman). Here there are beautiful houses and shops down both sides of the road, there are also buses and trams, pavements with pedestrians, and automatic fountains every 50 cubits. Clocktowers, theatres, cinemas and dance halls, civil and military courts, banks, printing houses, playing fields for tennis, hockey, and polo, a railway station, and people of every sort were there. It's a metropolis of the British empire.

The worlds of indigenous people and their spirits, and of the Europeans with their enchanting technology, *are* real, but they're not right for Agnidatta. He makes a number of suitable marriages with Hindu spirits. And he marries the four Hindu princes he saved to the daughters of the indigenous spirit kings. Thus, their kingdoms are taken over and Hinduised. Lecomte-Tilouine argues that the story is an allegory for how caste Hindus subdued a wild, alien world.

In the second phase of its encounter with British colonialism, the Himalaya was integrated to a global market in commodities such as timber, cotton, jute, indigo, sugar, cardamom, and tea. Wild tea was discovered by colonial botanists in Assam, in the eastern Himalaya, in 1823.[94] The British could produce for themselves a vital global trade good for which they'd previously relied on China. As a Britisher wrote, the unhealthy jungle of Assam would be converted into one continued garden of silk and cotton, of tea, coffee, and sugar.[95] Between 1870 and 1900, 750,000 labourers were transported from elsewhere in India to work in the tea gardens of Assam, in a draconian regime that was a kind of serfdom.[96] Darjeeling tea gardens started replacing the forest in around the 1860s, and from there tea spread to Ilam in Nepal.

The growth of railways, which arrived at the edge of the hills in the 1840s, not only served to transport goods but created the demand for Nepal's greatest export, which became timber, especially for railway sleepers. The trees also made ships' masts, chests for opium and indigo, rolling stock, and railway buildings. By this stage, the military anxieties which had motivated Nepal to maintain the Terai forests in a wild and impenetrable state had passed. At the end of the nineteenth century, timber exports may have provided 40 per cent of Nepal's government revenue.[97] In 1923 the British sent a forestry officer to advise the Nepal government on the exploitation of forests, and it was he who extended the railway a short distance across the border to carry the wood away.[98] Yet the commercial destruction of forests within Nepal was nothing compared to that in Himalayan forests further west, which were actually governed by the British.

※

I stopped to wait for Girish at a shop by the roadside in a village called Tandrang. The young girl who sold me a bottle of Coke told me she was a prodigious student, on course to pass class ten at an unusually young age.

There was an old man on the bench outside wearing rubber boots, with thin legs rising into brief shorts. He was muddy from working. He surprised me when he heard that I'm British by mentioning Horace Walpole, Lord Palmerston, and the Anglo-French wars in India. He was a retired headmaster who had specialised in Sanskrit, and he said he'd had a hard time from the Maoists during the insurgency. (The Maoists opposed the teaching of Sanskrit, which they associated with feudalism.) There were others sitting around too.

The people here were all visibly affected by the destruction of an enormous simal tree, which was lying shattered across the road in front of the shop. It had collapsed with a great sound at one-thirty that morning. They claimed that this tree had been 365 years old, and that it was famous even at holy places in northern India.

'It seems to be a god,' someone said.

'It did not cause any harm to anyone. Despite falling like this, no harm was caused.'

Someone else said, 'There must be some power within. There

are houses on this side, and also on that side. Anyone could have been harmed. It is indeed a god.'

'But has the power of Tandrang gone now?' the first speaker asked.

'Tandrang's power *has* gone,' replied the second.

Now they talked about the distribution of earthquake relief, and it went something like this.

'Bhandari's son brought relief, but he only distributed it to so and so ...'

'The Dahal family took great advantage. They did not give it to others ...'

'They distributed material at some places, but we weren't given any ...'

'They haven't distributed anything around here ...'

'Lamichhane distributed relief to everyone, he did it here at Simalkophed ...'

'Surya's son distributed the relief, but he gave it only to those who drink water from Sinsnegaira ...'

'Kukhure's daughter-in-law is a manager, or something, of the tin roofing shop ...'

'They did what their conscience allowed them to do!'

None of which interested me as much at that moment as the history of this village, and its ancient tree.

According to the old headmaster, whose name was Meghnath Banjara, there had been a profound astrologer named Durlabh Lamichhane, who lived here more than 200 years ago. There was some confusion in his account, because Durlabh cast the law-giving king Ram Shah's horoscope, and he also advised his descendant Prithvi Narayan. Anyway, according to Meghnath, Durlabh determined the auspicious moment for Prithvi Narayan to capture Nuwakot, and when Prithvi Narayan was victorious he offered his astrologer as much land as he could walk across in a day. 'So Durlabh set off, from his home up there among the pines, where you can still see the remains of the bricks and stone, and he walked a long way, trailing a thread behind him. Durlabh's descendants used to collect the land revenue in this village.'

'Does his family still live here?' I asked, and the old teacher gestured beside him and said, 'He is the family of Durlabh.'

'Yes, I am the family of Durlabh,' the next man said. I asked, 'Did you also collect the land tax?'

'No. Not now,' he answered. 'My father used to collect it.'

'Durlabh made a goddess temple on top of the hill called Tandrang Kalikot. At that time,' Meghnath explained, 'any place where a royal palace or temple stood was called a kot. Kot means arsenal, where the arms were stored. At that time kings used to live in high-up places. There is Arukot …'

By this time Girish had joined us, and he asked about Salyankot, and the story we'd heard the day before, about the Ghale raja who was chased off the cliff there on his horse.

'No no,' said the teacher. 'There's no war in the history of Salyankot. That was over in Ligligkot.'

If I had to choose I'd take the teacher's side on this one, over the old men the day before, but it's confusing. Part of what's going on is the compression of a process of many generations into a single epic story, which decided the current configuration of the land and its people. Here in Prithvi Narayan's heartland, even more than for most Nepalis, the position of these villagers socially and actually in the place they live has meaning because his conquests crystallised that process.

Girish and I walked on.

Gorkha district is unusual in these hills for having a small, longstanding community of Muslims. We passed through a village where there were many. They told us that they'd come here in Prithvi Narayan Shah's time, to make glass bangles for women and weapons for the king's arsenal.

Towards the end of the day, when we were well tired, we reached the large bazaar of Gorkha. The old Shah fortress was up on the ridge. We checked into the same hotel I used to stay in more than ten years earlier, when I was a journalist covering the Maoist insurgency. I discovered that my friend Nayan was staying there, working on a survey project relating to post-earthquake reconstruction.

According to Nayan, the main problems were these. To qualify for the Rs 2 lakh rebuilding grant (which was then worth about $2,000) people who'd lost their homes had to use an approved, safer design. But the cheapest designs cost at least Rs 7–8 lakh, if you were fortunate to live near where the necessary materials could be procured. Many people knew they wouldn't be able to comply with the building standards, and therefore to qualify for all three instalments. They were planning to take the first payment and then get by as best they could. Anyway, there were huge bureaucratic difficulties for anyone who needed to rebuild in a different place from where their original house stood. Which was not to mention the impossible situation facing people without land papers, obviously. Finally, people who'd long abandoned their village home to live in the city were trying to cash in by pretending to rebuild their old place, causing huge resentment among more worthy beneficiaries who couldn't get their claims recognised.

This flawed scheme, which was being implemented by the government but largely designed and funded by the World Bank, wasn't being rolled out in any notable hurry. It was only now beginning, more than a year since the quake. It's what our world's best expertise in responding to such disasters looks like. Obviously, it's difficult. Yet you might think that Girish and I would have walked through a building boom, fuelled by at least some share of $4 billion in foreign aid that had been promised for reconstruction. We probably could have counted the houses we saw being built, on a two-week walk, on the fingers of two hands. Certainly, our four hands would have been too many. If anything, the policy had prevented people from taking any initiative due to warnings that they'd disqualify themselves from receiving assistance if they acted independently.

I've said that the agrarian state is a recording and measuring machine. A year earlier, an historian named Yogesh Raj wrote a newspaper column titled 'Remembering to Forget', in which he pointed out that before the earthquake the government had been known to demand every detail of its citizens' lives, requiring to see their citizenship certificates and land registration documents innumerable times. However, as he put it, just when it needed to remember those details and relieve people of their misery, the state seemed to suffer a severe case of amnesia. The land survey office has digital topography and cadastral maps that link to the owner of every registered household, he pointed out. The election commission knows how many adult members any household has. The ward offices of the municipalities and villages have multiple sets of data. State agencies have been told about every significant event in the lives of Nepalis, and about every relationship umpteen times, and each time in a fully attested manner. Yet when the crisis struck, those very government agencies chose not to recognise their citizens. The Nepali state, Yogesh Raj complained, cannot remember what it has read when it moves to the next sheet of paper.[99]

In the morning Girish left early. After a more leisurely start I also checked out, and went looking for a bus to Kathmandu. When I got there, around the corner from my house, I visited a shop that sells the things people use in rituals, and I bought for my children an interesting stick, and a stone like a shiny black egg.

Western Nepal + Dolpo

Area of detail

DOLPO

TIBET

MUSTANG

BUDHI GANDAKI

TRISULI

MT. DHAULAGIRI

MT. ANNAPURNA

POKHARA

KALI GANDAKI

KATHMANDU

✈ NEPALGANJ

INDIA

Detail of Dolpo

SALDANG — KHOMA

SHIMEN

NANGUNG

TINJE

SHEY

CRYSTAL MOUNTAIN

CHHARKA

PHOKSUNDO

SANGDA

RINGMO

------ Route in Sept/Oct 2017

KAGBENI

✈ JUPHAL

PART 3

Architecture

'The mules were driven by human intelligence and commercial interests, expertise in breeding and bloodlines. Everything was human; the farthest wilderness was steeped with sociability, and the sketches they had made, in so far as they had any value, stood as records of this permeation.'

Cesar Aira

'Savage nature does not represent an ideal state in the Tibetan mind. It may even be said that part of the aspiration of Tibetan religious ideology is to eliminate wilderness by subjugating it.'

Charles Ramble

'If we find a mound six feet long and three feet wide in the forest, formed into a pyramid, shaped by a shovel, we become serious and something in us says "someone lies buried here". That is architecture.'

Adolf Loos

More than a year had passed since my first two journeys. My wife, Subina, was awarded a fellowship in America, so we'd been to live in Cambridge, Massachusetts, and had a fine time. Now we'd come back home.

In the autumn of 2017, with an old friend from Britain called

Conrad, I flew from Kathmandu to Pokhara in western Nepal to begin the next walk, which would be in a high mountain enclave called Dolpo. From the plane we could see brown vapours hanging in the green valleys all throughout the hills. Industrial pollution and stubble burning in Punjab and the north Indian plains was covering the country with smog. The next day we drove up the Kali Gandaki River. At first it was a fat land of ripening rice and millet. It was a gorgeous scene of bright green fields and dark green forests, and red cottages with blue window frames. Herds of mountain goats were being driven down the road towards us, ahead of the Dasain festival. The sky was bright and the Annapurna mountains stood brilliantly in it, covered with fresh snow, unbelievably high.

The land became rugged, craggy, and steeper as we entered the gorge. This is supposed to be the deepest valley in the world, which seems a vague sort of claim, but it makes sense on the basis that it runs between two of the highest mountains, the giant massifs of Annapurna and Dhaulagiri. Since prehistoric times it's been a primary trade route, giving access to some of the lowest passes on what's now the Chinese border. But it was a fearsome route nevertheless, until this road was quite recently built, and it's still easy to imagine the terrifying path above the river described in mid-twentieth-century accounts. Although the river is large, at some places the chasm is so narrow that you could toss an apple or a bunch of keys to a person on the cliffs opposite, and they could just stick out a hand and catch it as if you'd tossed it across a street. In ten hours the pedometer on Conrad's phone counted 29,000 bumps in the road, but we couldn't complete the drive because a landslide had closed the way ahead.

The rocky slope had collapsed onto the road where it crossed a cliff, far above the river. We spent the night nearby. There were several changes of plan as our information changed, and many phone calls to the porters who were waiting for us. We finally called them down the valley to carry our equipment around. As they arrived the bulldozers rolled the largest boulder off the road. All the people who were standing around got back in their vehicles, whose drivers started their engines and began manoeuvring to overtake each other. In a cloud of dust and black fumes we went through.

Not far beyond there the ravine broadened into a valley again. The air became crisp, the vegetation changed from broad-leafed plants to pines and thin bamboos, then to juniper and apple orchards. There was pink-flowering buckwheat in the fields. We were surrounded by arid mountains that Conrad compared to the set of a Sergio Leone film. The river was braided across a gravel bed, shining silver and pink as the sun went down, first striking the hills at the end of the valley, then picking up only the snow tops of the mountains, turning them cold yellow. We arrived at the famous village of Kagbeni in the dark.

Until two years earlier a syndicate controlled all the traffic on this road, asserting – with violence if necessary – a high-priced monopoly for its members' vehicles. The arrangement somewhat resembled the old monopoly on the Kali Gandaki salt trade, which was auctioned by the government to one local family or another between the late eighteenth century and 1927.

While I was hanging around Harvard the year before, I took a class in landscape archaeology. At the end of the semester the professor, to whom I'm very grateful, helped me download an enormous image of the upper Kali Gandaki catchment area. On 3 December 1964 an American spy satellite passed over from north to south and just let it roll, as Professor Ur said, exposing a strip of film about 9 inches wide and long enough to be divided into twenty-one square images labelled from A to U, each square containing well over a gigabyte of data.

Professor Ur, who studies Bronze Age Mesopotamia, had a multi-screen supercomputer on his desk with which he handled this kind of thing. 'I don't see any humanity,' he said as we looked at the first image. 'I have zero ground control, so I don't really know what I'm talking about here, but this all looks very natural. There don't seem to be any roads or anything.' Frame A was far up on the plateau somewhere. 'Woah!' he said, when we were scrolling around a vast enlargement of frame K. There was a square compound with corner towers beside a river. 'That really is a bloody outpost in the middle of nowhere!' (A Chinese government facility was my guess, for what it's worth.) In L we found the medieval royal capital of the upper valley, which is a walled city called Lo Manthang. Professor Ur fired up Google Earth on another monitor, and the colour image swung around and tightened futuristically, so the same place fifty-three years apart appeared on two flashy screens. Some fields had been abandoned in the interval.

The region of this old kingdom, which is called Mustang, is characterised by oasis agriculture. The settlements have an area of irrigated fields around them, but the land nearby looks completely wild from space. It's a lot of rocky mountains, and what seem like vast patterns made in sand by water. Yet down here we found paths. Professor Ur said that diffuse paths, in the Middle East anyway, often mean animal tracks. Human routes are more discrete. 'That seems like an interesting place,' he added, noting where two paths meet. 'Or at least, a lot of people are going there.'

The film spooled all the way down through the mountain system, into the world of mid-hill agriculture. 'It's a really remarkably different settlement pattern,' Ur said. 'Everything here's cultivated. Just every inch! I'd love to know how old some of this is.' It was somewhere on the south side of the Annapurnas, so it's not relevant at the moment. The environment and history of the inner-Himalayan world, and the plateau beyond, is completely different from the monsoon-driven life on the southern slopes of the mountains.

The treeless rangeland that exists today was made by people. Fossil pollen profiles from southern Tibet show that the region was once forested, and that there was a decline in tree cover associated with the presence of pastoralists beginning 4,600 years ago.[1] Other evidence suggests that in the second millennium BC the cultivation of barley, and also wheat, allowed the further colonisation of the plateau.[2] Because rainfall north of the mountains is low, these crops had to be grown in irrigated oases. Peach and apricot trees may have been brought to Tibet from Kashmir at around the same time. The domestication of the yak in this period was another breakthrough. This animal provides muscle power for transport, meat, milk (and therefore butter for eating and lighting), hair for making tents and coats, hides, and three times its body weight in dung annually, burning which provides more energy than any other fuel available. Other animals need taking care of, but yaks can be turned out to fend for themselves in most weather.³

Example of the petroglyphs near Kagbeni (courtesy of Perdita Pohle)

The first evidence of permanent human occupation in Mustang seems to be some centuries later than on the plateau. There are large stones near Kagbeni carved with hundreds of hoofprints, blue sheep, deer, human figures, axe heads, solar discs, labyrinths, and cup marks. They are attributed to the first millennium BC, although there's no really good way to date them and the writing surface seems to have been used for some time.[4] The site was largely destroyed in 2024 in a bungled attempt to preserve it.[5] What it meant isn't knowable, but the animals depicted suggest the area was at least partly forested when it was made.

From around that time the sequence of the upper Kali Gandaki's uniquely rich archaeology begins. Excavations at settlement sites, cut 6 metres deep, show phases of occupation back to about 350 BC.[6] Spectacular burials have been discovered from this early phase, in the galleries of caves that were dug into cliffs above the valley. The bodies, which are interned in wooden bunks, were naturally mummified by the dry air. They were accompanied by glass, shell, carnelian, silk, copper, and bronze objects which indicate trading links from Persia to China. These people were connected to the silk roads, running east and west through Central Asia. The archaeology of plant remains shows barley, buckwheat, flax, and apricots in the prehistoric period (1000–400 BC), the addition of wheat, millet, and peas in the period 400 BC–100 AD, and the presence of crops that must have been traded from the south, including lentils and rice. A thousand years later they had dill and coriander.[7] Trade enabled people to link one ecosystem to another. The people of trans-Himalayan regions such as Mustang benefitted from their intermediary position between lowland farmers who had grain, and pastoral nomads of the plateau who had salt, without which no one can survive.

Settlements came and went, and so did whole kingdoms, which over centuries ebbed and flowed through these valleys and across the neighbouring regions of the plateau. The salt-trading kingdom of Lo Manthang emerged in the late fourteenth century. In the sixteenth century the village of Kagbeni, where Conrad and I spent the night, was built at a controlling point in the valley, not only on the north–south route but also between passes through the mountains to the east and west.

After the establishment of the Nepali state, Kagbeni's importance was superseded by settlements slightly further south, where a customs point for the salt-trading monopoly I've already mentioned was established. Whoever held the monopoly was entitled to buy, and exchange for grain, all the salt that was brought this far by traders from Tibet. By the early twentieth century the cost of the licence was Rs 150,000, the equivalent of 56 kilograms of gold, implying a daily trade of almost 3 metric tonnes of salt.[8] Life never stopped changing, but it changed more slowly then. The Chinese takeover of Tibet brought more rapid developments.

In 1946 the first Khampas were seen in Kagbeni. These were women, children, and men with guns and swords, from a distant and strife-torn part of Tibet called Kham. The Khampas robbed people and caused terror by shooting in the air. During the 1950s Communist China asserted sovereignty over Tibet. In 1959 the Dalai Lama fled and the Chinese tried to close the border, which had scarcely existed until then. (Just as Nepal's southern boundary was only mapped after the British occupied the other side, the northern border was delineated after the Chinese occupied Tibet.)[9] Soon enough there was a flourishing cross-border insurgency in Mustang, in which a guerrilla force of refugees from Kham raided the People's Liberation Army. The days of the salt route were nearly over. Meanwhile, the first roads in southern Nepal began to spread iodised Indian salt in the domestic market, which the government subsidised.

When an anthropologist called Christoph von Fürer-Haimendorf visited Mustang and Dolpo in 1962 some salt was still being traded. But he found that yak herds were being depleted by what he called the marauding Khampas, and that there were encampments of Tibetan refugees leading to problems of overgrazing. In Kagbeni Haimendorf and the Khampa guerrillas drank chyang beer together and flirted with the young woman who served them. The Khampas came and went with an easy familiarity that Haimendorf raised an eyebrow at, and helped the woman with her brewing, while the anthropologist offered to take her as his junior wife. He wrote that he saw Khampas at every corner and looking out of practically every door and window. The atmosphere was that of a small garrison town, and when he went into a house (clearly the handsome old building now used as the Red House Hotel) he found himself in a courtyard surrounded by open storerooms, packed with sacks of rice flour and other provisions for the Khampa encampments in the hills.[10] They were not, he judged, a trained fighting force, but rather a rabble of young and middle-aged men bewildered by the turn their lives had taken. He learnt that they were funded by the Dalai Lama, using a relay of eight intermediaries from his base in India up the Kali Gandaki gorge to Mustang.

I don't know about the eight intermediaries. But the Khampas were being secretly trained at Camp Hale, Colorado, and funded by the CIA. When they captured a pouch of valuable Chinese documents the Americans gave their leader a Swiss watch.[11] This is why there's such a large spy satellite photograph of Mustang in 1964, now declassified for the benefit of science.

The demise of the salt trade, in part thanks to the Khampas, led to a decline in Mustang's population. Also in the 1960s, new laws from Kathmandu had the effect of fragmenting family landholdings.[12] And, when apples were introduced in 1966, a new means of livelihood emerged. By 2000 there were 40,000 apple trees in orchards throughout the lower parts of the district.[13] Now the weather is getting wetter because of climate change, which is causing disease in the apple trees. Orchards are being planted further into Upper Mustang, while vegetables and cereals replace orchards in the south. The year after Conrad and I were there, freak rains caused the worst flood in decades, sweeping away land and parts of the road.[14] A few years after that, thirty houses in Kagbeni were destroyed when half the year's rain fell in a single day.[15] At the same time, the shrinking snow fields and glaciers leave some villages without water for irrigation.

※

In the morning Conrad and I set out from Kagbeni towards Dolpo, on the route across the passes to the west – leaving the area covered by the satellite photograph, unfortunately. Our equipment was loaded onto five mules and we were accompanied by a guide named Ayita, a cook, a muleteer, and two porters who carried the kitchen stuff in two large baskets. 'It's like the nineteenth century,' Conrad said. 'We're heading into the Himalaya and I don't know who the prime minister will be when we come out.' Britain was more than a year into the national breakdown that followed Brexit at the time.

The sky was perfectly blue. The arid valley sides were eroded into organ pipes and chimneys. The ground was dusty, strewn with rocky fragments, and partly covered by pillows of thorny scrub. The few junipers and silver birch were twisted like bonsai. Below us, the silver river made a snakeskin surface on its gravel bed. Hillsides with grazing were covered by webs of animal tracks, like capillaries.

Where there were footpaths we could see how they made smooth arcs around the landforms. Where motorable roads were being cut they took theodolite-straight zigzags up the slopes.

Western travellers describing the Tibetan landscape have often marvelled at the subtlety and beauty of the colours. The mountains were orange, yellow, grey, olive, and aubergine, caused by minerals or by lichen on the rocks, I supposed. Without climbing

up there it was hard to say. The hills of Upper Mustang were still in front of us – red and purple – somehow looking like the primeval seabed that they are. They are quite different from the mountains we were climbing into. We crossed the shoulder of a hill and entered a staggering valley. Profile after profile of its steep sides plunged to the canyon below in receding inky shades. Glaciated peaks and imposing gendarmes stood above us. The scree slopes had been ploughed by boulders crashing off those pinnacles.

We passed the summer village of Sangda and the winter village of Ghok, which is actually at a higher altitude but preferable in the cold because it gets more sun. There is a deserted village on the other side of the valley, given up decades ago for lack of water and too many landslides. The disused fields around it looked like bars of music on the steep slope.[16] In fact, the whole landscape was covered by webs of lines. There were the tracks of crashing boulders and the strata in the rock. But especially there were paths, some of which were almost imperceptibly thin, gathering like fibres into twine. And as we walked and looked around it seemed to me that these lines showed people and livestock had reached every point in the landscape, however precarious or inaccessible seeming, in which resources could be found.

We sat in the sun and ate at the foot of what looked like a worrying section where the path climbed improbably across a cliff face. Conrad, who works in economic policy, suggested that the process by which viable routes are found, and valleys humanised, could be thought of as an error-correcting feedback loop.

At the base of the Sangda-la (la means pass) we saw the last trees we would encounter for a while. They had grains of rice lodged in their bark where pack animals had scratched themselves and snagged their sacks. These junipers were clearly old. They were gnarled survivors in a nook of the mountain. Their unsheltered upper parts were blasted bare grey spikes. Conrad proposed that the traces of humanity we were discussing, like the rice grains in the bark, the paths themselves, and the odd fire site or piece of plastic at the wayside, provided some kind of comfort in what would otherwise have been a desolate wilderness. So the skeletons of the mules that had perished on the route, though they seemed pessimistic, must have a similar meaning? The meaning would be that there's constant struggle here, to tame, adapt, and survive.

Rocks pierced the mountainside in jagged clusters, as if fistfuls of huge stone pencils had been twisted off and shattered. The path climbed through dusty screes. The stones we walked on were shaped like blades of many sizes, from swords and daggers to the bodkin our crew used to mend our gear. Some of these stones had been stacked together into cones. This was religious architecture. The monument, called a stupa, represents the funeral mound of a great teacher. The cairns or stupas had been erected to tame the route.

The top of the pass was a small saddle on an otherwise sharp and craggy ridge. There were prayer flags and thousands of hoofprints in the dry mud. Perhaps these were the goats we'd seen driven down to Pokhara. According to our map this pass was at 5,100 metres, but my altimeter disappointingly showed just 4,939. Our map claimed that the next pass – which was standing right in front of us – was lower than this one, but we could clearly see that it was higher. And it marked our path where it would have been deadly to venture. When at last we reached the top of the next pass we found another group of tourists resting there, while walking the other way. Together we produced as many variant altitudes as there were maps and altimeters among us. Our map seemed to be symbolic, a representation of the landscape that shouldn't be taken too literally. Then we descended into a bare valley and walked down it for several hours.

The walk I've just described took three days. We'd crossed the watershed from the Gandaki into the Karnali basin. We made our camp on the third night in that bare valley, which the sun soon left, and it was very cold. The little river gurgled on but spilt water quickly froze. The five mules, which we'd termed The Five Brexiteers and named Rees-Mogg, Johnson, Gove, Leadsom, and another that I forget, wandered away across the river, so the muleteer got freezing feet to bring them back. It was good to get the sun again when it reached us after breakfast in the morning.

※

On the afternoon of the fourth day we began encountering the outlying architecture of the village of Chharka. There were stone walls beside the path, quite broad and long but connected to nothing at either end. Dark slabs from the hills had been laid in the base and rounded white river stones on top. Every stone in these walls was carved with texts or mantras, especially the syllables 'Om mani padme hum'. Then there was a prismatic shaft of black rock emerging from the earth. People had heaped white calcite pebbles on and around it. Monuments like these bless travellers, or they're the shrines of gods who occupy the landscape, or they're offerings to them, or they mark the boundaries of the village and protect it, or they do all of those things.

The oldest part of the village of Chharka is on a mound at the junction of two rivers. This setting, along with the mostly windowless outward-facing walls, has led visitors to suppose that the site was chosen for security against other people. It was surrounded by fields of ripe barley, which looked warm and lovely in the evening sun.

Conrad and I wanted to buy a goat, but the villagers wouldn't sell us one — that would be a sin on the tenth day of the month, when they worship the pioneer and teacher Guru Rinpoche. We sat in the sun and drank a couple of cans of Chinese beer. The old shopkeeper sat on a camping mat, swinging a prayer wheel and rocking through the recitation of a manuscript. But the following morning we could make our purchase. The porters slaughtered the brute on the riverbank, and the jointed meat was hung up in the sun around our tent. This day — the eleventh, of the ninth Tibetan month — had been chosen by the village to begin the harvest.

The food economy, or political ecology of Dolpo, is based on an unusual combination. The people are farming nomads.[17] They grow barley in the fields around their villages (which are said to be the highest permanent settlements in the world), and they move their flocks and herds across extensive rangelands.

I chatted frivolously with half a dozen women who were cutting barley. They were mostly unmarried, and they wanted to tease me for not bringing my wife along.

'Our language is easy,' one of them claimed, referring to her Tibetan dialect, not the Nepali we were speaking. 'Everywhere else they talk up and down like a song. But here we talk straight.'

'In Saldang,' according to another woman, speaking of another village, 'they say *eee, ooooo*. They talk like that.' She tipped her head and rolled her eyes.

The harvesters were busy from shortly after dawn. First they concentrated on the fields that belong to the monks, beneath their ruined former monastery on the far side of the river.[18] That was mostly done by noon. At lunchtime there were two groups over there. In one group they were throwing hay at each other. The other was picnicking with jugs of beer. Occasionally a cry of female laughter carried across the valley.

For lunch we ate our goat's offal and blood. Then our crew played cards while Conrad and I went to wash in the river. The moon, which was waxing in its eleventh day, rose and sat in the eastern afternoon sky as it had throughout our journey so far.

Besides barley the village raises animals, whose most important product is milk, which is made into butter. Work is divided along gender lines. Women stay near their village, or at least in their home valley. (One of the harvesters I spoke with had never been to the next village, which is called Tinje, two days' walk away.) The men roam further afield. At this time of year the animals were close by, ready to be brought in to graze on the barley stubble. In the tenth month some male animals would be culled for meat. In the winter the animals used to be sent to the plateau to be kept by the nomads there, whose steppes are less snow-bound than these valleys, but that pattern has been disrupted now.

Subsistence and profit in this landscape produced partly insular, largely self-governing village polities. Rational choice theory, which claims that people will act as individuals to maximise their own benefits, also claims that there is an exceptional situation in small communities. These groups foster mutual trust, and concern for the common wheel, thus solving the problem of how social order could have emerged. It's an argument that led the anthropologist Mary Douglas to exclaim, 'Has no one writing on this subject ever lived in a village?'[19]

In the village of Te, in Mustang, men apparently used to wear their hair in topknots secured with long needles to prevent them from being grabbed in fights.[20] In the same village, a good way to exercise your antipathy towards a neighbour is to throw a handful of weeds in their irrigation channel. Then you can watch your enemy's family bent double, weeding their barley all summer. So the community oath of Te, which was taken every year by the villagers, includes this provision: May all those who throw weeds into the irrigation system be punished by the territorial gods.[21] It has other provisions on access to fodder; the protection of animals used for stud; and not entering into sexual relations, or even sharing any information at all, with neighbouring communities. May all who take information from the inside to the outside be punished by the territorial gods, the village law concludes.

An anthropologist called Charles Ramble has argued that the particular combination of Buddhism and the worship of local divinities, especially in connection with village governance and production, the selection of village officers, ceremonies related to cooperative activities, and the ritual affirmation of the community law, amounts to a distinct civil religion. The civil religion (which Ramble compares to the piety surrounding American government and its revered texts, national holidays, and sacred sites) relates to the governance of the community rather than theological principles, and in its specific features it belongs to a single village alone.[22] Like the politics of Te, the religion of Te is concerned with the terms and the limits of cooperation between households, and the management of natural resources.

Villages throughout the Buddhist Himalaya have their own territorial gods and their own traditions of government, which might – for example – impose a fine for every hoofprint when one household's livestock damages another household's crops. Crucially, the law divides access to scarce resources such as irrigation, fodder, pasture, and dung.[23] This often involves sortilege, which means making decisions by drawing lots or casting dice. By applying equal probabilities to the allotment of shares, sortilege removes human bias and divines the whims of the gods instead. In these ways, while herds are private property yet scarce resources such as pasture are common, they are successfully managed.

So the people up here provide a proof against the conventional dogma known as 'The Tragedy of the Commons'. Based on faulty claims about common grazing in European history, this influential essay of the 1960s argued that public property will always be degraded, so resources must be secured in private hands to preserve them from the ever-increasing masses. It's a claim that's been taken up as a truth about human nature, with the essay's title as a slogan, although it's just the expression of an ideology.[24] These days it seems the theory got the culprit wrong, and it's mostly wealthy private interests that destroy public property.

※

The day the harvest began was also the day that the sitting member of Parliament, and leading candidate in the forthcoming election, was planning to campaign in Chharka. I thought of the woman Girish and I had met, who said, 'They come around here when there's an election. The rest of the time, even if we want to bow to their feet we can't find them.' The candidate's staff arrived before him. The candidate, travelling by horse, was expected around three. By four a drunken villager was stumbling around, shouting at the harvesters that they were stupid to do today what they could do tomorrow. They should stop their work and come to hear the big man. So in an atmosphere of general levity they gathered, but there was still no sign of the politician by the time Conrad and I went for a drink.

※

In the morning the village was preparing to slaughter a goat, drink beer, and dance, sponsored by the politician. We walked on.

Not far above Chharka we reached the encampment of a family who'd spent five summer months grazing their herd far and wide. They'd been across the border in China, briefly. Now they were waiting to re-enter the village and graze on the stubble as soon as the fields were cut. They were burying food in pits to last the winter, because this campsite was frequently used by the family. It had simple stone furnishings that they'd erected their tents around.

In a striking phrase in an essay on the domestic architecture – including the tents – of Dolpo, the anthropologist Corneille Jest referred to the *courage* of the people, who make their life in one of the most difficult regions of the world.[25] We bought some dried cheese from the old couple and carried on. Soon we crossed another pass, at about 5,000 metres, and I climbed above it to take photographs. While I was coming down herds of sheep and yaks were being driven over in the direction of the village.

The Tibetan tradition naturally sees the wild environment as a threat to people's precarious survival, and their history is about unwilding it. Until the seventh century, when Buddhism first arrived, the entire land was occupied by a fearsome demoness. King Tongsen Gampo's Chinese wife showed him how to

pin her body down with a pattern of monasteries. In the eighth century King Trisong Detsen brought Guru Rinpoche (precious teacher), who is also known as Padmasambhava (lotus born), to evangelise Buddhism in Tibet. He is the Tantric magician from what's now called Swat, in Pakistan, whom the herdsman Girish and I met said had travelled up by Gosainkund. There's hardly a place in the Buddhist Himalaya where he isn't supposed to have been. But although he was apparently a real person, there's almost no trace of the historical Guru Rinpoche. He's a divine figure now, credited with taming wild spirits and implanting Buddhism wherever he went. The old shopkeeper who sold me and Conrad beer in Chharka said that, long ago, Guru Rinpoche had also been this way.

The Sino-Tibetan treaty of 822 AD is carved on a column in the Tibetan capital, Lhasa. It reads in part:

> A treaty that is made like this may never change. We invoke the three jewels [the Buddha, his teachings, and his followers], the various saints, the sun and moon, the planets and stars as witnesses. Having declared this with solemn words after the animals have been sacrificed and the oath has been sworn, the treaty is made.[26]

This shows that despite the arrival of Buddhism in previous centuries, animal sacrifice was still practised in Lhasa.

The Tibetan empire disintegrated in the following decades. A period of anarchy ensued, personified by the vengeful ghost of an assassinated monk called Palgyi Yonten, who appeared wherever the trouble was spreading, riding a wolf and beating the earth with his iron staff.[27] Then, in the eleventh century, the Tibetan world underwent a cultural transformation. Buddhism, which had a tenuous position since its first introduction, was rejuvenated and flourished, spreading quickly to enclaves including Mustang and Dolpo. Missionary teachers came from India, such as the Bengali monk Atisha, who defeated Palgyi Yonten.[28] Tibetan Buddhists travelled to India and conducted a vast translation project, transferring a huge corpus of Sanskrit Buddhist literature into the Tibetan language, in what has been called the wholesale import of one culture into another.[29]

One of the men involved was the Great Translator Marpa. He travelled from Tibet via Kathmandu to India and back three times. At home he sold his Tantric empowerments for a high price: 10 ounces of gold for the spell to protect children.

There was a man called Milarepa who lived in the Nepal–Tibet borderlands in the eleventh century. His case wraps together many parts of traditional Tibetan thinking on the landscape, it illustrates the historical development I'm trying to describe, and reference was made to him by several people we met, so I'll describe Milarepa's legend in some detail.

Mila was probably born in 1040. According to his fifteenth-century biography, that was his first ordinary deed: the deed of his birth.[30] It was a world of intense religiosity, where people had experiences of faith that caused the hairs on their body to quiver, and beautiful maidens appeared to address holy men before disappearing like a rainbow. From his boyhood Mila was known for his beautiful singing voice. His mother was a beautiful woman, skilled in worldly affairs, who loathed her enemies and loved her friends. While he was still a child his father died, and the family's field and other property were stolen by his uncle and aunt, leaving his mother and her children destitute. This was his second ordinary deed, the biography says: the deed of practising the truth of suffering in its entirety.

Mila's mother said, 'I would like to see you draped in a fine cloak and mounted upon a horse with your stirrups slashing the throats of our hated enemies. Such will not come to pass, yet success is still possible by means of treachery. So I would like you to train in black magic, curses, and casting hail. Then you should destroy all those who inflicted misery on us, villagers and countrymen, beginning with your uncle and aunt, cutting off their family line for nine generations. See if you can do that.'

Not at all the easy-going type, his mother concluded her speech by threatening to kill herself in front of Mila if he failed to return with black magic suitable for a desperate family. He set off.

Mila's first teacher was a second-rate lama, who promised him evil mantras to make heaven and earth tremble and crash. Would-be students offered him a manifest of precious trade goods (gold and turquoise, tea and silk, woollen cloth and butter, barley, horses, yaks, and sheep) in exchange for his teaching, but only Mila offered his body, speech, and mind. He constructed a cell on a mountain spur and in it he made a mandala, which means a kind of cosmic diagram. Mandalas represent ideas in Tibetan religion, and also in geography and building. They depict and also embody a principal deity in the centre, with sets of associated deities arranged in circles around him or her, mapping out the characteristics and sometimes the physical setting of the god at the centre.

On the fourteenth day of Mila's meditation, deities appeared at the margins of his mandala carrying thirty-five human heads and hearts covered with blood. 'This is what you wanted,' they said, and piled the heads and hearts at the edge of the mandala. Mila later discovered that thirty-five people had gathered at his uncle's house for a wedding. While he practised his magic the courtyard filled with spiders, snakes, tadpoles, and a scorpion as big as a yak. The tethered horses of the wedding guests stampeded, pulling the house down, and everyone inside was killed.

In an episode from the ensuing events Mila's mother connives to send him help by means of a wandering holy man. She offers to patch the itinerant's cloak, hides 7 ounces of gold inside, then embroiders the stars of Pleiades above the treasure with coarse white thread. Mila encounters the holy man, recognises the sign, recovers the gold and uses it to buy more magic. In the magical pit of his cell he gathers a storm. Lightning flickers inside the cloud. Simply by pointing his finger he can direct the hail against his enemies. But his teacher, the lama, tells him to wait until the barley is standing high before he acts. In fact, this has been an especially good year for barley. Mila returns to his region. He stands at the head of his valley. He summons the deities, gathers the clouds, and beats the hail down on his village. A mountainside is washed away. Seeing the loss of their harvest the villagers weep. This was his third and last ordinary deed: the deed in which he annihilated his enemies.

Mila is a great sinner, a mass murderer. He sets out in search of Buddhist enlightenment and redemption. He tries to persuade Marpa, the Great Translator, to accept him as a disciple. But Marpa treats him harshly, setting a series of hopeless and backbreaking trials. Mila is ordered to repeatedly reconstruct fortified towers, a task which suggests the insecurity of life in what the text calls the gloomy land of Tibet in this period. After endless ordeals, when anyone else would have given up long ago, Marpa accepts the young magician as his disciple. The suffering that Marpa has caused him redeems Milarepa.

Marpa transmits esoteric teachings. After long, devoted study and intense meditation he says, 'Son, I have introduced you to the truth that phenomena are like an illusion. Seek out retreat sites in the mountains, the snows, and the forest.' Marpa lists several mountains, rivers, and sacred lands. After naming each place he intones: 'Go there and meditate.' These are uninhabited places, where conditions are favourable for solitary self-realisation. The teacher sings:

In the rock caves of desolate places
You'll find the trade of life's round for transcendence.

There are no more ordinary acts for Milarepa, only supreme deeds. Life is short and death strikes without warning, so he dedicates himself to becoming a perfect buddha. He sets off again, begging for meat, butter, and cheese from highland nomads and barley flour from lowland farmers. One nomad tent he approaches turns out to be his aunt's. She recognises him and sets her dog loose.

Feeding on thin barley gruel he meditates, becomes intensely cold, and experiences a state of luminosity. Three years pass, and he finds some nettles to eat. His body, which is already like a skeleton, turns green. 'For seasoning, use nettles,' he says. 'For flour, too, use nettles. For salt, use nettles.' This is his cookery. 'I have sacrificed food, clothing, and conversation,' he says. 'There is no one in this world more courageous and high-minded than me.' His eyes are sunken in their sockets. His bones stick out. Fine, bristling, greenish hair grows from the skin hanging off his bones. The hair on his head is in frightful disarray. His own sister mistakes him for a ghost.

Milarepa's biography, his worldly youth, followed by renunciation, awakening and liberation, teaching and a remarkable death, parallels that of the Buddha on which it's based.[31] In certain respects Milarepa is a bit like Jesus, too. He's an earthy, rustic, ethical teacher whose historical reality is slightly out of reach. He's known through accounts that began to be written by disciples and exegetes shortly after his death. In Milarepa's case, there's also a large number of songs he purportedly composed and sang on apposite occasions (that sweet voice he'd had since boyhood), and these were compiled by his most famous biographer in the fifteenth century. Anyway, Milarepa's charisma has held people in its power since his lifetime until ours. Both men were concerned with redeeming corrupt humanity and solving the problem of mortality. Both meditated in the wilderness. Although Christian commentators have often seen the desert of the Holy Land as an environment conducive by its nature to monotheism, Milarepa naturally found cohorts of spirits in what he supposedly called the world's broad and vast northern quarter.[32]

Milarepa's first attempt to overcome the miseries of physical nature is by abnegating his body, and he fantasises about his own oblivion:

> My death unknown among people
> And rotting corpse unseen by vultures –
> If thus I can die in this mountain retreat
> The aims of this yogin will be complete,[33]

he sings. But after years in the cave he becomes reconciled to the senses:

> This body, so hard to obtain and easily broken,
> Found something to eat and now feels quite well,[34]

he sings later. He wanders through the whole universe, from top to bottom, in his dreams. 'I continued to meditate,' he says, 'and gained the ability to actually fly through the sky.' As he flies he hears the people below talking about him. This reminds me of what I read somewhere else, that hot-air balloonists who've flown over the Tibetan plateau report that the voices of people, and dogs barking on the ground, carry upwards with remarkable clarity through the desiccated air.[35]

In a certain sanctuary Milarepa sings the 'Great Song of the Snow Ranges'. In another place he sings the 'Song of Wild Asses'. And in a certain cave he teaches his followers the 'Cycle of the Pigeon'. He teaches hunters not to kill. Through this long phase of his life he gathers disciples and tames places by meditating in them. He's asked to identify the sites of all his retreats, so that future members of his doctrinal lineage can also gain merit by meditating there.

Milarepa's life ends with a betrayal, and his own self-sacrifice. A wealthy and dissolute lama sends his lover with a gift of poisoned curds, and Milarepa, although he understands the ploy, eats it. Thanks to his amazing spiritual strength his death is prolonged, allowing time for final teachings, miracles, and poignant last meetings with his disciples. He says that as a result of their previous sinful deeds worldly people experience a host of miseries, such as birth, ageing, sickness, and death. Nothing whatsoever can avert them – not the power of kings, not the skill of the brave, not the bodies of beautiful women, not the wealth of the rich, not the speed of cowards, not the joking of the sharp-tongued. 'But I have an effective rite for avoiding misery and experiencing everlasting happiness,' he says.

'Please give it to us,' say his followers.

'Very well. It is certain that you will experience the miseries of what's called life's round: everything accumulated is exhausted, everything constructed is destroyed, everything united is separated, everything born dies. Since life is short and the time of death is uncertain, devote yourself to meditation. Act in such a way that you will not be ashamed of yourself.'[36]

His killer repents and is forgiven. In his eighty-fourth year, at sunrise on the fourteenth day of the last winter month of the wood-hare year, under the constellation of Ashlesha, Milarepa demonstrates the act of dissolving his physical body into the sphere of reality. A great mandala appears in the sky, where there are lotuses, rainbows, clouds in the form of umbrellas, victory banners, curtains, canopies, ribbons, tassels, streamers, and the like. Stupas formed by five-coloured clouds adorn the mountain peaks and a crystal stupa fills the sky with light.[37] This description, extending through his extraordinary cremation, lasts several pages.

In a more firmly historical way than the even more mythical Guru Rinpoche a couple of centuries earlier, Milarepa mastered the local demons and claimed the landscape of the Himalayan borderlands for Buddhism. Many of his places are still important pilgrimage sites. The most famous among them is Mount Kailash.

✳

Conrad and I met another trekking group passing the other way, which was composed of recently retired French people. Being gourmands they'd also slaughtered a goat. The man I spoke with said he found Dolpo sad. Although he had no way to speak to the people, he'd looked into their eyes and seen that they were sad. Conrad's observation, following this conversation, was that Dolpo is full of Western baby-boomers using their over-endowed pensions, subsidised by the young, to pursue their generation's characteristic devotion to personal experience, and that in a few years, when they're too old to walk, the trekking firms will offer horse-borne tours. So the entire encounter touched upon the same questions of sensuality, suffering, and mortality that Milarepa grappled with.

Our path descended into a broad valley of coarse grass and pillows of low, thorny scrub, at about 4,700 metres. Loosely woven paths flowed over the valley floor. This valley had gentle forms, except along the western side where black crags and pinnacles stood hundreds of metres above us. Over there, the strata in the cliffs had been turned right over and curled backwards like a mountain-sized wave of rock. I fell behind to photograph the wavering tracks with my new large-format camera, which took some time to set up, and then I enjoyed walking alone for a while through the great space. The others had disappeared somewhere and it felt very fine to be here with no one in sight.

As the valley sank, shrubs appeared on the riverbank, turning from green to yellow, and gold to red. The ground became thick with the heathery forms of low and varied bushes. Compared to the earlier bareness it seemed soft and pleasant. Finally, our stream joined a larger one, which was the headwaters of the Karnali River. We hung our boots around our necks to wade across and reach our campsite, which was already in shade at the end of the afternoon. It was lovely to see the pleasure of the mules – Johnson, Rees-Mogg, and the rest – rolling in the dust when their packs were taken off, the bells pealing around their necks.

There were a few fireplaces, which showed that travellers sometimes spend the night here. Our porters collected dung and made a good fire for us after night fell. We crouched around it so close that the flames leapt in our faces, and the porters dipped their hands right into the flames to warm them. Conrad mentioned the stars, many of which were visible despite the nearly full moon, and Ayita – our guide – said reflectively that the sun and moon and stars go around the earth. The others murmured their assent. In the black beyond our circle the Karnali made its gentle sound. The mules' bells chimed. The flames rushed. I translated Ayita's remarks for Conrad.

'Do you want to break it to them?' he said.

Every village has its own sacred landscape, in the notional centre of which sits a holy mountain whose god was tamed by a hero such as Guru Rinpoche or Milarepa. He opened the land, incorporated the god and the mountain in the Buddhist pantheon, and made it a protector of the village. He tamed the place. This type of primal, local divinity is called a yul lha (lord of the land). The yul lha are often concerned with matters of daily survival, like the fertility of the fields, the village's water supply, the orderly management of the community, and sickness and health. The worship of the yul lha still occasionally retains pre-Buddhist elements, such as blood sacrifice, which is suggestive of their ancient origin.[38]

Buddhism seems to have first reached Dolpo during the period of growth roughly coinciding with Milarepa's career, in the eleventh century, when the monastery at Bicher was established. In the twelfth century, Druptop Senge Yeshe (1181–1255), a follower of Milarepa, came from Kailash to Dolpo and opened the Crystal Mountain at Shey as a site of pilgrimage and meditation. According to an early biography written by his own disciple, Druptop Senge Yeshe lived in a cave at Shey called the Vajra (thunderbolt) Fortress.[39] He identified the Crystal Mountain as the home of the Buddhist god Cakrasamvara, and engaged in conflict with a local (pre-Buddhist) sorcerer. In the course of this struggle Druptop Senge had dreams in which he flew through the air, and frightening scorpions and tadpoles also featured. At length his opponent died. In other words, he accomplished the victory of Buddhism over pagan magic that his master Milarepa embodied in his life, and he did for Shey what Milarepa did for Kailash. I was reminded of Druptop Senge a couple of years later while on holiday in the islands of Scotland when I picked up an early biography of the sixth-century Irish missionary Columba. On the first page I read that when countless hosts of horrible devils were making war against him, Columba, with God's help, repelled them. He curbed the raging fury of wild beasts and confounded the wizards of the Picts.[40]

The first biography of Druptop Senge Yeshe includes realistic descriptions of travel, featuring sick horses and brigands. But in the later traditions Druptop Senge doesn't just dream of flying, he actually takes flight on snow lions, and there are dreadful descriptions of Shey before he tamed it, haunted by non-human beings that ate people. In one account Druptop Senge sees the rocks transform into the joking and dancing embodiment of Cakrasamvara's consort Vajravarahi, with four faces and twelve arms. In a state of high realisation he dwelt in her vagina for twelve days and experienced the joys of bliss and emptiness. The mountain became a mandala, or the elaborate palace of the god. The snow lions he conjured left footprints in the rocks, which became part of the itinerary now visited by pilgrims. The pilgrims dance at the place he danced.

But the process of settling the region took time. Several of the men who tamed Dolpo were born in the fifteenth century and their biographies were written by their own contemporaries, who knew them personally.⁴¹ Lama Sonam Lodrö (1456–1521) came to Dolpo when his home in Mustang was consumed by war, the devil had blessed the minds of men, there was famine, and all sentient beings were given to suffering. He retreated for years into mountain caves, abnegated his body by mixing sand in his food, and tried to deny the reality of the physical world. The freezing rocks around him were replaced by ecstatic visions of flaming gods. These gods in their mandalas, rather than the snowy land afflicted by hatred and robbery, were the ultimate reality. Sonam Lodrö maintained ongoing personal relationships with the yul lha around him. By entering that level of realisation a great lama could magically intervene in the world of outward appearances, to produce rain or to cure people when the gods inflicted smallpox.

Sonam Lodrö's younger contemporary Chyökyap Pelzang (1476–1565) was a landscape magician in the same mould. From the age of three he wanted to go into the mountains, to defeat the wild animals of false doctrine.⁴² These prelates' personalities come through in the records. Chyökyap Pelzang had a peer and contemporary of equal stature called Panden Lodrö (1467–1536). He was a different type of character, more sober monastic administrator than wild mystic.

You can see the local gods in action in a prayer from Mustang, which implores the yul lha: When we go forth, be our escort, and receive us when we return; … if we go onto the crags, be our steps and ladders; if we pass through water, be our bridges; if we walk on the trails, be our props; if we travel in darkness, be our lamps; kill our enemies who are hostile to us; subdue the obstructive demons who harm us; reverse the misfortunes caused by hindrances.⁴³

Over the years the monks and teachers tried to persuade the villagers to abandon pre-Buddhist practices, such as blood sacrifices to the yul lha, and give up unholy activities like hunting.⁴⁴ At the same time, village-level sacred geographies that arranged the yul lha in a pattern (a mandala) around the village became connected to a sacred geography that encompasses the whole

Tibetan world. The prayer I quoted above, which appeals to the local gods to be our steps and ladders when we go into the crags, begins with the famous gods of faraway places such as Mount Kailash and Kashmir (in the barbarous lowlands, as it says). Then the recitation circles in through successively closer regions, until it concludes by addressing the gods around the village where the appeal is made.

Before I end my summary of Tibetan sacred geography, there's another thing I should mention. There may have been a tendency since early times to bury religious treasures during periods of strife, to be recovered in better days. By the thirteenth century a movement of treasure-seekers (tertons) had emerged. They cultivated meditative states and received supernatural signs that helped them to discover encoded texts hidden in temple walls and statues, and also to literally unearth them from mountainsides and caves. These texts (called terma) had apparently been concealed throughout Tibet by Guru Rinpoche, to be retrieved when they were needed.[45] They introduced all sorts of new material, including new yogic techniques, liturgies, architectural principles, statements of philosophy, and references to contemporary politics – contemporary, that is, to the period of their discovery, couched as the prophecies of Guru Rinpoche. The text of this sort that is most famous in the West is known as *The Tibetan Book of the Dead*. So, just as the supply of Indian Buddhist scriptures to translate into Tibetan was drying up, a new class of apocryphal Buddhist writing was discovered that could literally be extracted from the landscape.

Guru Rinpoche had also left another gift in store. In the fourteenth century, when Tibetan society was under pressure from the Mongols, a millenarian movement began identifying hidden lands (bayul) among the valleys of the Himalaya. They had been rendered inaccessible by Guru Rinpoche's Tantric magic, to be opened and serve as refuges for Buddhism in times of crisis.[46] They would be like lifeboats in the storm. The Langtang Valley, which Girish and I looked down on from Gosainkund, was one such hidden land. These were earthly paradises, where a yogin could achieve remarkable visions, and ordinary people could obtain eternal youth, strength, beauty, and fertility.

※

It was an icy morning in the camp. We packed up and walked on down the valley. For many minutes two enormous eagles flapped and cavorted around the crags above. By the time we stopped for lunch there was a heat haze flickering between us and the mountainsides.

This part of Dolpo is accessible by an easy pass from China. We saw the track of a motorcycle on the footpath. On the other side of the river a motorable road from the border was even being built. So wheeled transport has penetrated this valley, and it has arrived not far behind the potato. When the Tibetologist David Snellgrove was here in the fifties there were neither potatoes nor hens' eggs. There are still no hens, but we bought potatoes in every village. I wondered if this is one of the very last places in the old world to grow American crops. Potatoes had been introduced to Bhutan, which is not very far away, two centuries earlier.

Outside the village of Tinje the people were celebrating the opening of a new footbridge. When the dance broke up we walked on, passed on the broad, dusty track by motorcyclists and horsemen. The village stood beneath a black hill, which was catching the last of the sun. We entered it by a picturesque wooden bridge across a tiny gorge, then crossed the fields, which had been harvested three days earlier and were now being grazed by sheep, yaks, and horses. The field walls were made from white river stones but the village was built from dark slate, the same colour as the hill above it. There was firewood stacked on the flat roofs of the houses, draped with loosely twisted ropes of hay. The bushels of barley were collected in the yards. This village is the home of Dolpo's great modern landscape painter, Tenzin Norbu.

※

It might seem surprising that while Tibetan painting is always religious, and the landscape is so important to the religion, the environment as it actually appears seems to be absent from the paintings. The various schools of art over the centuries either hardly show any terrain at all, or they show green and rolling hills that don't exist. Months after we were in Tinje I went to see the artist Tenzin Norbu at his home in Kathmandu, and explained that I was trying to write a book about the relationship between people and the landscape. Since he's a famous landscape painter, could he please tell me how he sees it?

'I think many artists, not only in Tibet, but in all the world, earlier, they didn't care about everyday life,' he said.

Since his young days in Tinje he'd been interested in history, but he realised there was no history of everyday life. 'There's only the history of high lamas. If you look for the history of my village you'll never find it. You have to look at important people's history. You know Milarepa? Milarepa was very famous, and his story is very true. He made mistakes, afterwards he was sorry, he made a very good practice every day, and he became a buddha. I like this very much. You can see everything in his life. So I did a lot of work on his story, his life. I learnt from him.

'Also,' he said, 'though we had many lamas in the village, one lama was special. He was a storyteller. In the winter time, when there was not so much to do, he went to every village and he told stories. And he needed illustrations. I worked for this man.'

'How old were you?' I asked.

'From twelve or fifteen I worked for him.'

'How old are you now?'

'Now I am forty-eight. I learnt, and I liked it very much. I had to study the history of everyday life.' This was stuff like driving yaks and having trouble in the snow. 'Everything is there, and I had to find it,' he said, but he was especially inspired by the story of Milarepa. 'You can find everything in his story. That's why I am a landscape artist. And I took care over the landscape. I looked at the shape of the snow in the melting time. And which colours are in the rocks of Dolpo.' In 1991, on his first visit to Kathmandu, Tenzin Norbu saw the work of Hokusai, Van Gogh, and Monet in books. 'They do exactly what I want,' he said. 'Then I got stronger. I said, "Yes, I would make a good artist." And I was right, I found.'

His father was a traditional painter, of the scroll paintings called thangkas. 'He liked to do it the traditional way,' said Tenzin Norbu.

He summarised the history of Tibetan painting for me. The first dominant influence came from Kathmandu. These paintings have a reddish palette. The main god, or Buddha, or high lama, is in the centre with associated figures in a grid of niches (or caves) around him. 'Beautiful!' said Tenzin Norbu. 'I like it very much.'

Later (around the sixteenth century) Tibetan painting came under the influence of Chinese art, which often depicts landscapes, but these aren't Tibetan landscapes. The paintings have a blue and green palette. The figure of the primary subject is still in the centre, surrounded by a host of associated figures which are more freely arranged. And behind them there's a scene of green hills strewn with lotuses and jewels, and various creatures. In the sky there might be banners and ribbons like those that appeared at Milarepa's death. Tenzin Norbu said, 'In the corners of these thangkas there are beautiful waterfalls, that kind of thing. When I was small I was so happy to see this. I like this Buddha [the main subject] but I am more happy here [in the corner of the painting]. I think my freedom was there, my real heart was there. From here I get my big space. Like democracy, let's say.' (It was an obscure remark, but it's how he put it.) 'It's wonderful,' he continued. 'Then I always looked at the landscape. I looked at the colour changing in each month. Rocks! Ah! So beautiful.'

He made many sketches and photographs of rocks.

'The moon is very important,' he said. 'You can see so many moons in my paintings, and also snow, because in my life I grew up with the snow and moon, and blue sky, and I have a very strong memory in my mind. The full moon is very important in Dolpo life. We had no light, no electricity, you know.'

His wife brought green tea for us in a Chinese teapot with matching tiny cups.

The style of Tibetan painting with fanciful green scenery is named after a high lama called the Karmapa. 'These landscapes are completely imaginary,' I said. 'So what do they mean?'

Tenzin Norbu said, 'I think the Karmapa went to China and he saw many Chinese [painted] landscapes. He got this idea. Why don't we put this landscape in thangkas? The Karmapa had power. Nobody could say "don't do that", you know. If I am a small artist and I take this idea from China, higher people would say "you've made a mistake".'

'What about the idea that it's a symbol?' I asked. This reading has been a useful resort for Western scholars. It's argued that the demonic figures clothed in human skins, festooned in skulls and dripping blood, represent the need for horror supposedly felt by Tibetan peasants because of their cruel environment. Or they represent the feudal monks' need to terrify the populace.[47] The copulating divine couples, which are apparently so hard to take literally, don't represent sex but some metaphysical dialectic. And this completely made-up backdrop of pleasant hills and lotuses represents purity of mind.

'It's possible,' he said, and referred to the representations of elephants. 'Of course this is imaginary. The painter knows it has a very long nose and big ears. It's very funny for me. I like it also.' He liked realism, he said, but sometimes what's perfect is boring.

'In my monastery when I was small I had one Cakrasamvara.' This was a painting of the Buddhist god Cakrasamvara with his consort. 'The male is blue and the dakini is white and they are together, naked. It was a very strong one. I think I was seven, eight, nine years old when I asked my father, "What is this?"

'He said, "This blue buddha is the sky and this white dakini is the cloud. It's not really sex. This is about interdependence." If you don't have this cup you can't be drinking tea,' Tenzin added. 'It's beautiful for me. My father said, "Cloud and sky together, they become rain." I was really interested at that time. I think it's true.'

Padmasambhava and the Eight Great Mahasiddhas, a nineteenth-century painting on cloth in the Karmapa style from Kham Province, Eastern Tibet (courtesy of the Rubin Museum of Art). Padmasambhava (Guru Rinpoche) is in the centre. Milarepa is shown in a cave at the bottom right.

When I was in Dolpo I had a sketchpad with me, because I wanted to ask people to draw pictures or maps of their villages. In Tinje Conrad and I settled down in the tent of a trader with long hair across his back named Purba Lama, and we drank a couple of cans of Lhasa beer among his other merchandise. Purba showed us videos on his phone: of a celebration at a Tibetan home in China, of a Tibetan wedding in the Chinese language, and of a Chinese woman in Tibetan costume singing a Tibetan song. She broke down in giggles then bent towards the camera. Eventually I asked Purba to draw me a picture, and one of the other men in the tent, who was called Karma Tashi, reluctantly agreed. He hovered over the page for a long time before making the first mark, then he drew a perfect scheme of Tinje village, filling the entire sheet without making a mistake, although he said he didn't know how to write his name at the bottom. His picture shows the river, the bridge in the little gorge, the fields, the clusters of houses beneath the hill, two monasteries, the positions of the yul lha marked by cairns with flags on top, and the profile of the mountains.

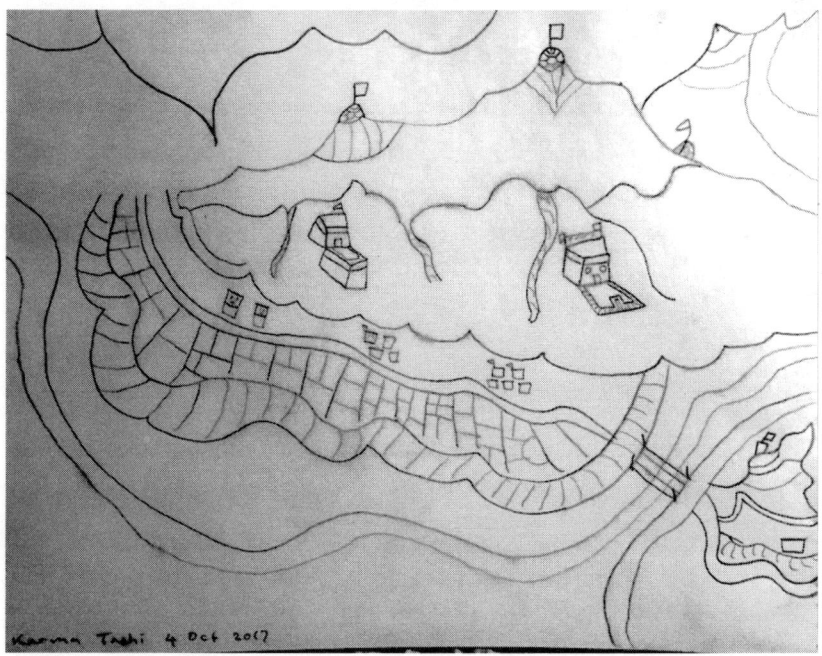

I said to Tenzin Norbu, 'In Dolpo last year I asked people to draw pictures for me. A guy in your village did this one.'

He chuckled. 'Hm-mmm, ha ha, yeah yeah yeah. Very nice,' he said. 'This is my monastery. This is the other monastery. This is the village. This is the bridge. It's true. Before, when I was in this village, I thought this is one of the biggest villages in the world. Then I came to Kathmandu and I thought this is the biggest city in the world. There is no big and small for the eyes. It depends on your mind, I think. Buddha said it also, and I think it's really true. I think when he drew this he thought, "this is the best village", and he tried to do it, you know.' There's more laughter on the tape.

And then Tenzin Norbu described what sounds like a wonderful work of art that's gone. 'I did maps before, too,' he said. 'My village map. When I was small I had white chalk. Inside a Dolpo house it's almost black, because of the smoke, you know. And I made a lot of white marks everywhere. The same as this. This is the monastery. One of the biggest houses is there. This is the village. I thought my place is best.'

Despite what I've just written, there are other ways traditional paintings contain the landscape. For instance, a mandala can be thought of as a map. Also, the paints are made of minerals. In America I visited a restoration laboratory at the Boston Museum of Fine Arts where they work on Tibetan thangkas. They kept the powdered pigments in glass vials: azurite, malachite, turquoise, cinnabar, and pearly ground mica, which is applied to give the work a sheen. 'Beautiful dirt,' the conservator called them.

In the morning, when Conrad and I were in Tinje, I got up early – which is easy to do when you're sleeping in a tent – to take a photograph of the sun striking the hills that face the village. The animals were grazing the stubble, and a few people were collecting dung. Mastiffs with frost in their coats, which had guarded the herds all night, lay with one eye open. I set up my big camera on the tripod. While I waited for the light to spread down the hillside I showed passing people the upside-down image on the glass back. Then I inserted the film holder, removed the dark slide, got the exposure wrong, and I screwed up the development when I got home.

The people of Tinje were preparing to travel to the Chinese border to collect rice, which is provided as food aid by the Nepali

government. It's easier to transport goods by road through China than over the trails through Nepal. Our own mules were loaded, and we walked out of the village past rows of women threshing barley.

The young Karnali River made a small gorge. The mantra 'Om mani padme hum' was carved on the cliffs in many places. After some time we reached the stupas that mark the outlying architecture of Shimen. There was a wide expanse of stones carved with prayers. The whole place was strewn with offerings of words, which must be part of Shimen's mandala. They are landscape art, in the sense of being huge sculptures in which the landscape is the subject as well as the medium.[48] Being addressed to the gods, the landscape is actually the audience as well. The village itself is of reddish houses beneath enormous reddish cliffs, with poplar trees among the buildings. They were the first trees we'd seen in a week.

Almost everyone from Shimen had also gone to the border to collect rice, leaving just a couple of mothers looking after many children. We pitched our tent beside the house of a brawny, garrulous woman who was keen to find fun in us. Her husband had died when she was pregnant with her second child. Conrad called her the Merry Widow.

The Merry Widow had a fierce dog tied in her yard. Herdsmen keep them to protect their animals, and they make them vicious by keeping them chained. At night they're let loose to patrol the camp.[49] You can get charms to protect yourself from these terrifying creatures. The dogs wear spiked collars, to protect them in their fights with snow leopards. Foreign travellers have always paid careful attention to the big dogs of Tibet. Even Marco Polo, who didn't come this way, heard that the region has mastiffs the size of asses, which he believed were used for hunting yaks. Later visitors have described Tibetan dogs as something between a wolf and a bear, and very dangerous, with a bark that makes everything shake.[50]

At the beginning of the colonial period the foreign authors were surgeon-scientists or pragmatic soldier-diplomats, who were often reticent about publishing their observations because they didn't see them as having general worth.[51] George Bogle, a late eighteenth-century British emissary to Tibet, didn't romanticise the people or the places he visited. His landscape descriptions aimed at objectivity, mixing geography with botany. But once the colonial genre of travel writing got going it was driven by romantic adventurers. Journeys would be justified as the pursuit of some archaeological or mountaineering obsession, or as a spiritual pilgrimage. Those books, full of laconic observations and comic dialogue, are imaginative or half fictional, even when they purport to be straight reportage.

Between the late eighteenth century, when the first British travellers still had no word for Buddhism, and the flight of the Dalai Lama in 1959, Tibet became a kind of sacred landscape in the Western imagination. The period coincides with the European craze for mountains, from the early Romantics to the tedious obsession with Mount Everest. For a century Tibet was closed to outsiders, enhancing the country's allure.

At the same time there were also strategic motivations. In the second quarter of the nineteenth century, British security concerns in Afghanistan, Punjab, and Nepal heightened the importance of Himalayan exploration. By the end of the century the Royal Geographical Society, which was founded in 1830, had given more gold medals for Himalayan exploration than for any other region.

Rousseau, who was a citizen of Geneva after all, helped to inaugurate the European taste for mountain scenery. He wrote that he must have mountains to go up and down, fir trees and black forests, torrents and rugged paths with precipices on either side to frighten him.[52] The European Alps provided an aesthetic model for comprehending the Himalayan landscape. Even so, the Himalaya presented a spectacle more intimidating and bleak than Europeans were prepared for. A visitor in 1818 wrote of deep chasms he could scarcely view without shuddering. I never saw such a horrid-looking place, he declared.[53]

My own reaction on first seeing the Himalaya was similar. At the age of nineteen, with two friends from university, I spent seven weeks hitchhiking and walking in Tibet. We spent a few nights camping at Everest base camp with no one else around, and a few days scrambling over the moraines and glaciers there. I'd never imagined such an alienating place, so inimical to the presence of tiny people as those vast and shifting heaps of debris, which we could always hear rumbling and collapsing nearby, and which crumbled and slid as we clambered over them. How cold we were when we fell in a torrent of water where it disappeared into a cavern under the Rongbuk Glacier. Rather conventionally, we narrowly escaped being savaged by an enormous dog.

From the get-go the imperial adventurers drew a connection between the environment and the culture of Tibet. The pure and rarefied mountain air was supposed to promote spirituality, unlike the putrid and noxious vapours of lower altitudes. The rugged terrain was supposed to promote vigour and honesty. Very much like the Gurkhas, and the Sherpas whom the British would encounter in the twentieth century, Tibetans were attractively robust and had positive moral qualities. The implicit, or sometimes explicit, comparison was to the people of the plains of India, of course.[54]

John Ruskin laboured to develop the link between landscape aesthetics and morality, although he had the Alps rather than the Himalaya in mind. For example, he noticed that there's greater purity in all things wherever the rocks are made of granite. Fence posts don't rot, hands and faces are always clean, and there's a wholesomeness in people's homes which it would need the misery of years to conquer.[55] Digging deeper, he thought that mountains have two moral consequences upon people.

The first is Mountain Gloom. Ruskin took notice of medieval depictions of the danse macabre at Lucerne, in Switzerland. These are hellish images of people being pierced by demons of disease and dismemberment.[56] They are inspired by the fact that beauty in the mountains is continually mingled with the shadow of death, he thought, and they reflect the squalor of the peasants' homesteads, and a gloom of spirit which possesses the whole land due to the bad air, unwholesome food and excessively severe labour. As I've already mentioned, Western interpreters of Himalayan art have offered the same explanation for the horrifying figures, dressed in garlands of heads and human skins, which appear in Tibetan paintings. Obviously it's all a bit arbitrary – it seems the character of the homes and the quality of the air could be whatever Ruskin needed it to be.

On the other hand, Ruskin says, there's Mountain Glory. The mountains of Greece and Italy are the wellsprings of European culture, and the mountains of Scandinavia inspired the Gothic of the Normans. Terror, inspired by mountains, leads to devotional thoughts and stern reasoning.[57] The processes of deep time that make the mountains also stimulate reflection on the absolute. The existing precipice, says Ruskin, is wrought into towers and bastions by the perpetual fall of its fragments. In what form did it stand before a single fragment fell? The builder of the temple forever stands beside His work, appointing the stone that is to

Smashana Adipati, Lords of the Charnel Ground, a fifteenth-century Tibetan painting on cloth (courtesy of the Rubin Museum of Art)

fall, and guiding all the seeming wildness of chance and change into ordained splendours and foreseen harmonies.[58]

Both of these opposite ideas were applied to Tibet.

Seen through a mood of mountain gloom, the millions of prayers carved on the stones of mani walls were a benighted waste of labour, and Buddhism was described as a filthy esoteric doctrine of the Tantric philosophers, full of sex and violence.[59] The theocratic government of the monasteries was despotic: crucifying, ripping open the body, pressing, and cutting out the eyes were by no means the worst forms of punishment, according to an author writing in 1885.[60] (Compare that to the phlegmatic attitude of George Bogle in the 1770s, who simply said, Let no one who has been to a public school in Europe cry out against the Tibetans for cruelty.)

In 1904, alarm over Russian ambitions, combined with curiosity and hubris, led the British to invade Tibet. They were full of Romantic lust to unveil Lhasa, the last forbidden city of the Orient, but they were appalled to discover the existence of so-called buried anchorites, monks who had submitted to be bricked inside caves, sometimes for life. The leader of the 1904 invasion, Francis Younghusband, whose Maxim guns confronted warriors in chainmail wearing charms to stop the bullets, happened to be among those who were especially inclined to be impressed by mountain glory. After signing the peace treaty he walked alone up a mountainside and found the scenery in sympathy with his feelings. I was insensibly infused with an almost intoxicating sense of elation and goodwill, he wrote.[61] When he died years later his daughter placed a Buddha on his coffin. Another member of the expedition, Perceval Landon, wrote that the colour of Tibet has no parallel in the world. Neither in Egypt, nor in South Africa, Sydney, Calcutta, or Athens is there such constancy of beauty, night and morning alike.[62] Tibetans were said to pray a lot because they live close to heaven.

If you saw things that way, then the Dalai Lama wasn't a medieval tyrant but a philosopher king. By now, an appreciation of extreme wildness on the scale of the inner Himalaya and the plateau was established within Europeans' (and Americans') frame of reference. According to an author named Amaury de Riencourt, who visited Lhasa in 1947, the awe-inspiring landscape of Tibet, the severity of the climate and the remoteness of the valleys, the majestic silence and solemn peace in which the Roof of the World is bathed, are certainly responsible for the existence of psychic knowledge.[63]

It was wildness that inspired ideas of the divine in these Westerners, which is quite the opposite of the struggle to tame nature that's sacred to Tibetans. Nevertheless, this type of reaction can end up with feelings like those of Alexandra David-Neel, who in 1912 became the first Western woman to meet the Dalai Lama.

I am one of the Genghis Khan race, she wrote, who by mistake and perhaps for her sins, was born in the Occident. So I was told by a lama.[64]

By the end of the century, the Dalai Lama had been a guest editor of Paris *Vogue*.

*

In 1933 the novelist James Hilton published *Lost Horizon*, which is said to be the first bestselling, mass-market paperback. It begins with a strangely assorted group of Westerners, including the hero, Conway, being rescued by plane from an outbreak of disorder somewhere in northern India. Through the portholes of the cabin the evacuees can see range upon range of snow peaks. It's a fearsome spectacle of raw and monstrous ice cliffs. As the little craft drones over the abyss it dawns on the passengers that they're being kidnapped. Conway can't quite bring himself to care. He feels a glow of satisfaction that there are such places still left on earth; distant, inaccessible, as yet unhumanised. The very namelessness of the peaks has dignity. Those few thousand feet by which they fall short of the known giants might save them for eternity from climbing expeditions, Conway reflects, because although it's been suggested that his character is based on the Everest-obsessed George Mallory, he finds record-breaking mountaineers vulgar. The plane crashes on the plateau, and the dying pilot directs the bedraggled party to a nearby monastery. This is the first appearance in any language of the word Shangri-la.

The monastery of Shangri-la is a group of coloured pavilions, as superb and exquisite as the petals of a flower, clinging to the mountainside beneath the dazzling slopes of Mount Karakal. The thin air has a dreamlike texture. The new arrivals come under the direction of a monk named Chang, who explains that the rule of the order is moderation, including moderation in virtue. They rule over the villagers in the valley below with moderate strictness in return for moderate obedience. Their subjects are moderately sober, moderately chaste, and moderately honest. (The monks engage in a sufficient, but not excessive, amount of fornication with them.) They're not dogmatic. Many religions are moderately true, says Chang.

Shangri-la is not marked on any map. It's stocked with masterpieces of Chinese art, and supplied with every modern comfort, such as hot baths. The inmates, who include at least one beautiful woman, cultivate themselves in the library or by playing European classical music on a harpsichord. Soon enough Conway meets the high lama, who explains that Shangri-la was founded in 1734 by a Capuchin missionary from Luxembourg named Perrault. By the time his monastery was complete Perrault was already full of years. He began to study Buddhism at the age of ninety-eight, then he got into drugs and yoga. His life went on and on. Conway is sensitive, so he realises that the old man he's talking to is Perrault. Shangri-la's residents are a catalogue of lost explorers, living forever alongside those Tibetans, Chinese, and Japanese people who've also strayed there somehow. To preserve Shangri-la from the contamination of the world, those who enter can never leave.

Conway is intellectual, reserved, and contemplative. He's talented, but he has few friends and no ambition. 'I don't know whether you classify the people who come here,' he tells Perrault. 'But if so you can label me 1914–18.'

Back in 1789, when Perrault first thought that he was dying, and was reflecting on his already long life, he foresaw the future. The nations would strengthen not in wisdom but in vulgar passions and the will to destroy. Machine power would multiply, and when man had filled the land and sea with ruin he would take to the air. 'Exulting in the techniques of homicide, mankind will rage so hotly across the world that every precious vulnerable thing, the small, the delicate, the defenceless, will all be lost,' says Perrault.

'I share your opinion of that,' says Conway.

The purpose of Shangri-la is to outlive the doom that gathers round on every side. In other words, although I don't think James Hilton would have known about the concept of a bayul, or hidden valley, he reinvented the idea. Shangri-la is a single lifeboat, the book says, riding the seas in a gale. In this storm there will be no safety in arms, no help from authority, no answer in science. It will rage until every flower of culture is trampled, and all human beings are levelled in vast chaos. Now Perrault knows he really is dying. Conway has been chosen and brought here to keep the hope alive. But Conway decides to leave. The last we hear of him he's half mad, wandering the Far East, desperately trying to find his way back to Shangri-la.

It's a good story and a good book. Nevertheless, by this stage the realities of the Tibetan world had been replaced in the Western imagination by a fantasy, represented ever since by the name of Shangri-la. It's a sacred landscape of physical beauty, spiritual refinement, and happiness, a place that's an antidote to modernity, outside history.

A much worse book also marks the same destination. In 1956 *The Third Eye: The Autobiography of a Tibetan Lama* was published by a monk named Tuesday Lobsang Rampa, and became a global sensation. Exasperated specialists hired a private detective

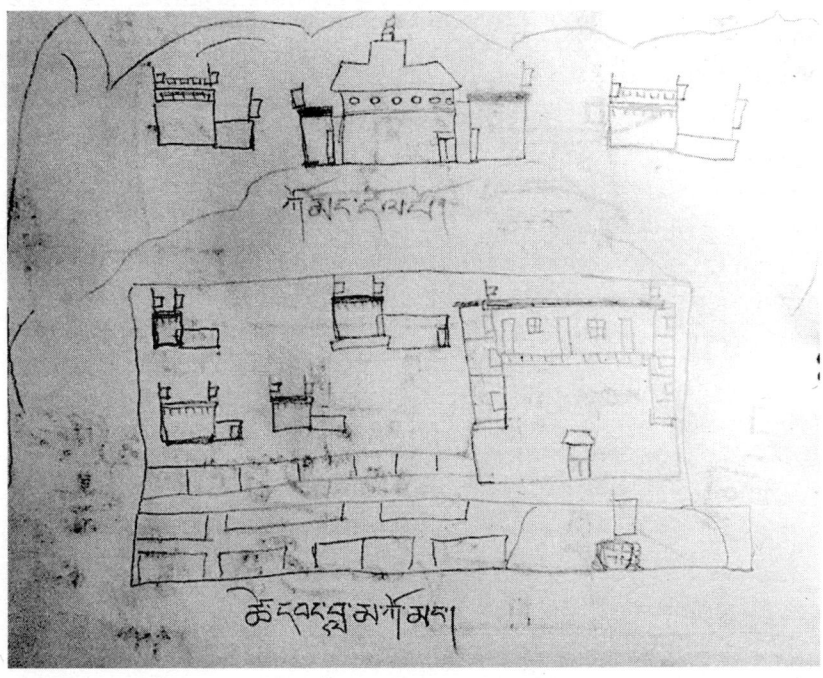

to expose the real author as Cyril Hoskin, a plumber's son from Plymouth, England. Nevertheless, its fanciful account of secret rituals in caverns beneath Lhasa, where the golden bodies of the prehistoric gods are stored, and of the purported author having an all-seeing third eye surgically opened in his forehead, is still in print in several languages. An American professor of Tibetan studies introduced the text to his students without explanation, and they found it credible and compelling, all in all the most realistic and comprehensible item on their syllabus.[65]

The night we were at Shimen was the full moon. The next day we walked to a village called Khoma. I asked a monk there to draw a picture of the place, and this is what he did. The monastery is above and the village is below, but there the obvious resemblance to Khoma ends. I had hoped that I could use these drawings to think about how people conceive their environment. Conrad found them hopelessly unrealistic. Back in Kathmandu, the artist Tenzin Norbu, when I showed him this one, said: 'I think he tried to do the best for his village. There is a lot of mistakes actually, in a village. In a natural way. He's done it very perfectly. He tried to respect his village. He tried to make his village the best.'

'More formally organised?' I said.

'Formally organised, yeah yeah,' said Tenzin Norbu.

A day later we reached Saldang and were put up in the house of an elderly traditional healer, known as an amchi. I asked him to draw a map for me.

Tenzin Norbu identified the author immediately. 'This is Lambrang Tunduk's home,' he said. 'This is the monastery. I did this monastery's paintings. Here is something very important. And this is Shey Gompa. He gave you a kind of map of his own stuff. He's an old man.'

'He's a famous old man,' I said.

'In this area he's very famous.'

I asked about the important place.

'There you see the yul lha,' he said. 'Every year the village people come here and put flags. This is Shey-la pass. Between Saldang and Shey there's a big pass. And there's Namgung

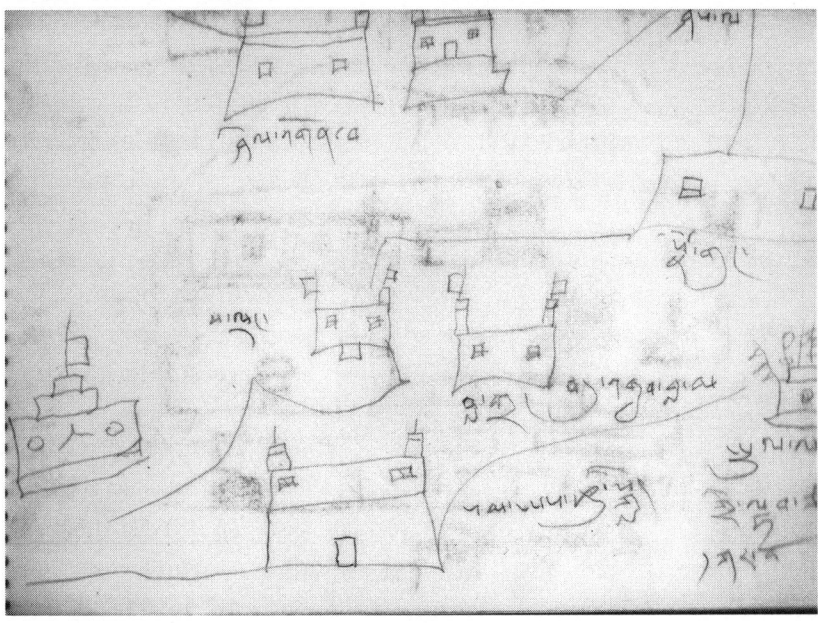

monastery. After Shey-la, coming down, you see a monastery. This is realistic, you know. He gave his heart.'

❋

The old amchi, Lambrang Tunduk, took us to see a yul lha. There was a stone cube decorated with flags at the edge of a precipice. He also took us to the monastery, where we saw Tenzin Norbu's murals. Milarepa, who's easily identified by his white robes, is shown among the rocks. And we went to the village clinic, where Lambrang Tunduk keeps sacks of medicinal herbs and iron dental instruments. A government health worker is posted there for six months of the year.

Lambrang Tunduk's maternal uncle was a man called Nyingma Tsering. He was an important figure in the region in the 1950s, who defeated brigands from the plateau and was a key informant of the Tibetologist David Snellgrove.[66] Nyingma Tsering provided several of the manuscripts Snellgrove copied and translated. So I was able to show Lambrang Tunduk his uncle's photograph in Snellgrove's book, and he took it away to take a photo of it.

I asked Lambrang Tunduk about local history and he produced a manuscript of eighteen long, thin folios, which I photographed. He said it was written so long ago that he had no idea by whom, but it describes the history of his family at a time when there were no houses in this village. When I got home I wrote to the anthropologist Charles Ramble to ask if he could recommend anyone to translate it. Charles very kindly offered to do it himself. The manuscript is fascinating.

This is an unusual, secular history: the type of thing which Tenzin Norbu said you don't find. It seems to have been written by a series of authors, who occasionally refer to themselves in the first person, or to some time or another as the present time. It begins with this statement: I have set down here in writing the history of my forebears, both bad and good, in their successive generations, and the story of how we came to settle in this place.

On one side, the family is descended from a man of southwest Tibet, who was called the King of Tiger Gorge. He was suckled in the wilderness by a tigress. His descendant came to work for the king of Mustang, but fell foul of court politics. He fled to Dolpo by a route called Lonely Pass and was received at a monastery. The people there told him, 'There are plenty of villages here, but no nobles.' So the fugitive courtier settled down, became a chief, and married an abbot's daughter. Meanwhile, a child was discovered being suckled by a black goat in a cleft in a mountain. He was named Man Cared for by Black Goat. Man Cared for by Black Goat married the chief's daughter, and the lineage the manuscript describes is descended from this couple, who were somehow derived from a goat and a tiger. From Man Cared for by Black Goat and his unnamed wife, down to the last people who appear, I reckoned nineteen generations.

Notwithstanding these animal origins, the history is pragmatic. Members of the family found mates and had children. They built houses in various places. The dynasty quickly produced an eminent cleric.[67] In the fourth generation the first son inherited the family home and the second son, named Kunga, entered Namgung monastery. The passages involving Kunga are quite personal and in the present tense. Having become a monk, it turns out that he's not the religious type. He thinks, 'These days, even if you're a monk, there isn't anyone who fully accomplishes the religious path, and yet the door to worldly affairs is closed to you. It would be much more secure to have a proper married life.' So Kunga sets off in search of a wife and a place to build a house, frankly explaining to the people he meets, 'If the religious life doesn't turn out well, at least the secular world seems secure.'

In his search Kunga comes to three communities, each of which has been settled for a generation, so he keeps going. Then he comes to Saldang, where he tells the people, 'I'd originally set out to be a monk. But as the saying goes, and it's true, if you think about things too much you're lost. If the goal is happiness without being reborn in the lower realms, there is less risk involved in being a man of the world. That was my thinking.'

The people in Saldang say, 'Why should we not let you stay? Not only do we all agree to this, but which of us is native to this place? If you can manage it by yourself, you are free to take as much land as you need.'

They were all settlers there. So Kunga moved to Saldang, driving his two yaks before him. He gathered timber and built his house.

In the ninth generation, by my reckoning, a daughter of the family named Paldzon shacked up with an abbot.[68] The couple had two sons and two daughters.

Paldzon's nephew, named Rabgye, lived in secret with a nun.

By now this was a substantial family, occupying four households. They enjoyed great prosperity and hosted many visitors. They commissioned the copying of scriptures and the construction of sacred objects. And they delighted in making offerings to the gods above and giving alms to those below. Later there would be a rotten son, who ran the estate down, failed as a trader, then went to live in northern Tibet. Yet the family seems to be doing well enough by the time the account ends. Blessings and good fortune, it concludes. This is the story of how the members of our family were born, and how they came to settle. May virtue flourish.

The manuscript is obviously complicated. It's beyond my means to attempt a close reading. At face value, the early mention of the Mustang kingdom implies a date sometime after the late fourteenth century for the beginning of the story. Not surprisingly, the Mustang king is cast as a villain. Perhaps some of the early settlers of Dolpo were refugees from strife in neighbouring kingdoms.

Dolpo was always an out-of-the-way place, on the route between nowhere and anywhere else, but it wasn't immune to the changing relations of neighbouring powers. The Khasa-Malla kingdom in Jumla was to the west, the Mustang kingdom rose up to the east, and the Gungthang kingdom was on the plateau to the north. A song by a man named Orgyen Tenzin (1657–1737) recalls troubled times:

> In the valleys of Mustang, [and] Dolpo,
> Hundreds of soldiers hack at hands and feet and die.
> Consider well impermanence, mothers.[69]

Maybe so, but (unlike the biography of Sonam Lodrö) this chronicle doesn't mention any violent conflict.

Although there had been permanent settlements in Dolpo

(the monastery at Bicher) since the eleventh century, by the time of Kunga's generation, apparently several centuries later, parts of Dolpo were still settler country. The new settlements included what's now the old and important village of Saldang. Kunga established the branch of the family that preserved this manuscript, so he's bound to be important. Nevertheless, from the length and intimacy with which he's described it's nice to imagine that a layer of the text was created by someone who lived in Kunga's time.

It's interesting that the family participated in the seemingly quite open sex lives of some clergy. Presumably that sometimes related to Tantrism, as well as ordinary human nature, because (despite the idea that images of copulating gods are merely symbolic) yogins certainly practised sexual yoga. Celibacy is a monastic ideal, but Tantric practitioners need to copulate.[70] Most interestingly to me, the chronicle records irreligious attitudes attributed to Kunga. His views are represented as reasonable common sense, in comparison to being a monk which involves thinking too much. He rejects the frightening abstractions sought by lamas and yogins and opts for the more reliable life of a pioneering householder.

Now Saldang is one of the most substantial villages in Dolpo. The pioneers' descendants were threshing barley when we were there. The men and women stood on opposite sides of a circle and beat a rhythm with their flails, which they swung alternately, the women then the men. Peals of song and laughter were laid over this beat. I showed the video to Tenzin Norbu.

'This is Saldang, not my village,' he said. 'You need a woman, especially a Saldang woman, to understand it.' Then he said, 'It's a love song, I think. I understood that one. She said, "There's a river coming, but it's not special water so I don't care." Ha ha. "There is water everywhere, but it's not very clean so I don't care." Ha! Maybe the men are trying to get something.'

The rhythm of the slapping flails continued, sometimes

overlain by the soaring women's voices, shrill, like the women in Chharka told me the Saldang women are. Then hoots of laughter. The men were whistling to call the wind, to blow the chaff away.

Conrad and I walked on, towards Kunga's Namgung monastery, the Shey-la pass, and Shey, on the route the old amchi had drawn. As we climbed above the valley we saw the brown ocean of hills spread out across all of Dolpo. For a while we were in step with a woman leading a white pony. I tried to talk to her, but she only smiled at me.

When we rested in the shelter of the slope, and laid on our backs looking into the blue sky, Ayita said he could hear the karang kurung. Far above us the bar-headed geese, whose honking means cucumber and pumpkin, were migrating south again. 'Can't you hear them?' he asked. But though we strained our ears, the geese were almost impossible to discern. Then Ayita showed us how to see them. High, high up, almost at the edge of sight, the flock was visible when it turned and caught the light. They seemed to be going round and round up there. Like a ball of fish, I thought, which brought to my mind the image of a giant, cosmic whale crashing through the sky with its gullet open. Ayita believes that the geese go to Kailash in the summer, and that they're a god, the vehicle of the goddess Saraswati. 'For the winter,' he said, 'they go south to the sea.' After a minute they were gone.

I fell in again with the horsewoman and a train of mules from Saldang. In single file we crossed the sheer side of a chasm, with the houses and monastery of Namgung right below us like a map at our feet. That afternoon I took a bath in the stream, which cut deep enough to be private. Then I sat drying on a rock in the sun, in a state of nature, feeling very good.

At night we watched the sky. Wrapped in coats and gloves, we lay on our backs on our sleeping mats, stuck to the earth, and looked down into endless space. There was a lightening in the east, then a cold glow spread all around the horizon. The Milky Way dimmed and disappeared, leaving only the brightest constellations. The eastern sky turned inky blue. Moonlight hit the highest points, then worked down the slopes in the opposite way that the shadows had spread four hours earlier. The furrows and canyons in the land returned. I watched it for hours, estimating when the light would reach me and I'd see the moon rise. I thought about the poet Kalidasa, who wrote of time's dividers the sun and moon, alternating their tides of light across the earth, across the pastoralists' camp far off somewhere, where I could hear the dogs barking, guarding the flock from what?

※

It was a wonderful walk in the morning from Namgung over the high pass to Shey Gompa. This famous monastery stands alone in a broad valley, beneath the Crystal Mountain. A prominent Californian Buddhist, whose recent travels in the area I happened to be aware of, had left a photograph of herself with her arm around the Dalai Lama on the main altar. The place has a bit of the Shangri-la mystique about it, largely thanks to Peter Matthiessen's famous hippy pilgrimage book *The Snow Leopard*. We were told that from the summit of the Crystal Mountain (where no-one ever goes) you can see Mount Kailash about 210 kilometres away.

'With their third eye, maybe,' said Conrad.

The summer settlement of locals' and tourists' tents was still set up beneath the monastery, for maybe one more week before the season turned. Conrad and I had encountered other tourists at Saldang and at Namgung. Here at Shey we studied a group of elderly Australians through my binoculars. A lean, stooped man was loping towards the monastery, pursued by children selling trinkets.

'Ah mate! Ah mate!' Conrad lamented, like an Australian cricket commentator. 'Still. He's got a nice steady rhythm.'

In one of the tents below the monastery we found the horsewoman sitting with her mother. We took our seats on the Chinese carpets and drank a can of Lhasa beer each. The horsewoman was combing her hair beside the stove. There was an old woman there too, who I took to be the grandmother of the family, and two porters from another group, who borrowed some tape to stick a banknote together. The horsewoman put dung in the stove, moved the kettles and pans around, and hacked at the ends of her hair in a bar of golden light.

'What long hair you've got!' I said.

'How long's your wife's hair?' said the old woman.

We started drinking home-brewed chyang, and after some time the old woman said: 'You and me, tonight. We'll sleep together and we'll fuck.' She made the gesture with her fingers and repeated her proposal – or prophecy – several times, while the horsewoman twinkled and filled my cup. The crone tossed her cigarette in the fire, stood up, brushed herself down and strode out. The other two were quick to say, 'She's just an old woman from our village.' When we finally left, the lovely equestrian said she'd give me my change in the evening. Conrad called it adroit saloon-keeping.

The valley at Shey is bitterly cold when the sun leaves it. That night the last part of our goat was served. This was the head, which is supposed to have warming properties. After dinner we returned to the horsewoman's tent, where it was dark and smoky, and we took our seats among the other customers and sacks of merchandise. There was a trekking guide from eastern Nepal, who was happy and surprised that I guessed he was a Kulung Rai. We talked about the holy lake Salpa Pokhari. When the food was cooked the women asked if we'd have some goat's-head soup.

I was pleased to say, 'No, thanks. We just had some.'

They ladled heaps of grey boiled meat and smashed bone onto slabs of rice, and served the others, who ate with noisy relish. The women spoke Tibetan and laughed among themselves, while the trekking staff spoke Nepali and we spoke English.

When they'd finished eating, one of the guides tried to tease the young hostess charmlessly by calling her his old woman, telling her not to eat too much because it would make her sleepy later, and saying that his colleagues could go to their tent and he'd stay here, daughter and son-in-law on this side, and mother over there. The mother laughed along, while the horsewoman made no response at all. The guests shared tobacco, and their jokes turned to the subject of belching. Then the mother declared it was time for bed and kicked everybody out. We pulled our hats on, fastened our coats, and stepped outside.

In 1961 the anthropologist Corneille Jest, along with three more-or-less local companions, set off on a pilgrimage around Dolpo.[71] Among this group there was a Tibetan nomad who told stories on the way, which Jest recorded. Jest's account is also laced with proverbs he collected, such as this: In the day, it is hot three times and cold three times. In life one is happy three times and unhappy three times.

One of the nomad's stories involves three young friends who have three magical objects: a saddle bag which produces any food you wish for, a whip that will transport you anywhere you want to go, and a hat of invisibility. In the course of a convoluted story the chief character, Trangdrug, arrives at a nomad camp where a young woman is living with her mother. He introduces himself to the daughter as Chachatiwa ('it's raining') and asks for a place to stay. She tells him to ask her mother. He tells the mother that he's called Chochichi ('make love'). That night as they are lying in the tent it begins to rain. The hero shuffles down to where the girl is sleeping and begins to caress her. She wakes up and cries, 'Mother, Mother! It's raining!'

'If it's raining,' says her mother, 'get close to make love.' They make love all night, and for the rest of the week.

In another story a woman becomes pregnant because, being thirsty, she ate a hailstone that fell from a clear sky. It had been ejaculated by the bird-god Khyung. Creatures such as him stand at the beginning of many notable lineages.

There's a pair of matching tales to demonstrate the wickedness, callousness, and treachery of men and women respectively.

There are absorbing details, such as that a loom must not be left set up overnight because demons will weave their own patterns.

Much of this material is familiar in one way or another. There's the story of a junior queen who wanted to kill the king's child by his first marriage. She hired a hunter to do it, but he took pity on the victim and deceived the queen by returning with a goat's heart.

In another story there's said to be a black-and-white rock in

Dolpo, which will purify your sins if you can squeeze through a narrow opening. It's a bit like an account I read of a mosque in Cairo where there are two pillars too close to pass between, but they'll move apart for a man who's never told a lie.[72]

There was once an attempt to poison a monk who tried to end the practice of animal sacrifice. (He saved himself with a scarf of invisibility.)

And there are stories of people who discovered cracks in the rock that lead to palatial caverns inside mountains, with succulent dishes laid out in gold, silver, and turquoise chambers. In one instance the trespasser was turned to stone. In these stories there are echoes of Rai mythology (the insemination of Miyapma), of Snow White, even a premonition of Harry Potter (the garments of invisibility).[73] The palaces of gods inside mountains, which are such a big thing in the Tibetan tradition, resemble the palaces inside mountains as they're described in the courtly Hindu literature of late nineteenth-century Kathmandu. Some of these correspondences are obviously the result of a common ancestry, but others stretch across wide gulfs. Ruminating on how stories of distant origin can be alike, Nick Allen, the anthropologist of Rai mythology, cited Jorge Luis Borges who wrote: it may be that universal history is the history of the different intonations given to a handful of metaphors.[74]

Here's another proverb from Jest's pilgrims: To say there is no truth to a proverb is to say there are no wrinkles on the arse. This is weird, because there are no wrinkles on an arse. Is it a poor translation of the crack in the middle, or a self-deprecating proverb?

✳

The waxing moon, which had stood in the eastern afternoon sky at the beginning of our walk, became the waning moon in the western morning sky in the last few days. We left Shey, heading north. The valley became a canyon of jagged towers and bastions. There's a small monastery built into the cliff around Druptop Senge Yeshe's cave.

Every twelve years there's a major festival at Shey. According to Ayita (it must be an exaggeration), 3,000 foreigners attended the most recent iteration, and there were even more locals present. There was steady helicopter traffic to remove the tourists suffering from altitude sickness. As we walked Conrad speculated that the attraction of Buddhism to Westerners is that it offers a spirituality which, unlike other religions, doesn't obviously contravene scientific knowledge, and that there are similarities between some of the claims of the philosophy of mind and Buddhist teaching on the self. I wondered whether Buddhism might appear untarnished to foreigners, coming from so far away that its purity is preserved from history. So the notion that Buddhism is a religion of peace (any more than other religions are) is able to escape the actual records of all the Buddhist countries, which are as full of blood and cruelty as any other. Chatting like this we walked anti-clockwise around a section of the Crystal Mountain. We came into a world of bare spiked peaks and deep abysses below us. The moon was hanging above. It was like looking at the moon from another moon.

For a mile or more the path was scratched onto a sheer mountainside, and I had to concentrate on keeping my composure. I knew the most important thing was that my hat did not blow off. If a gust of wind should lift that piece of cloth from my head and send it swimming over the void I'd lose my shit completely. We laboured up to a pass with huge views of Kanjiroba Himal, then down the valley to a campsite that kept the mountain in full view. The crew collected dung and made a fire.

In the morning there was ice inside the tent and in the stream. Our boots were frozen. It took a long time for the sun to reach us, so we needed the fire again before we ate and continued down the valley. We could see horrific tracks on the cliffs around us, which are used by those who gather yarsagumba, a dreadful trade. Then we saw birch in the valley below us. It was the first forest of our trek. Bottle-green juniper covered the ground at our feet. There was red berberis. The path went into the trees. We turned a corner and saw the valley plunging below in forested canyons of dark green conifers and white-barked birch, their bright green leaves turning gold. Down there was the confluence of torrents that roared out of the high valleys we were coming from. The white peaks of Kanjiroba were in the cloudless sky, and in the distance we saw Lake Phoksundo. Our lunch place was under trees, where wild walnuts lay in the warm grass.

We descended to the river and walked beside the blue water through canyons of orange stone. As the valley broadened we were beneath towering mountains again. Blue and white glaciers hung right over us. Changing light, caused by wisps of cloud that gathered round the peaks, varied the effect of the autumnal trees. All this colour, after weeks of austerity, made me feel that these two days' walk from Shey – at first so cruel, then so gorgeous – were the most beautiful and dramatic two days' walk I'd ever had. Our campsite was on the north shore of the lake. Huge quantities of bleached driftwood had collected there, from which we made a fire of timbers as big as ourselves.

※

Lake Phoksundo is amazing. It almost glows a kind of chemical blue, like an underlit swimming pool. 'That's exactly it,' said

Conrad. 'Like a giant overchlorinated swimming pool that a terrible investment decision has put in this wilderness.' Something remarkable happened at dawn. The water was grey at first, with a thin sheet of mist floating over it. The sun pierced a gap in the hills. A shaft of light moved down the bank. When it reached the water the light made a thin white stripe in the mist, which seemed like a breaker way out across the middle of the water. As the light spread the lake turned turquoise. Conrad said, 'Look at that!' The mist had begun to spin in a clockwise pattern that filled the whole north end.

The path around Phoksundo was notoriously frightening before being widened in recent years, and it's still alarming. At its highest point my altimeter showed we were 400 metres above the surface. The lake was blue like pool-coloured glass. The cliffs that enclose it are unbelievably high in places, and they go straight down through the water. I asked Ayita why no one uses a boat to avoid this disturbing trail. He said this lake is so deep the boats would simply sink.

I threw a stone from the path. After waiting a long time we heard the splash, and a minute later I had the stomach-churning thought: That stone is still falling in the black depths.

You might imagine that such a remarkable lake, which looks so unreal, so literally supernatural, would be sacred and the focus of some kind of worship.[75] In fact there's a demoness in there. The lake's evil, and mostly ignored for religious purposes.

We swam in it the next morning (it's extremely cold), and after a day's rest we carried on.

Again we entered a different world. The deep valley was forested with coniferous trees, including some very handsome junipers. There were thorny jungle creepers, and many other broad-leafed plants. At the tea house where we stayed there were chrysanthemums and marigolds in the garden, and hens pecking around – things we hadn't seen for weeks. Two days in that gorge brought us to the airstrip at Juphal, where every room was occupied by people waiting for a flight. We had a booking. After a day our turn came.

The person in the seat next to mine was a child, who'd been attacked by a bear some days earlier while gathering firewood. He was being sent to town for treatment. I thought I could distract him from his fear and obvious pain by making conversation, but a foreigner trying to chat seemed a new experience too far.

The tiny craft rattled and swayed between the mountains, over the mid-western hills, and the protected forest in the plains. Within twenty or thirty minutes of taking off we were landing in the plains bazaar called Nepalganj.

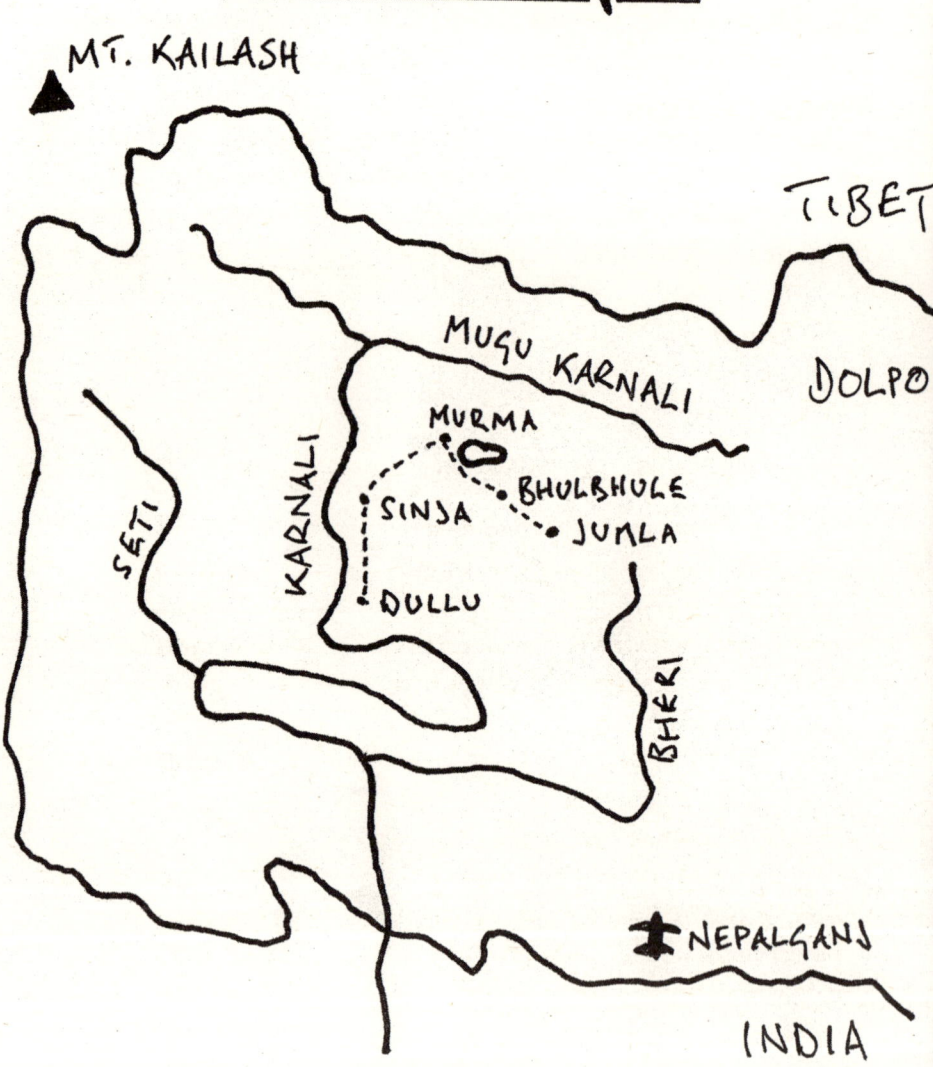

PART 4

Conservation

'In virtually all of its manifestations, wilderness represents a flight from history. Seen as the original garden, it is a place outside of time.'
William Cronon

'... a growing number of people had come to find man's ascendancy over nature increasingly abhorrent to their moral and aesthetic sensibilities. This was the human dilemma: how to reconcile the physical requirements of civilization with the new feelings and values that the same civilization had generated.'
Keith Thomas

'... the vision has never been clearly understood: a democracy for the people, who are intrinsically good and pure of heart; a democracy in which poverty is honourable, power innocuous ... not nature as it really is, cruel and disgusting, but nature sanitized, majestic and above all good.'
Ruth Scurr

'It is said that man is the chief environment of man.'
D. H. Lawrence

By now it was 2018, the year I attained the age of forty. For the last walk I was joined by my wife, Subina. On the day we left, our son decided to take his interesting stick to school. As I walked the children to the bus stop a guy passed us, and he said, 'That stick's dangerous. It's shaped by black magic.' While we waited for the school van other people glanced at it too.

'That stick might be more interesting than I thought,' I said.

'It's just a legend,' said my son.

The van came. They climbed in. Both their parents travelled for work quite often, but rarely at the same time. My sister-in-law would look after them while we were gone.

❋

We were going to the Karnali in winter. This region is the backwater of a backwater now, notorious for its poverty and conservative social practices. Once it was the heart of the Khasa-Malla kingdom, which stretched from the foothills to the plateau, where the proto-Nepali state was founded on irrigated rice cultivation. On the plane we passed white mountains rising from white clouds on our right, and ridge upon ridge of inky hills to our left. In a couple of places the forest was on fire, smoke streaming off a hillside and filling the valleys with brown vapours. Roads, which had been carved across the hills in recent years, were seeping down the slopes everywhere. In the recent election campaign roadbuilding had been one of the most frequent demands in the villages, and one of the most freely given promises of the candidates.

We landed at Nepalganj. The following morning we flew between the snowy mountains into Jumla, where Rajendra was waiting for us. It was good to see him again. I asked if he'd got a new power bank yet.

'No.'

'After one and a half years?'

'Mine was stolen, and I haven't got another.'

❋

According to tradition, rice was brought to Jumla from Kashmir by a yogi called Chandannath, to whom a shrine in the town is dedicated, and it was Chandannath who's supposed to have established a strict timetable for cultivation. The paddy fields are ploughed in February or March, depending on snow conditions. Jumla is said to be the highest region of rice cultivation in the world, at about 2,700 metres, and it's famous for a red-grained variety which is regarded as a delicacy. The seed beds are watered on the second day of Chait (March–April). All irrigation channels must be repaired by the eleventh.

From our first meetings onwards we heard anxiety about the weather. The staff at an international organisation in town said that water sources were drying up because of climate change. Whereas there used to be several feet of snow in winter, this year snow had fallen for just a couple of hours two weeks ago. Only the fields that are irrigated by river water give two crops a year now.

On the path out of town we met an old man who told us, 'We used to have snow up to here.' He gestured to the top of his thigh. 'The snow would melt and water would flow down. The source has dried up. There's no snowfall.'

'But why is there no snowfall?' I asked him.

'It concerns the gods. What can we do? We don't know where they took Guru Maharaj Dattatraya Baba's statues. We've been crying. They stole the statue we were supposed to do the puja to.'

'Who took it?' Subi asked, but he just answered, 'They took it last year. If gods give water then there's life. If not, there isn't.'

'Hmmm,' said Subi.

'I'm happy we met,' the old man said. 'I went to Canada last year.'

'To Canada?'

'To see my son and daughter-in-law. In *Wodbedan* in Toronto.'

'I'm British.'

'Ahh,' said the man. 'A baba-jee has come,' he continued. 'He's been living in a cave since December. I'm on my way to give him food. Happy to meet you,' then he turned to another passerby and asked, 'How's things?'

※

We walked past dry fields that were neatly tilled and manured, but bare. Thorny bushes were planted around the field boundaries, and particular trees had been planted on the banks of the dry streams. Our path climbed through orchards, pines, and rocky parts, then through pastures, and reached an isolated homestead high up the valley.

In the evening the guests gathered by the kitchen fire, where a man and woman were cooking. A younger man was grinding chillies on a stone. An elderly couple sat against the wall, in shadows left by a weak electric light. They would reach their home the following day. Two weathered men sat on the bed behind me. They'd come to cut timber. Everyone was bundled up in scarves and woollen hats. There was a jug of moonshine. 'Hey sister, give it to me. I'll pour,' said Rajendra. The owner of the place said that he's a jhankri, a shaman and traditional healer.[1] 'I can only summon the spirits when I drink. Not in the morning,' he claimed.

Subi said, 'You can't summon without drinking?'

'The drunker I am, the better it is.'

'This jhankri must cause a lot of trouble,' Subi said.

'You don't have a cup? With a handle?' asked the elderly traveller in the corner.

'So, where do you all come from?' Subi asked.

'We're here working,' one of the woodcutters said. The conversation turned to the price of timber.

'Machines have ruined everything in our area,' said Rajendra. 'Before, we used fire. Now they use petrol- and diesel-run machines and *ghui! ghui!*' he revved an imaginary chainsaw. 'They cut through trees this big very quickly.'

The conversation turned next to water, and so it went on. Swirling fireside chatter. We talked for a while about the trail ahead towards Rara Lake. We learnt about a snowstorm forty years ago, which killed a lot of horses. 'There was enough snow to drown us!' said one of the woodcutters.

'Now there's no snow.'

'We'd kill wild boars up in the mountains,' said a woodcutter. 'We'd kill twenty or twenty-five wild boars in a year. Some would just die, and we'd go with dogs to kill the others. There used to be that much snow!'

'Now there's no snow,' repeated the elderly traveller in the corner. 'There's a motor road and vehicles now. And electricity.'

'Forests have been destroyed,' the jhankri noted.

'The temperature went up,' one of the woodcutters said. 'The water's gone because the forests have been destroyed. You'll see in the morning. It's just parched.'

'It rained all through Kartik.'

'It rained too much between Asar and Bhadra. It hasn't rained since.'

'This year, the rain didn't let either harvest flourish.'

'We used to plant beans, mustard, buckwheat, and things like that in Asar, after harvesting barley and wheat.'

'I haven't grown barley or wheat for three years now,' said the jhankri.

'I still grow barley and wheat, but I've stopped growing millet,' the elderly traveller said.

'Maize is scarce now too,' said a woman in the shadows. The grains they used to grow have been substituted with white rice which is imported from the south. It doesn't taste good and gives everyone gastritis. 'That rice?' someone said. 'Don't even talk about it!'

It might seem there was a mood of misery and complaint in the inn that night, but in fact it was quite convivial. They were sharing knowledge and memories in an atmosphere of spreading warmth, thickening woodsmoke, and deepening drunkenness.

'These clothes are not our traditional clothes,' the jhankri explained. 'These are plastic. Men like us wore wool.'

'Handknitted too! It was warm enough, however much snow there was. Now the fashion's like this and the food's the same. That's why people get sick.'

'Sister, pour me more raksi,' someone said.

'Raksi's a painkiller. It soothes my legs. Madam, would you like some more?'

'No, enough for me,' said Subi.

'Millet is good to drink. Millet, wheat alcohol, it's all good.'

They passed boiled potatoes round, which we peeled with our fingertips and dipped in the paste of salt and crushed chillies the young man had made. 'If nothing else, the potatoes are good,' Subi said in English.

'Nun khursani piro, khane manche hero,' rhymed the jhankri. Salt and chilli's spicy, whoever eats it is a hero.

'Don't sit too close to the fire. Your jacket will wrinkle up like a ball!'

'This liquor soothes my leg.'

'We consume liquor. It's about to consume us! What to do?'

'Sister, can I have a cigarette?'

'I thought you were quitting?'

'This is the wrong time to quit. This is the best place to smoke,' I said.

'The brother gets on quite well with this group.'

'That's why I married him,' said Subi.

'Oh, *that's* why?' There was laughter.

'Why marry someone who doesn't match?'

The shaman said something about eloping with someone else's wife.

'Whose wife?' asked Subi. 'Why?'

'You talk to them and they say "okay". You say "let's go", and you take them,' the shaman explained, as if Subi had asked him how to do it.

'You can't do all the work alone,' someone agreed.

'How many wives did you bring?' asked Subi.

'Three. Four, if you count the one who left.'

'And how do you take care of them?'

'He's joking.'

'No, it's true,' said the woman at the back of the room.

'I still have three wives.'

'It's because he has no kids,' someone whispered.

'You can start serving the rice,' the jhankri said.

'So where are the other two?'

'One has gone to her parents, after an argument. The other

one was summoned by her sister. So now it's just the two of us here.'

'Where did you get your wives from?' asked Subi.

'Mine?'

'Yeah.'

'From three different places.'

'And they trusted you?'

'If not, why did they come? I'm not lying to you. I herd sheep. I have buffaloes. I keep bees. I do agriculture. This is what I look like, this is what I wear. Look,' he said, and indeed his clothes were full of holes. 'This is how I eat. I have ghee, honey, milk. That's what women are after. Food!'

There was more laughter.

'So why did you marry him?' Subi asked.

The woman handing out plates of rice and potatoes just laughed.

'We sing in our culture,' the old shaman said. 'You sing to win or lose. If she wins I'll be her servant, doing her dishes, all sorts of things.'

'So you brought them here by singing?'

'He's not lying.'

'But I have to understand …'

'Back in the day, it did happen,' said one of the woodcutters. 'On market day they'd sing songs and bring wives. Our grandfathers told us.'

'Do you guys need spoons, or you'll eat with your hands?'

'Not so much rice! That's enough for me.'

'We sing a deuda,' he said, referring to a tradition of folk song in the form of a freestyle duet, in which men and women sing alternate rhymes.

'Teach me how to sing a deuda.'

'We are very shy in our culture,' the jhankri claimed.

After we ate our dinner Subi and I stepped outside, and we saw the stars.

'Oh wow!' I said.

'It's like an explosion!'

The biggest stars were exceptionally bright, and the endless tiny ones emerged as our eyes adjusted.

'You can see *all* of them. I should have brought the star book,' I said. 'But what a story!' I'd hoped that, with Subi along, someone might divulge a heartbreaking love story. This wasn't the kind I had in mind.

'He seems to be infertile so he kept bringing more wives,' she said. 'He insists he got them in a deuda. It's a competition, and if she loses the girl has to come with you. And I was like, Are you *insane*?'

It was very cold outside. We went in and laid down in the draughty upstairs of the jhankri's inn, wrapped in sleeping bags, covered with unfresh blankets, steeped in the smells of smoke and the feet of the woodcutters, who were lying nearby.[2]

☀

In the morning we went to visit the baba, who was living in a cave nearby. It wasn't so much a cave as a cell that had been dug into the slope, and covered with a tin roof, which had smoke rising around the edges. He had a deeply lined, smiling face and he wore a heavy woollen smock, with further woollen layers beneath it. When he pushed his hat aside we saw his bald pate. The whole Jumla Valley was spread out below his place, mist still lingering in the bottom.

We said we'd met an old man yesterday who was bringing him food, so we thought we'd drop by.

'Oh. Pandit jee,' the baba said, and offered us a seat, tea, and dried apples.

The baba was born in Benaras to Nepali parents, and for the first part of his career he travelled around India, from the edge of Lanka to Pakistan, from Kashmir to Manipur, to Dhaka, to Lhasa. 'I walked to as many places as I could,' he said. 'I haven't been on a plane or ship. I do take trains. I can't get in a motor vehicle.'

'Do you get sick?' Subi asked.

'I puke my guts up.'

He had an older sister. 'She must have gone,' he said. 'She's probably no more. Her children might be alive, in Bombay maybe.'

Travelling around down there was fun, but in the end there was something lacking. Like milk without butter. 'Do you know what I mean?' he asked. The mountains are more suitable for spiritual practice. For a long time he based himself at Badrinath in Garhwal. Now, for many years, he's spent his winters here, and in the summer he'll roam again. Especially, every year he walks for about fifteen days through Dolpo to the shrine at Muktinath. 'Let's see where I end up this year,' he said. 'Maybe I'll end up in Kailash. Have you been to Kailash?'

I said I had, about twenty years ago.

'As a child? Haha. Kailash has changed. There are buildings everywhere.'

'Back then there were only tents.'

'It's not like that anymore.'

'It's so nice here in the sun,' Subi said. 'I feel very sleepy suddenly. I hardly slept at all last night.'

'This nature, I think it's decreasing,' said the baba. 'The old things in the world are decreasing day by day. It is because of people's hearts and minds. Science got popular.' According to him, nature and science are as different as day and night. 'Some people like nights, and some like days. When days get longer nights automatically get shorter,' he said.

Of course he mentioned the weather, and how there's much less snow. We'd have been deep in the stuff here, once, at this time of year, although the sunny aspect made it bearable. Now the drought means the apple farms can't irrigate. 'There'll be hunger,' he said. 'It's a kind of crisis.'

'My mother's uncle always tried to run away and be a hermit,' Subi said. 'And my grandmother caught hold of him and got him married. He'd made it to Janakpur when they caught him. Poor old man! He used to talk about it until the day he died.'

'Nothing ever goes the way you want it to,' the baba said. Eighteen or twenty years ago he was passing by this way while coming down from Rara. 'We spent the night near that pine tree,' he said. 'We heard music, the kind that ties a knot in your heart. There was nothing else. And just like that I got attracted to this place. I had no other reason to stay. This is not a pilgrimage site.

The water source is far away. It's difficult to live here. I've been here for eighteen or twenty winters in the hope I might encounter that goddess again.'

'Hmmm,' said Subi.

'Nothing happened. I only heard it once. Five seconds and that's it. I've felt that the words sometimes float in the air. Apparently the words we speak are also reverberating in the sky. But because the sky is huge, the words disappear. Will you walk again today?'

'The porter already left carrying our bag.'

'Go now,' he said. 'You won't get there today.'

'I'm so sleepy, and sitting here the sun is making me sleepier,' Subi said. But we gave our goodbyes and set off up the slope. 'A sweet old man,' she decided.

The trail passed through a coniferous forest, where we found the woodcutters cutting planks for doors and windows. Subi put her earphones in and listened to *Sense and Sensibility*. 'It's quite amusing and it distracts me from my pains,' she said. I'd look back occasionally and see her tramping along behind: like the victim of some disaster, unlikely to go the distance, I wrote in my notebook.

The track emerged onto a craggy ridge above the trees, with traces of ice and snow, and I sat down to wait for her with a view of the soaring white flanks of Kanjiroba Himal in front of me. It was the same mountain Conrad and I had seen from the other side a few months earlier.

At times on this trip I put my own headphones on and listened to an audiobook of *The Prelude*, William Wordsworth's verse memoir in which he describes his discovery of natural beauty as a child. A few days after we met the baba, when I was lying in bed, I came again across a passage that made a direct connection to what the old man said. Wordsworth recalls coming upon a ruined church when he was riding with a boyhood friend, and he summons the memory of

> ... that single Wren
> Which one day sang so sweetly in the Nave
> Of the old Church, that, though from recent showers
> The earth was comfortless, and, touch'd by faint
> Internal breezes, sobbings of the place,
> And respirations, from the roofless walls
> The shuddering ivy dripp'd large drops, yet still,
> So sweetly 'mid the gloom the invisible Bird
> Sang to itself, that there I could have made
> My dwelling-place, and liv'd for ever there
> To hear such music.

Throughout this book I've tried to trace parts of the relationship between people and their environment in history. One way of thinking about it is Wordsworth's statement that nature is the mirror of the moral world, which correctly implies (though he didn't mean it this way) that people continually find their values reflected by what they perceive in their environment. I've tried to keep sight of Western ideas where they intrude, or where I found an attractive point of comparison. Often the different traditions have seemed like variations on a handful of themes. As we walked towards the national park at Rara, global history and Western environmental ideas collided with local life.

For centuries Europeans believed they had a biblical mandate to subdue the earth and have dominion over nature.[3] People feared the wild, found it ugly, and celebrated the hard-won domestication of the landscape. I mentioned that Christian settlers in the hostile Massachusetts forest thought that the natives – who didn't seem to cultivate the land – had no right to own it. It's nothing unusual: Himalayan rice farmers had a similar outlook. In another way, Himalayan indigenous peoples also feared the wild forest. Rousseau's fantasy of the wild, natural life was a novelty in Europe, and it doesn't have any attraction to followers of these Himalayan traditions.

For Europeans, but not only Europeans, the original nature of people themselves was also something to be managed, domesticated, and overcome. As John Donne put it, How happy is he which hath due place assigned to his beasts, and disafforested his mind.[4] (Think of Chyökyap Pelzang in Dolpo, battling the wild animals of false doctrine.)

Early modern Christian scientists thought they could better understand the Creator's magnificent arrangements by reading nature as God's book. Their discoveries vindicated social hierarchy, political institutions, and economic processes, providing examples of the division of labour, the abhorrence of waste, the guidance of an invisible hand, and the metaphor of the economy of nature. Since Roman times at least, Europeans had observed that bees are governed by a king. As the historian Keith Thomas wrote, it is an enduring tendency of human thought to project upon the natural world (and particularly the animal kingdom) categories and values derived from human society, and then to serve them back as a re-enforcement of the human order.

In his later years Rousseau developed an extreme sensitivity to the opinions of others, which made his life miserable. Although his writings were widely loved, he became paranoid that his enemies and former friends (who found him insufferable) were engaged in a vast conspiracy to destroy him. In fact some of them did want to. He found relief from social hell in solitude, botany, and Romantic communion with the landscape. I cannot believe I am the only one to possess so natural a taste, he claimed in his final work, though I have never yet encountered it in anyone else.[5] In a series of essays framed around a series of walks, he described himself immersed in what he called the great ocean of nature. His faculties were most alive when he was walking, his mind working only with his legs.[6] Apparently, people who saw him collecting plants thought he might be a sorcerer.[7] He loved lakes, of course. The shores of Lake Bienne, he judged, are wilder and more romantic than those of Lake Geneva, because the rocks and woods come closer to the water.[8] I scale rocks and mountains, he wrote, or bury myself in valleys and woods, so as to hide as far as I can from the memory of men and the attacks of the wicked. Deep in the forest shades it seems to me that I can live free, forgotten and undisturbed as if I no longer had any enemies.[9]

Rousseau and his heirs advocated the liberation of our individual natures, and believed that people could solace themselves in the wild. There were sympathetic developments in science, which instead of seeing nature as a machine began to speak of the earth as something like a single organism – instead of a supreme engineer there was an anima mundi. These insights entered the Romanticism of people like Wordsworth, Goethe, Alexander von Humboldt, and later Henry David Thoreau, who were attracted to scientific thinking, but feared that industrialisation and urbanisation were alienating humankind from nature. They wanted to discover themselves by encountering wildness. The new appreciation for the beauty of mountains grew and grew. God is everywhere! exclaimed Samuel Taylor Coleridge after climbing the Kirkstone Pass in a storm.

Not enough attention has been paid to the fact that some of these men were partly inspired by the European discovery of Hindu thought.[10] Early, influential texts translated from Sanskrit into English included the Bhagavad Gita (1785), and William Jones's translations of Kalidasa's play *Shakuntala* (1789) and the *Laws of Manu* (1796). These writings supported the growing view in Europe that India's philosophical tradition was ancient and pristine. As William Jones put it, Pythagoras and Plato derived their sublime theories from the same fountain as the sages of India. It was a view that seemed to be confirmed by his discovery that Sanskrit is related to Latin and Greek. For some European intellectuals, an idealised view of Indian culture emphasised ideas of harmony between people and nature.

Kalidasa's play *Shakuntala* tells a story from the great epic Mahabharat, of a king who meets a beautiful woman – Shakuntala – while hunting in the forest. They are married, separated, and ultimately reunited. It was the perceived ethic of the text, which contains vivid descriptions of natural beauty and injunctions against killing animals, that was more important than the plot for some European readers. Jones's translation of the

Prologue, for example, captures the holistic and animated view of nature that the Romantics embraced. It reads in full:

> WATER was the first work of the Creator; and Fire receives the oblations ordained by law; the Sacrifice is performed with solemnity; the Two Lights of heaven distinguish time; the subtil Ether, which is the vehicle of sound, pervades the universe; the Earth is the natural parent of all increase; and by Air all things breathing are animated: may I'SA [Shiva], the God of Nature, apparent in these eight forms, bless and sustain you![11]

Goethe responded to the play in rapture:

> Would'st thou the young year's blossoms and the fruits of its decline,
> And all by which the soul is charmed, enraptured, fasted, fed,
> Would'st thou the Earth and Heaven itself in one name combine,
> I name thee O Sakuntala! And all at once is said.[12]

Separateness is the illusion, one and many are the same, Goethe wrote.

I am myself identical to nature, declared the philosopher Friedrich Schelling, who also engaged deeply with Sanskrit literature. The explorer, botanist, and polymath Alexander von Humboldt, whose brother Wilhelm was an Indologist, spoke of nature as one whole, animated by the breath of life.[13] His recognition of patterns in ecology spanning the globe (although the word ecology did not exist yet) was revelatory to the young Darwin. Unfortunately, Humboldt's repeated applications to visit India and the Himalaya were rejected by the directors of the East India Company, who distrusted his anticolonial politics.

Meanwhile, geology opened up a vast extent of time in which gradual processes accrued. Nothing can escape what went before, the geologist Charles Lyell said.[14] In Britain, political radicals, taking their cue from France, were attracted to new ideas of biological evolution.[15] Because of the subversive implications of making man into a beast, Darwin cultivated his views in private. He realised that human morality descends from the social and sexual instincts of animals, which, he wrote, are our brethren in pain, diseases, death, suffering, and famine. He argued that shame, wonder, humour, reverence, curiosity, magnanimity, mutual love, and sympathy are shared with lower species from our origin in one common ancestor. Moral behaviour was not at odds with wild nature, but evolved from it. It's a beautiful insight. But he shuddered at the cruelty and waste of the process by which nature makes improvements.

By the time Darwin revealed his discovery of evolution by natural selection he was able to put it not into the hands of radicals but a rising capitalist class. It was a theory of meritocracy and rational competition. Power wasn't shifting from landowners (and botanising country vicars) to the masses, but to industrialists and merchants. Nature was a competitive marketplace. Evolution was the law of progress. Darwin himself was perfectly aware of the social and political implications of his biology. Marx called *The Origin of Species* a bitter satire and quipped that Darwin recognised his English society among the beasts and plants.[16]

The day's walk brought us into a valley of bare trees and bare tilled earth, and finally to a village called Nyaurighat, which is nestled by a river. We stayed there in the home of a young widow and her four daughters.

A cloth trader, who wore a shiny grey suit, was in the kitchen when we arrived. 'The problem with this country,' he said, 'is that Nepalis don't work with their brains. It's all hard labour. We should get on with *smartworking*. I don't see any future in *hardworking*. When I tell people we should do *smartworking* they tell me I'm stupid. They toil up and down, but the land isn't in our favour. People don't listen when they're given good knowledge.'

He offered to organise a ride for the widow and her daughters, who were preparing to head out.

'We don't need a jeep when we have legs,' she said.

The shiny-suit guy left – we'd hear of him again. Then the widow and her daughters left us too, because one of the girls had a stomachache and they needed to consult a jhankri. 'Help yourselves to the food that's cooked,' she said. 'The raksi's here. Let me know what you've had in the morning. Don't lock the door.'

We helped ourselves to her wood pile and got the fire roaring, then settled down on the wooden floor, glad to enjoy such undemanding hospitality. Rajendra started searching the bare kitchen for spoons. 'It's so hard to find stuff in someone else's house,' he said.

'I wonder what caste they are,' I said.

'How can you ask people what caste they are?' Rajendra objected, which seemed to be a change in attitude since we were in the east together. He'd given up drinking, too. He never did drink, not really, he said. And now he had a wife and two sons, the oldest fifteen.

'Tom said you were teasing all the girls along the way,' said Subi.

'It's nice to talk to people,' said Rajendra.

Eventually the kitchen became so hot and smoky that we opened the doors onto the cold night outside, and the barking dogs put their pleading faces in.

In Subi's analysis, it would be a matter of honour for the community to protect the widow and her daughters, so (besides our respectable appearance) she had every reason to feel comfortable leaving us in her house, and us going upstairs to sleep with the door unbarred. At breakfast we learnt that they got home at one in the morning. The girls were preparing strips of cloth to tie to a shrine. The jhankri had been consulted for the daughter's stomachache ('a witch afflicted her,' the mother said), but because she didn't have diarrhoea we didn't mention the antibiotics in our first-aid kit. Instead, we put a dressing on her sister's arm, where she had a gruesome gash from falling on rocks the day before.

And Subi gave our hostess a ticking off about her business model. 'Where's your margin for salt? Where's your margin for oil in these prices? The next time tourists come here you don't charge 100 for the room. You ask for 500.'[17]

The woman was astonished. 'We don't do that!' she said.

The dogs had guarded the hens in the night and killed a nyauri, which is the animal that gives this place its name. A nyauri can be any of various mongoose-like creatures, in this case a Himalayan marten – I think – which is even capable of hunting small deer.

The mid-nineteenth-century Massachusetts naturalist and moralist Henry David Thoreau was an earnest admirer of the Gita and of the *Laws of Manu*, than which he believed there is no grander conception of creation anywhere. He gave extended commentaries on them in *A Week on the Concord and Merrimack Rivers*, and he wrote in a letter to a friend that he saw himself as a yogin. In *Walden* he sits like a yogin in his doorway from sunrise till noon, rapt in revery. He called the muskrat his brother, and the bream his neighbour and contemporary. However, Thoreau's appropriation from Indic texts was selective, rejecting the principles of caste which he found in Manu's laws. Thank God, he wrote, no Hindoo tyranny prevailed at the framing of the world, but we are freemen in the universe, and not sentenced to any cast.[18]

American transcendentalists like Thoreau saw the woods as God's first temples, but he could see the forest and its creatures disappearing before his eyes.[19] Is it not a maimed and imperfect nature that I am conversant with? he asked.

Starting with Niagara Falls, followed by the Catskills, Adirondacks, Yosemite, and Yellowstone, places of beauty in the United States were designated for preservation and recreation – Yellowstone becoming the first national park in 1872. This movement was not only about a new appreciation of natural scenery among a growing urban middle class, and the protection of the environment from damage by humans. It was also part of a nationalist celebration of the majesty of the land, and especially of the wild frontier. National parks got going right after the end of the Indian Wars. The parks erased the history of native Americans, who had inhabited and altered those landscapes for thousands of years and were now expelled, their homes declared a virgin wilderness.[20] National parks became sacred landscapes in America's civil religion, and they were sacred because they are wild.

The word 'ecology' was invented in the late nineteenth century. One of its early propositions was that after going through a series of phases, an environment – such as a forest or prairie – reaches an ideal, final, climax equilibrium. That view is no longer accepted, with major implications for considering what a perfect state of nature could be, if environments never stop changing.

Wilderness is not quite what it seems, according to the historian William Cronon, who goes so far as to call it a human creation.[21] He writes that only a people which is already alienated from the land could hold wilderness up as an ideal. The opposition between what's natural and what's human is false, to the extent that the word 'natural' has little meaning. The goal of environmental history, Cronon says, is to show that we can't escape into an imagined wilderness, and nor can nature escape from humans: we are the gods, and we might as well get good at it.[22]

A new ideology of nature conservation was born in the particular conditions of nineteenth-century America, then exported around the world. National parks became part of the material and mental colonisation of the world by Westerners. The first national park in Nepal was established in 1973. By 2020, Nepal had over 34,400 square kilometres of protected areas, covering over 23 per cent of the country.[23]

It was a crisp wintry walk from Nyaurighat under a grey-white sky, between neatly tilled bare fields, leafless birch, and bottle green firs. The only plants in leaf – except the firs – were occasional bushy evergreen oaks, and sometimes a stand of the small bamboo. The river was a broad, quick, shallow stream. There was ice at the edges and icicles on the cliffs above. The path rose on the cliff, then descended to a watermill in a side valley, where there was a dwelling in a cave. The old man who lived there had dogs, cats, fleas, hens, rabbits, goats, and bees.

Of course he said despairing things about the weather. There used to be so much snow, and after that the crops would grow. 'It's stopped snowing now. It used to be cold, but it's not cold anymore. There used to be a lot of trees. The forest's been destroyed. There's electricity and roads. Water sources are drying up.' Instead of barley, wheat, and potatoes, people eat white rice which is brought here from the south. 'Why doesn't it rain?' he asked. And answered himself, 'The scientists must know.'

Expecting the gods to come into it I asked him, 'Do you do pujas when it doesn't rain?'

'Pujas don't do anything. The scientists must know why it hasn't rained,' he said.

But the young men with whom we ate a lunch of spinach, chapati, and fried eggs said they pray for rain. 'May it rain! May it rain!' they pray. 'Hey Lord, we don't have enough to eat!'

In the village up the valley the women were sitting on sheepskins and crushing walnuts. They'd planted barley two months ago but the fields were bare. The sky darkened and a breeze picked up. 'You've brought the rain,' they joked, and it looked like it. Before we left we bought plastic sheets to cover our backs. But all afternoon, as we walked on towards Bhulbhule, the blackening clouds failed to open.

At Bhulbhule, which is a village at the boundary of Rara Lake National Park, we found accommodation in a house that was in crisis.

It was a simple stone and timber place by the roadside, where a young couple were operating a hotel. There was a stove in the bare ground-floor room, and hard wooden beds upstairs. We put our bags down and sat by the fire.

A truck stopped outside. It was the first vehicle we'd seen. The cab was packed with passengers, and the back was loaded with rice bound for Mugu district. Away it went. 'How many have died on that road, how many?' asked our hostess rhetorically. She was called Lakshmi and she was twenty-four.

'In the old folks' days they had to sing songs to fall in love,' she mused, by way of making conversation. 'Now we use phones.' She told us about the man in the silver suit who we met the night before. 'He's got so many kids from different wives. When I see the kids I want to cry! What will happen to them?' she asked. 'If I run away, what will happen to my kids?' she added, as if to herself.

She said she'd made a love-match at seventeen.

'What does your husband do?'

'Nothing, except play cards,' she said. But when he showed up he seemed to be a clean-cut guy, a few years older than her but still youthful, and he busied himself cooking the meal while Lakshmi sat telling everyone's stories. At some point the subject of joining the Indian army came up, and the husband by the stove, whose name was Bhim Bhandari, said that he once thought of joining the army.

'You get married young and that's it, finished,' Subi remarked bluntly.

Then they told us their troubles. The family had recently received a letter from the national park authorities, requiring them to demolish their house. 'They said we'll go to jail if we don't comply,' Lakshmi said. 'They said we have to move out in the next few days.' According to the park, they'd encroached upon park land. But the couple said their family had owned this land for years, and the authorities refused to even look at their documents.

While they were talking they served the meal. Then three soldiers arrived, so we stopped discussing the park. The soldiers ordered drinks and behaved rudely. They took everyone's attention, and it seemed there could be an unpleasant situation if they weren't handled carefully.

Three inches of snow fell overnight, and it was still falling when we woke. At breakfast we asked the couple again about their situation. The letter from the national park had arrived thirteen days after it was dated. 'What's the date today?' Bhim asked. We told him. 'We only have six more days,' he said. 'We have to throw this house away in six days.'

It had been built a few years earlier, at the side of the road after the road was built, but the family had the land for decades, and they had various papers going back to the period of the park's foundation in the 1970s, such as land tax receipts and government gazettes describing the park boundary, which it seemed to be outside. They did not have complete papers though. 'Nobody here has land certificates, but they're only asking us to move,' said Lakshmi. Anyway, park officials were staying in the village when the house was built and they'd raised no objections.

'It cost us 10 or 12 lakhs to build this. To level the land and build,' Bhim said. 'We invested all our income. We're yet to pay our debts.'

'Have you been paying taxes for this?' asked Subi.

'We have!' said Lakshmi.

'It sounds difficult,' Rajendra observed.

'Yeah. Only six or seven more days in this house.'

'We don't know where to go after this is dismantled,' said Lakshmi. 'We should go to Kathmandu. We'll have to go to Kathmandu and work as labourers. With two kids!'

A few days earlier Bhim had visited the park headquarters and met the chief warden. 'He didn't even take our letter,' he said. 'An educated man like him should have at least looked at the documents. He said to us, "Don't try to be smart." And I said, "Sir, this is a buffer zone according to the 2034 [1978] gazette. So how is it within the park?" When I said that, he said, "I've read a lot of gazettes like this. I've read more gazettes than you."'

'Who said this?'

'The boss. The main boss.'

'Tell us everything, and show us everything,' said Subi.

'They act like we stole their father's property,' said Lakshmi.

'*Don't talk here. Just leave right away!*' Bhim croaked, in the chief warden's voice.

'They might do something to us, after you talk to them,' said Lakshmi.

'They're threatening to destroy your house anyway. What more will they do?'

'She's scared!' said Rajendra. 'Why are you scared? Tell them your grievances and they'll pass them along. Why are you uncomfortable? Why be scared?'

※

It was half past ten when we set off for Rara and the snow was falling again. We'd have to walk nine hours by the circuitous route of the motorable road, since all the footpaths were hidden. The clouds were low. Everything was white, unless the snow hadn't stuck to it yet, in which case it was black. At the army checkpoint outside the village, where we registered our entry to the park, a soldier remarked, 'It will be difficult to mount a search and rescue in this weather.'

'What's all that training for?' asked Subi.

We tramped along the road. We'd be lucky to get in before dark, even if we weren't so slow. The snow was about 6 inches deep now, but not freezing, so it was slippery. Subi and Rajendra both slid and fell. Each time I walked for a minute and turned around I'd see her 30 yards behind me, shuffling along, listening to *Pride and Prejudice* on her headphones. After about an hour we decided to turn around. As we came back towards the village we found that our footprints had been covered already.

It snowed all day. The question changed from when we would reach Rara to when we would be able to leave Bhulbhule at all. News came of the rice truck we'd seen the night before. While it was returning from Mugu in the dark, driving by the light of a mobile phone because it had no headlights, it went over a cliff. No one died.

Sometimes there was a *whumf* as snow slid off the roof. Instead of being shooed out of the kitchen, the hens were allowed to stand inside the door.

'Poor things,' said Lakshmi.

Bhim and Rajendra passed part of the afternoon fussing over the stove to produce a chicken stew and fried beans. By three in the afternoon there was audible drunkenness in the other houses of the village. At five it seemed about time that we started drinking too.

'It makes my stomach burn. I've stopped drinking raksi,' Rajendra said. 'In my village, my grandfather would give me raksi from early on, and if I didn't drink he'd give me a slap and say, "This will give you energy when you take the oxen out." After a glass of it, when your head was ringing, you could do anything.'

Bhim and Lakshmi melted ghee in a pan, burnt some rice in it, then topped it up with liquor and poured glasses.

'It's snowed for exactly fifteen hours,' said Rajendra.

'It's just light snow,' said Lakshmi.

Occasionally we'd hear the rumble of a small avalanche nearby.

'Later, there'll be a storm that feels like it'll send the house flying,' Bhim said.

'Those storms scare me so much!'

'We've burnt two logs in the fire so far. That kept us going all day.'

Bhim's father turned up. He had a handsome, craggy face. The old man told us his stories, about how he was orphaned and ran away to India when he was still young. How he met his wife's family, who were also Nepali migrants living there. How his brother died while gathering fodder when he fell off a cliff. We were sitting in a pool of weak electric light around the hearth. A new batch of raksi was warmed and the drinks were topped up.

'Just a little for me. Enough, enough. That's enough,' said Subi. 'If I drink more than this I'll fall asleep right here.'

'People have certain habits after drinking this stuff,' Rajendra observed. 'Some get sleepy. Some start fighting. Some like to walk.'

'I drank a lot while building this house,' said Bhim, coming in from the cold. He placed a tap, encased in ice, beside the fire to thaw. He'd pulled it off the pipe outside. 'It was heavy work, carrying stones and building walls. Hard labour and drinking. It didn't agree with me, so I stopped.'

'It's good to stop,' said Rajendra.

'I know you were walking around drunk the last time,' Subi told Rajendra, referring to our journey in the east. She addressed the room at large, 'It is written that he walked drunk!'

'I think Sir forgot about that.'

'He's written it! Oh mother! Rajendra told everyone he was unmarried. And flirted with everyone on the way. Drunk!'

Everyone laughed.

'I was joking with the jhankris on the way. I was joking with the women in the bazaar,' Rajendra said. 'It's okay to joke in my culture. Nobody gets mad. And there were all these Rai women. I told them that they're Lahures' [Gurkha soldiers'] daughters. And they said, "Yeah, we are." I asked if they were married and they said, "We're not". I told them I was aiming for a Lahure's daughter. One of them said, "I'm here!"'

He talked about the festival at Salpa Pokhari. '"Sai raja sai sai, Sai rani sai sai." All the Rais there sing it. And they sing, "This year you come with nothing. Next year you'll return with a cradle." That's the song there.'

The door opened to show a white world and ink-black sky, as Bhim went outside again to feed the animals and closed it behind him.

'Don't women drink round here?' asked Rajendra. 'In my village men and women drink equally.'

'It's really different in the east,' said Subi. 'Women have a lot of freedom. It's easy for women in the east. Husbands do everything. Husbands wash clothes. Men do everything.'

'Oh!' said Lakshmi.

'That doesn't happen, Madam,' Rajendra corrected Subi,

then turned to Lakshmi. 'You can admire Madam. Other women have to wake up, cook, and get kids ready for school. She wakes up, dresses, and goes to a meeting!'

Lakshmi gave a short laugh.

'It's really difficult for girls in the west,' said Subi. 'It's difficult in Khas-Arya communities. It's much easier among Rais, Limbus. It's very difficult even among us Newars.'

'Oh really?' said Rajendra. 'Even there?'

'We work around the house,' said Bhim, who was back inside again. He actually seemed a pretty unusual guy. 'But look at Mugu!' – the next district. 'They come home at night and drink. They beat their wives. They don't do any work.'

'In Accham, Doti, the men don't do anything.'

'It's usually Thakuris there, and the women suffer.'

'I've never seen such useless men!'

'They don't do any work.'

'In our village women have started ploughing the fields,' said Rajendra. 'It's not a woman's work, but they started ploughing the fields themselves.'[24]

For hours we sat around like this. We learnt that all this snow meant the crops would germinate. It would be a late harvest, and a low yield this year, but 'they'll grow'. Subi laid down under a blanket to read a novel. Dinner ready and put aside, Bhim set about making the fried bread called namkin. He kneaded and rolled. He held lumps of dough in the flames, because the cold made it stiff to work. He cut it into strips and dropped it in boiling oil. The guy just loved cooking.

'Well, this is a lucky girl, I have to say,' Subi murmured in English.

☀

Nepal's first national park was established in 1973 in the lowland forests of Chitwan. It had been a hunting ground for the royal family. Foreign consultants working for the United Nations drew up the plans. Local people, many of them from indigenous groups, were driven out of the new nature reserve at gunpoint.

Their homes were set on fire or trampled by elephants.[25] That attitude hasn't left us. National park authorities in Chitwan also used fire and elephants to destroy the homes of indigenous people, whom they accused of encroaching on park territory, in 2020.[26]

The 1973 National Parks and Wildlife Conservation Act has been celebrated as a pioneering piece of legislation, which stands at the beginning of a progressive and successful conservation history, but it also contains repressive provisions.[27] Wildlife officers are empowered to search people or arrest them without a warrant, to impose fines equivalent to years of a villager's income, or to imprison them without trial. Entering national parks, which were people's ancestral homes, or exploiting resources like wood and fodder (which households relied upon) became forbidden. Like Chitwan, other new parks were established in areas occupied by indigenous communities, and they were guarded by the army.[28] Nevertheless, entrepreneurs were licensed to operate hotels inside.

Rara National Park was established in 1976 in another place that was dear to the heart of the monarchy. The old King Mahendra (d. 1972) had dedicated a poem to the lake, which kids had to learn at school. The royal family associated itself closely with national park management, which meant they could access substantial international funds controlled through the King Mahendra Trust for Nature Conservation. And they could cultivate an image that was both traditional and modern, pursuing kingly pursuits in the national landscape while scientifically conserving it. Until 1990, when multiparty democracy was established, royal visits to national parks involved encampments of sixty or seventy tents and a retinue of up to a thousand people, including courtiers, generals, and so on. The royal tradition of hunting inside the parks continued, although royal hunts were no longer photographed out of consideration for the new conservation values.[29]

❉

The following morning we set off for Rara Lake, guided by Bhim. The snow was a foot, or knee-deep in places. After the army checkpoint the path left the road and climbed a small valley to pass between two hills. We were surprised and thrilled by the view when we reached the top at about 3,500 metres and saw snow-covered mountains spread out to the north framed by a snow-decked forest. There was a frequent whoosh and patter of snow falling from the branches as we waded down the other side.

Bhim saw tiny figures on the road far below and called to them, 'Eeeee-Oooooo.' We saw them stop and listen. 'I cut the path! I cut the path!' Bhim hollered, but if they could hear what he said we didn't hear any reply.

Bhim said that more than twenty years ago a gang of robbers operated in this forest. They murdered a tailor, stole his earnings, and left his body under a pile of cloth. There were other killings. People became too afraid to pass this way alone or even in pairs. The gang was never caught, but Bhim said that they were men from Mugu. He took a wary view of the people in the neighbouring district, which we were entering now. Last night he'd accused them of fighting with knives too often, as well as beating their wives.

Once we regained the motorable road Bhim left us. The slippery path climbed through a squalid village called Jyaria, where the people were raggedly dressed. There was a shrine under a cedar tree. These giant, isolated trees, which usually have a shrine below them, are said to be remnants of old forests that are gone. Then we mounted a ridge to reach a group of hotels built from planks and tin sheets among pines.

Here we found a family of tourists from Kanpur in India. The husband was a correspondent for the Press Trust of India, but mostly he traded in bicycle parts across the border to Nepalganj, where he'd hired their car and driver. He was joined by his wife and their college-student son, and they'd brought their Pomeranian dog with them.

'The dog is mostly very angry,' they said, while it yapped around our legs. 'She is called Queen Victoria.'

The gorgeous lake was only two hours' walk away but they hadn't made it, 'because we are fatties', the son explained. We urged them to give it a try in the morning, but they said Queen Victoria couldn't walk in the snow. They'd been trapped here for two days.

That night I slept well, but Subi said Queen Victoria kept her awake, and at breakfast the woman of the place was fed up. 'That dog bites,' she muttered. 'Would it really die in the snow? I'm sick of it.' It had bitten her toddler.

'When our dogs misbehave we hit them, so they don't bite people,' her husband said.

'We don't hit our dog,' said the guests.

They asked for electricity to plug in their heater, but there was none. Already they were wearing as many clothes as they could. For a while they considered moving to another hotel, and the couple who ran the place grew hopeful. They changed their minds four times and decided to stay.

'This is hilarious,' Subi whispered. By seven-thirty we were gone, crunching through the frozen snow.

There was a sensation of specialness that morning that I compared in my notes to walking down to Phoksundo a few months earlier. Glittering crystals covered everything. Low light was slanting through the pines. The dark waters of the lake came into view, and as the sun rose over it the lake turned blue. At the edges we could see every pine needle and pebble in its own colour through the perfectly clear, still water. The water changed to turquoise as it deepened. Out in the middle, where we could only see the surface, the lake gave back the exact colour of the forested slopes, white mountains and clear sky.

Rara National Park is a beautiful tragedy. In 1976 a foreign expert was employed by the United Nations to design it.[30] The aim was to reduce human impact as far as possible, while promoting recreational activities for visitors and maintaining good relations with local people. The locals would be okay, the expert judged, because the creation of the park was not likely to seriously increase animal damage to adjacent crops or livestock.[31]

The planning document shows that only a small area inside the new boundaries was cultivated, yet the text declares that

> the continued existence of the villages of Chapra and Rara is totally incompatible with the purposes of the park ... The removal of these villages and the resettlement of the inhabitants is therefore a prerequisite to the success of the Lake Rara National Park. The residents, in discussion with senior project staff, have stated their willingness, indeed readiness, to leave Rara provided that alternative farming land is provided and appropriate compensation is paid.

These people were relocated to the plains, where several died. It's said that this experience contributed to the decision not to expel Sherpas from the new national park around Mount Everest when it was created the same year.[32]

It is claimed that the villagers of Rara may have been descended from courtiers of the Khasa-Malla kingdom, but if so their social capital had long since dissipated.[33] There are two heavily eroded steles, or engraved stone slabs, standing by the lakeshore near the national park offices, which show that the Malla kingdom did operate here. A little further on there's an area of young pines growing on disused terraces.[34] Among them there are three mighty trees that once stood in the cultivated landscape of the village. There's an elaborate stone tap. Then the lakeside path becomes a hollow way, which suggests the route of the old thoroughfare from the village to the fields. The houses of Rara were slightly further up the slope, and it's a scramble through bush to find them. The undergrowth where they stood is strewn with rubble. Down beside the lake the temple of Rara Mahadev still stands.[35] Because it houses their ancestral god, the expelled villagers return to it sometimes, which requires a journey of several days.

As I was walking back along the path a wild dog stepped out of the trees in front of me. It turned its head on its thick, shaggy neck, to look at me. With an easy bound it disappeared back into the forest.

At the national park offices, Subi – who is a journalist – interviewed the chief warden on camera about Bhim and Lakshmi's case. (We heard from them months later that the national park had backed off, for the time being at least, and they were still in their house.) And we interviewed an old man named Hari Bahadur Rokaya on the sunny bench outside the park office, with the glittering lake behind him. His village is Murma, which is only a couple of miles away, but it's outside the park so it survived the clearances.

'There used to be wheat on this land. It was all agricultural,' he said. 'It's become forest. It's barren. It became a national park. You can't do anything here, so it's just like this now.'

According to Hari Bahadur, each person who was displaced forty-two years earlier received 500 rupees for transportation. 'They were paid and removed from here. They didn't know how to close their doors and leave this place behind. They cried, they slaughtered goats, and they left knowing they wouldn't come back. It wasn't fun to watch. There were three villages along here: Rara, Chharu, and Murma. Two villages left and one remained.'

On the lakeshore beside the national park office there were two tourist hotels. This duopoly was controlled by the local bosses of two of Nepal's leading political parties, the Maoists and the Unified Marxist Leninists. One of them was the local MP. We phoned him up and asked how the park benefits local people.

'It doesn't. It benefits animals,' he said.

These days the general fashion is to take a less heavy-handed approach, although Nepal's Department of National Parks hasn't got the memo. It's increasingly recognised that protected areas that deprive people of their rights and deepen their poverty are not morally or practically sustainable. Anyway, such parks do nothing to protect biodiversity outside their boundaries. A quarter of Nepal is under draconian environmental regulations, which have undoubtedly been successful in protecting wildlife, while much of the rest of the country is being severely damaged by unregulated road construction, sand mining, and the deforestation of the Chure hills, all of which are related to official corruption.

The people of Hari Bahadur's village, Murma, said they are locked up or fined by the park authorities if they collect firewood or fodder from inside the park. They are even fined if their animals stray into the river that forms the boundary there. They're not allowed to take water from the river, so they have to walk far to collect it. They're not compensated if wild animals, such as boar, leave the park and eat their crops. Bears from the park plunder the village's apple trees, and when people tried to diversify their incomes by keeping bees, the bears wrecked the hives before they hibernated, leaving the villagers feeling hopeless. We met a young man called Rup Bahadur Rokaya who was attacked by a bear while herding sheep. Due to the absence of public services in the district, it took him three days to reach a functioning hospital and his left eye could not be saved.[36] For that injury he qualified for $500 compensation from the park. 'I've nothing but hatred towards the national park. Everyone in our society hates the national park,' he said.

A man from Murma called Lok Bahadur guided us when we walked on. We set out early, because we'd have to go the long way round in these snow conditions. Not that the snow was all that bad, Lok Bahadur said. Twenty years ago it would fill the bottom of the small valley we were walking along, many metres deep. Murma would be snowbound for weeks. Due to the changing climate, according to Lok Bahadur, you can grow vegetables such as cauliflower up here these days, and there are bird species people never saw before.

For the last five winters Lok Bahadur said he'd gone to India, and worked as a street hawker selling hats and scarfs in Gorakhpur and Allahabad. One year he used the proceeds to buy some sheep, but there was no grazing because of the park, so he sold them. He tried his hand at apples and honey, but that didn't work out because of the bears.

The route turned into a ravine, with trees spectacularly poised on the cliffs above us. After some time we began to climb. Here the pine forest had been destroyed by people cutting spars from the base of the trees. According to Lok Bahadur they burn the resin for light when they work in the watermill at night. Separately, he said, the grass had been burnt to encourage the growth of a certain herb. The fires caught the resin suppurating from the wounded trees and consumed them.

We traversed a high slope. It was pleasant up here. We were warm in the sun. Even the earth smelt warm. The snow had gone, except in a few shaded parts where we fell through the crust to our thighs. Gaining the top of the ridge we looked back towards the north, where Lok Bahadur pointed out the distant cave of the gods Shiva and Parvati in the mountains above Murma.

'With so many gods around here, you'd think the place would be rich,' said Rajendra.

'There are valuable herbs in the forest that no one even knows about,' Lok Bahadur said defensively.

We climbed to a pass, from which we could see white hills and mountains into the very distance, both north and south. Finally we descended in slippery mud to reach the village of Gothijyula in the Sinja Valley – more than ten hours since we set off, with no lunch on the way. We completed the walk in a moonless night full of stars, by the light of our mobile phones.

At six or seven the next morning Lok Bahadur drank a quarter bottle of vodka and set off back to Murma. So we were told, when we finally made it downstairs.

The woman who ran our hotel was called Challibudha. (Challi means chick; it had been her nickname since she was a child.) She married a man from this place, and initially everything was fine. Their first child was a daughter. During her second pregnancy Challibudha fell out of a tree while cutting fodder. She miscarried and never became pregnant again. Her marriage soured. Her husband took a second wife down on the edge of the plains, where he lives now. He only visits his old home, and the hotel she keeps there, to collect the earnings. She can't stop him because there's no bank here to keep her money safe.

Tinny folk music was playing on the radios, or more likely on the mobile phones of the shopkeepers in the bazaar. They were sitting around in the sun. All over the village women were working. Women carrying rocks, women laying paving, women sifting rice, women crushing apricot stones for oil, a woman feeding grain into the spinning stone in the water mill, little girls carrying water. When we stopped to chat or take photographs Subi complained that the women here do all the work, and suggested that the men should stir themselves. She was told that nothing would ever change, or she was met with embarrassed silences – from the women in particular.

We bumped into the driver who'd been working for the Indian tourists and Queen Victoria. He'd deserted them and walked down here. The road from Rara wasn't expected to open for days. He said the couple who ran the hotel were going crazy. His employers still refused to attempt the short walk to see the perfect lake. They seemed to be having a terrible holiday.

✳

We'd seen Malla steles at Rara and there were many more of them here. Several seemed to be in the process of getting lost or damaged. The Sinja Valley is littered with relics of the old kingdom.

The Mallas flourished until around 600 years ago, and their existence was not well remembered, leaving the stones that are lying around in need of an explanation. They're conflated in local memory with a story in the Mahabharat of the mythical Pandava brothers' journey into the Himalaya. One of the Pandavas was called Bhimsen, so the stones are known as 'Bhimsen's burden', because the epic hero is supposed to have left them here.

We were told to talk to Deependra Upadhyaya if we wanted to know about the history of Sinja. We found him in his stationery shop, a man in his early thirties who lived for the study of history and culture. 'Wherever I go, I have a camera and a recorder with me. I have one in my pocket right now,' he said.

Over the past ten years Deependra had collected tens of thousands of photographs, videos, and audio recordings of documents, artifacts, rituals, and folk stories, which he had stored on his laptop and several hard drives. 'Sinja is like the mother. It's a place of origin. It's the birthplace of everything,' he said. There is a place near Jumla called the motherfield (mulkhet), where the first rice in these mountains was planted. A ritual is performed when it's planted there again each year, he told us.

The Sinja Valley seems to have been the capital, or the summer capital, of the Malla kingdom. (The winter capital was further down the mountains in Dullu, where Subi and I would end our journey.) A copper plate recording a royal grant of 1393 AD reads:

> In the best of towns named the illustrious Sinja, which is lovely for the songs of women on the roof terraces of whitewashed palaces abounding in good fortune ... the glorious [king] Madinivrahma ... who is a swan in the hearts of women, like the swan on Laka Manasa ... [gives land and tax relief to two Brahmins] ... The witnesses are the sun and the moon ...[37]

In fact, to speak of a town was an exaggeration, and it seems the palace was quite modest. An archaeological excavation of a likely palace complex showed that its few rooms were accumulated over a period of time and that its stone blocks were bound by mud mortar. The crude pottery fragments at the site date it to the same period as this poetic inscription.[38]

'There's a lot we haven't understood,' Deependra said. Almost all the work remains to be done, but the materials are abundant. He's found texts engraved on copper plates, documents on paper, writing on clay. A hoard of gold coins was found in a potato field and removed to the National Museum. Six statues were recently unearthed when a house was built, 'just down there', Deependra said. He once took a text he'd found to Kathmandu, but the archaeology department couldn't decipher the unusual characters, or they couldn't be bothered. 'You call them to ask, "Sir, did you do it?",' he recalled. 'They'll say they will. You ask ten times but it won't get done.' After staying for a month in the city, and spending all his money, he returned to Sinja empty-handed.

All the time the antiquities are being removed or stolen. If an object looks impressive or valuable the government takes it. 'Our stance is that they should be kept here. They should be preserved,' Deependra said. 'Whoever comes, looks, sees something, and takes it.' Documents disappear. Foreigners even buy the old-fashioned wooden ladders from the houses. 'There are old things everywhere,' but people hide them because outsiders will interfere. Only the history that's still in the ground is safe, Deependra said. 'We'll be left with nothing but folk stories, and no proof.' At least he wasn't discouraged. He was preparing to set off on an independent research trip at the end of the month, to collect data from three neighbouring districts.[39]

✳

In our own condition of environmental anxiety we might not credit the environmental anxiety of the nineteenth century. In 1884 John Ruskin described the onset of climatic disaster. He could see that the strange weather was an indictment of his entire society. He'd noticed a new type of cloud, which

> looks partly as if it were made of poisonous smoke; very possibly it may be; there are at least two hundred furnace chimneys in a square mile or two ... It looks more to me as if it were made of dead men's souls ... Sun through the plague-cloud is blanched and colourless, like a bad half crown in a bowl of soapy water ... Remember, for the last twenty years, England, and all foreign nations ... have done iniquity by proclamation, every man doing as much injustice to his brother as it is in his power to do ... The Empire of England, on which formerly the sun never set, has become one on which it never rises.[40]

As early as the 1820s, alarm was raised within the administration of India that the wanton destruction of Himalayan forests was changing the climate.[41] Colonialism, of course, was based on the exploitation of cheap nature. Deforestation wasn't new, but it was taking place on an unprecedented scale as Himalayan timber entered an economy that stretched around the world. At the same time, global travel by Europeans such as Alexander von Humboldt was revolutionising the understanding of natural history. These scientists drew a connection between the deforestation of tropical islands, the drying of water sources, and changes in the islands' climates – a theory that became known as desiccationism. In India the idea was taken up especially by East India Company surgeons, many of whom were botanists. They saw a connection between forests, atmospheric humidity, climate, and health.

In the following decades those concerns gained traction among the highest colonial authorities, who had an interest in averting droughts as well as ensuring a reliable supply of timber. A circular issued by the Court of Directors in 1847 stated that the links between deforestation and the climate had a strong bearing on the welfare of mankind, and they were anxious to obtain extensive and accurate information about it.[42]

Climatic concerns, heightened by repeated droughts, led to

the regulation of forestry.⁴³ The Indian Forest Department was established in 1865, and in 1878, the third year of the Great Famine, the colonial state passed the Forest Act, nationalising forests.⁴⁴ It sought to control deforestation by penalising local people, who were prevented from collecting even a blade of grass within forest boundaries. The Forest Department still promoted commercial logging though, so deforestation continued, accelerated by the expansion of the railways.⁴⁵

An understanding of global weather patterns put an end to desiccationist theories by the early twentieth century,⁴⁶ but the colonial regulation and exploitation of Himalayan forests continued. The situation in independent Nepal, compared to regions that were governed by the British, was different but not completely: Nepali forestry was exposed to the same colonial markets.⁴⁷ Nepal's Forest Department was established on the Indian model in 1925.

After independence the Indian government continued to promote commercial forestry in the Himalaya, while penalising local people for denuding the environment. In the early 1970s a peasant movement arose in the hills of Garhwal and Kumaon (just across the border from Nepal) to defend traditional forest rights to fuel and fodder against the Forest Department, which was in thrall to commercial loggers and resin tappers, and in connivance with timber thieves.⁴⁸ The movement was called Chipko, meaning to hug, because the protestors vowed to hug the trees even if axes split their stomachs open, although in practice little actual hugging went on. Women took a prominent role in the Chipko movement, because they did so much of the work that relied on access to forests. Over a number of years Chipko brought commercial logging to a standstill and became a template for other environmental protests, such as those against big dams.

Nepali forests, which had belonged to feudal landowners, were nationalised in 1957. Draconian laws were introduced, such as the 1961 Forest Act, which aimed to prevent people from entering forests at all, and the 1967 Forest Protection Special Act, which empowered forest guards to shoot unauthorised forest users.⁴⁹

In 1973 the biologist George Schaller visited Nepal and wrote that upland deforestation was destroying the soil on which villagers depended. Nepal will soon be derelict unless it protects its watersheds, he reckoned.

> Interestingly, early this year several villages in the Gharwal [sic] area of the Indian Himalaya have shown how private initiative can protect the forests. Having finally realised the misery which total deforestation ultimately brings to the lives of hill people, villages began a Gandhian movement to save their trees ... True, in Nepal the villager himself is often an important agent in his own destruction, for he circumvents laws that prohibit the cutting of live trees by ringbarking them ... Perhaps some day the hill people of Nepal will also develop an ecological conscience.[50]

Beginning in the 1970s, and causing increasing alarm in the 1980s, a view took hold that the Himalaya was suffering an environmental super-crisis. According to this theory, which became known as the Theory of Himalayan Environmental Degradation,[51] advances in healthcare had led to a population explosion, creating massive demand for firewood, fodder, and agricultural land.[52] This had led to the loss of half of Nepal's forests between 1950 and 1980, and by 2000 no accessible forests would remain.[53] The destruction of forests on marginal slopes led to massive erosion and the loss of productive land, driving further deforestation while causing siltation and catastrophic flooding in the plains. The increasing scarcity of firewood necessitated the burning of animal dung, meaning there was less manure to maintain field fertility, further driving the vicious cycle. Numerous articles appeared in the international media describing the disappearance of forests from the Everest region and so on, and in 1987 Rajiv Gandhi blamed Nepali deforestation for disastrous flooding in Bihar. As the authors of an early critique wrote, the arguments seemed so reasonable it was hardly surprising they were widely accepted as fact.[54]

Obviously dire predictions are made to avert their own

fulfilment, but the theory of Himalayan degradation got a lot wrong. By the late 1980s, a growing body of research showed that the amount of forest cover in the Nepal hills hadn't changed much in decades, or even since 1900.[55] Government land policies and agricultural expansion, which were already established by the late eighteenth century, had been responsible for much of the deforestation that had ever occurred in earlier generations. Abandoned terraces showed that, if anything, agriculture had retreated in some areas in more recent times.[56] The fact that landlords and the government no longer collected most of the harvest in rents and taxes meant the land was able to support population growth without expanding the area under cultivation. What's more, the physical mechanics connecting deforestation to landslides, erosion, and siltation were a lot less straightforward than previously assumed. Critics were careful not to dismiss the possibility of any connection, contenting themselves with pointing out that there's no evidence to demonstrate the processes that had been claimed.[57] Anyway, there have always been a lot of landslides in the Himalaya, even on forested slopes, as anyone can see. But perhaps the theory's most striking shortcoming was social, or political. It blamed the poor for over-exploiting what the powerful despoiled. While peasants were excluded from forests by coercive states, state and commercial interests cut forests in India, while in Nepal logging was a monopoly of corrupt politicians.[58]

The theory of Himalayan degradation created a sense of urgency though, and even as some of its precepts were increasingly questioned in the 1980s it contributed to better policies in Nepal, with support from foreign development agencies.[59] A fourteen-volume Master Plan for the forestry sector was produced in 1988, which advocated putting forests under community management. The 1993 Forest Act replaced the punitive and exclusionary approach of the 1961 act with management by local users' groups. Over 11 per cent of Nepal is now community forest, and the policy is widely regarded as a success, for helping to improve people's welfare, as well as to enlarge Nepal's forested area, and improve the quality of the forests. At the same time, urbanisation has depopulated the countryside, reducing the pressure.

The doom of the Himalaya turned out not to be true, but now it seems to be true again. The place is nothing like a lifeboat in the storm. Recent temperature increases are greater than elsewhere in the world. The winter snows fail and the monsoon is coming in more concentrated deluges. A large share of a locality's annual precipitation can fall in a single day, causing devastation.[60] During the 2023 monsoon there was drought in some parts of the country, which struggled for drinking water, not to speak of irrigation.[61] It was something unheard of. Glaciers are disappearing, and the thawing mountain permafrost increases the incidence of rockfalls and lethal debris flows. Millions of Himalayan people are vulnerable to the manifold and uncertain consequences. Needless to say, they are responsible for only a tiny fraction of the world's carbon emissions. It seems likely that the Himalayan rivers will swell as ice melts, then dwindle, with implications for the billions of people throughout Asia who rely on them. Himalayan forests are being tied to global carbon markets through a mechanism called REDD+. Although one may guess, it remains to be seen for certain who will benefit and who will bear the cost of that scheme.[62]

I'd hoped to walk from Sinja down to Dullu, but we took the bus instead. All the passengers turned up at the scheduled time, which was seven in the morning, and we left three and a half hours later due to a rivalry between operators. The road was in a dreadful condition as far as the Kalikot district border, where we'd arranged to be met by a private jeep. From there, we continued our journey in that.

The scenery of Kalikot is terrible. Massive black hills plunged into the valley, the bottom of which was invisible somewhere far beneath the road. I have a friend in Kathmandu who calls this road the Karnali Death Highway. At one cliffy stretch the driver pointed out an accident blackspot. 'Many people have died here,' he said. 'Buses, trucks, tractors. A sacrifice was demanded and a temple was built.' After that the accidents decreased slightly.

Subi suggested drunk driving might account for all the carnage.

Partly so, the driver was willing to concede, but mostly it was the river demanding a sacrifice. Later he pointed out where a jeep had gone over the edge. 'The driver was new,' he said. 'The car was new too,' he added.

And where a cascade of boulders had been partly cleared from the road he said a motorcyclist had stopped to record a video and been killed by a falling rock.

In the late afternoon we entered the Karnali gorge, the low sun shining on the glassy river below us. Two dugout canoes were sliding over the surface. It looked perfect for fishing. We were coming into warm mid-hill country. Winter wheat was standing in the fields and the orange trees were in leaf.

We kept driving in the dark, at one point stopping while a wrecked jeep was loaded onto a truck, which made a stark spectacle in our headlights. At another point the driver swerved momentarily. 'I fell asleep,' he said, turned the radio up loud and drove more slowly on. Eventually we arrived at Dailekh Bazaar. He ate, then drove away again to collect his next passengers from Nepalganj in the morning.

I'd been to Dailekh once before, a few years earlier. That time it was for work, in a big white Landcruiser with the letters UN painted on the sides. The old Malla centre of Dullu is nearby. After my friend and colleague Ramyata and I had finished our meetings, we passed some time visiting archaeological sites. This visit followed a similar pattern. We had an introduction to the deputy mayor, so we called on her at her office. Then set we set off in a pickup truck provided by the hotel, joined by the driver's wife, for a day out. This book ends with relaxation and sightseeing.

We knew that a group of Raute had camped nearby. I'd seen one of them in the bazaar earlier, easily recognisable in his white cape and turban. This population of a few hundred people, who live in a couple of separate bands, might be the last hunter-gatherers in the Himalaya.[63] Neighbouring farmers call them forest

people, and they describe themselves (when they explain themselves in Nepali) as the subjects of trees, or alternatively as the kings of the forest, or the children of god.[64] The Raute range over mid-hill and lowland forests in western Nepal, coming to lower altitudes in the cold weather, and they told us they reached as far north as Rara in the summer. According to the anthropologist Jane Fortier, they would rather cut their own throats than live as farmers.[65]

They'd made their camp on a strip of open ground between trees and a pleasant stream, where villagers were doing laundry not far from the road, with farmland all around. Their tents were made of arched bamboo covered with dark, heavy cloth. The men were dressed in sheets of cotton and the women wore blouses and skirts with heavy metal jewellery, so there was no mistaking them for members of any other community. Colourfully dressed village girls walked through the camp carrying fodder or leading goats. There were some local tourists here too, who'd arrived in a car like us. They had soot and tika on their foreheads and they were looking around imperiously.

Of course we tried to talk, but the Rautes were cagey while it felt to us that we were participating in a distasteful tourist spectacle. 'Government officials, journalists, foreigners, people from organisations,' all come to see them, they said, and they were obviously only humouring us in the expectation of some money, which we did give them before we left. I also gave them some fishhooks and line, which they seemed very pleased with. They do all their fishing with cast nets, but there are no fish any longer in a stream like this, they said.

'What about in the Karnali?' I asked. I was going to stick around the next day and fish the Karnali after Subi and Rajendra left. There must be some fish left there?

'Maybe in the Karnali.'

Now that these journeys were ending I'd been thinking about how they began. Remembering Rajendra's remarks about lightning deaths I'd asked Deependra Upadhyaya if that happened much in Sinja. 'Yeah, it hasn't been a year since Tilak and all his sheep were killed,' he said. 'There are many incidents.'

I asked the Rautes the same question. They hadn't heard of anything like that.

We drove on to Shreesthan, the temple down the track, where the priest put soot on our foreheads. This was a charming place. It seemed to me the very epitome of settled village culture. A stream ran through the precinct. Colourful bunting and shiny-leafed banana trees made the scene delightful. Children in blue school uniforms were making a cheerful, disorderly queue for tika. There were steles and fragments of masonry lying around, which showed that the place was sacred to the old Malla kingdom. Inside the shrine a small orange flame flickered. It's one of a group of several fire temples in Dullu where flammable gas leaks from the ground, the height of the flames varying through the year with the water table.[66] These temples were on a pilgrimage route that once extended as far as Baku in Azerbaijan. Since the decline of local kingship the temples have become obscure, but at one time it was claimed that the fire of Dullu would destroy the universe in the end. Where bubbles rose in the stream our driver showed us how to roll a leaf into a cone to trap the gas and light it from the tip.

Another mile downstream there was another wonderful temple, with more stone fragments lying around. There was a

huge pipal tree, several metres in circumference, which we clambered up inside to see a protuberance on the trunk that looks like Ganesh, and to receive tika on our foreheads. As we climbed out the schoolkids arrived and swarmed in.

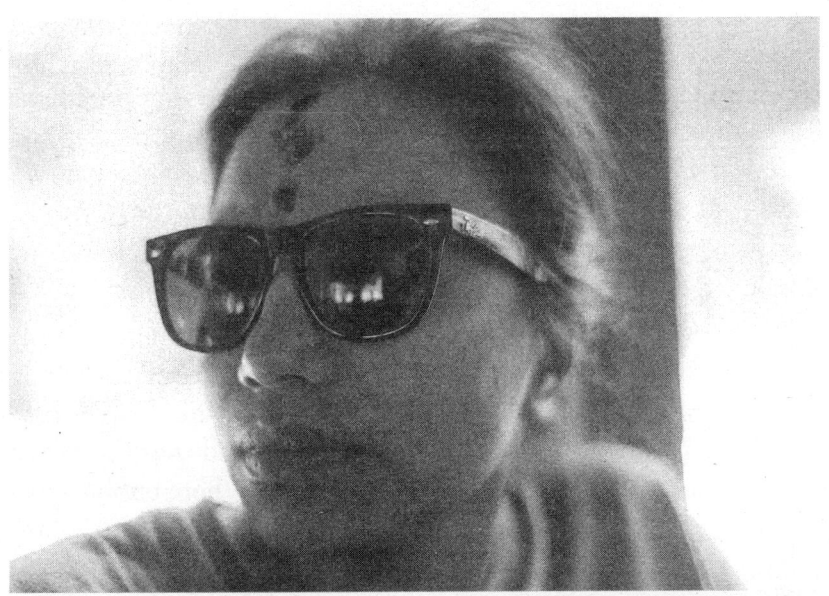

So the last hunter-gatherers were camping near the remains of the first agriculturalists. We had a cup of tea. Rajendra asked the tea seller, 'How much are these priests making from Shiva's offerings?'

We drove on. The first time I was here we visited impressive ruins on a hillside, but though I thought I could find them again it seemed I couldn't. We kept asking for directions. The area was so littered with antiquities we were being sent all over the place. The sun was low, and we were on the point of giving up when we parked the truck and were led through fields to a cluster of five neglected temples overlooking the valley. A beautiful spot! Each temple was a small stone allegory of a holy mountain. As the angle of the light slid lower, we stood for a long time amid the crops there.

Acknowledgements

Some of those who gave me their time, knowledge, and hospitality appear on these pages. I'm grateful to them all. I am especially grateful to Rajendra Sunwar, Girish Giri, Conrad Smewing, and Subi, who accompanied me on these walks. Era Shrestha and Nikita Tripathi translated and transcribed recordings of conversations that I made along the way. While we were in the United States I benefitted from the extraordinary opportunities given to the partners of Neiman Fellows at Harvard. Several professors kindly allowed me to audit their classes. Among those who taught me things that entered this book are James Engell, Jinah Kim, and Jason Ur. Michael Witzel allowed me to ask questions for several hours. Part 2 was written during a generous Paul D. Fleck Fellowship residency at the Banff Centre for Arts and Creativity. Thanks in particular to Joanna Croston at Banff. Rabindra Puri lent me a flat in Panauti when I needed somewhere to concentrate. Thanks to my friend Samden Sherpa's Snow Leopard Trekking for introducing me to Rajendra. I'm grateful to Sam Cowan, Duane Clifford-Jones, Dinesh Devkota, Mike Hutt, Arun Rana, Mike Searle, Bimbika Sijapathi, Mark Watson, and John Whelpton, among others, for information and suggestions, and especially to Charles Ramble who translated the family chronicle I photographed in Saldang. I hope he will publish it one day. Several people read part or all of the manuscript at various stages and provided valuable comments, which is no small favour. They include Aditya Adhikari, Prawin Adhikari, David Gellner, Shradha Ghale, Kabir Heimsath, and Julia Lovell. Only I am responsible for the remaining errors and vulgarities. Katrin Hagen, Perdita Pohle, the Philadelphia Museum of Art and the Rubin Museum of Art kindly gave permission to reproduce images. I'm very grateful to my agent Jessica Woollard of David Higham Associates for her patient advice. Thanks to Manasi Subramaniam, Milee Ashwarya, Shubhi Surana, Purva Dua, Saloni Mital, and the wonderful team at Penguin Random House India. Finally, and most of all, I'm grateful to Subina and our two children. The writing of this book sprawled across eight eventful years. They were obliged to endure my intermittent absorption in a task that took much longer than I'd imagined.

Notes

Preface
1. Jean-Jacques Rousseau, *A Discourse on Inequality* (1755), translated by Maurice Cranston.
2. 'Today when trade, travel and conquests bring various peoples closer together, and when their ways of living become constantly more alike as a result of frequent communication, one notices that certain national differences have diminished ...' But to say that 'men are everywhere the same ... is as reasonable as saying one cannot distinguish Pierre from Jacques, since they both have a nose, a mouth and eyes.' In Rousseau's footnote (J) to *A Discourse on Inequality*, pp. 154–61.

Part 1: Migration
1. The map I had was Panchthar, Ilam, and Tehratum (2003) in the Helvetas District Transport Infrastructure series, which was published to show the network of footpaths and trial bridges.
2. Bombax ceiba, also known as the cotton tree, silk-cotton tree, or kapok.
3. Corneille Jest, 'The Kushwar of Chaithali (central Nepal)', *Contributions to Nepalese Studies*, vol. 4, no. 2, 1977.
4. Shankar Koirala, 'Koshi Pradesh Ka Majhi Jati', *Ancient Nepal*, no. 3, 1968. Translated as 'The Majhi Community of the Koshi Region' in *Regmi Research Series*, year 12.
5. Joseph Hooker, *Himalayan Journals*, pp. 148–9.
6. Lil Bahadur Chhetri, *Basain*, translated by Michael Hutt as *Mountains Painted with Turmeric*.
7. Hooker, *Himalayan Journals*, p. 178.
8. Philippe Sagant, *The Dozing Shaman: The Limbus of Eastern Nepal*, translated by Nora B. Scott.

9. The classic account of this is in Fernand Braudel's *The Mediterranean and the Mediterranean World in the Age of Philip II*. Braudel asks, 'Can we define the mountains as the poorest regions of the Mediterranean, its proletarian reserves?' (p. 30) and notes later, 'The mountains have always been a reservoir of men for other people's use' (pp. 51–2).
10. Rousseau, *Confessions*, p. 320.
11. For a British account of the pilgrimage site at Barahakshetra in the early nineteenth century see Francis Buchanan Hamilton, *An Account of the Kingdom of Nepal*, p. 152.
12. From *The Prelude*.
13. This passage is based on the translation by Larry Hartsell.
14. Eric Hobsbawm, *Bandits*.
15. The case is different in the plains, where banditry and adjacent practices have a deep tradition.

    Of the elite-based criminal networks often described as 'mafias', which have become pervasive in Nepal since the advent of multiparty democracy, Hannah Arendt's saying sometimes feels apposite: 'Whatever political organization men may have achieved has its origins in crime.'

    An instance of social banditry of the type described by Hobsbawm is recorded in the culturally Tibetan region of Mustang in western Nepal by Charles Ramble. He quotes a letter to the authorities written in 1956 by the people of Chötsong, a community near the Tibetan border, which reads: 'The one called Dobdob Yeshe Zangpo has stolen property from within Nepal: 800 yak-loads of salt, and from seven households with [a population of] approximately 30 people within Nepal (or: with his retinue of thirty men [living in seven tents]) [he has taken] 2,000 sheep, 800 goats, nearly 1,000 yaks and thirty mules and horses ... the only person who causes trouble is Dobdob Yeshe.' According to Ramble: 'Dobdob Yeshe Zangpo was a well-known borderland bandit of Tibetan origin ... In his old age, Yeshe Zangpo became devoutly religious, gave away his property to good causes and died in the Tibetan refugee camp in Dhorpatan, in Nepal. He is reported to have passed into the post-mortem meditative state known as *thugs dam*, an indication of spiritual achievement that caused his enemies great annoyance. He is now remembered in Mustang as a kind of folk hero, and there are even songs about his adventures.' See Charles Ramble, 'A Century of Trade and Tension: Stakeholders in the Kali Gandaki Salt Route, Mid-19th to Mid-20th Centuries', in Jeannine

Bischoff and Alice Travers, *Commerce and Communities: Social and Political Status and the Exchange of Goods in Tibetan Societies*.
16. Compare Hesiod, writing in Greece around the eighth century BC: 'Take heed when you hear the voice of the crane from high in the clouds, making its annual clamour; it brings the signal for ploughing, and indicates the season of winter rains, and it stings the heart of the man with no ox.' (*Works and Days*, p. 50 in the Oxford World Classics edition, translated by M. L. West.)
17. Charles Allen, *The Prisoner of Kathmandu: Brian Hodgson in Nepal 1820–43*.
18. The common hawk-cuckoo, *Hierococcyx varius*.
19. A paathi can be a unit of weight or volume, equivalent to between 3 and 4 kilograms, or about 4 litres. There are eight manas in a paathi. So the woman may have carried about 24–32 kg of salt.
20. I have used AD not CE because this is not the 'common era' in Nepal. The primary calendar in common use is Bikram Sambat, in which 2024/5 AD was 2081.
21. N. J. Allen, *Miyapma: Traditional Narratives of the Thulung Rai*, pp. 150–3.
22. Allen, *Miyapma*, p. 153.
23. This account is based on Nick Allen's study, *Miyapma: Traditional Narratives of the Thulung Rai*, with some details from Martino Nicoletti's *The Ancestral Forest: Memory, Space and Ritual among the Kulunge Rai of Eastern Nepal* as well as Nicoletti's *Riddum: The Voice of the Ancestors*. The traditions of these two neighbouring Rai groups are very similar, although for example the names of some characters vary. This summary includes only those parts which are the same or similar in the two versions, and uses the names given by Allen.
24. Allen, *Miyapma*, p. 31.
25. The earliest evidence of human habitation in what's now Nepal was discovered by Gudrun Corvinus, who found Palaeolithic stone tools at two sites on the edge of the hills, in Mahottari and Dang. Differences in the tools showed that these were distinct cultures. She was able to date charcoal deposits in Mahottari to 7,000 years before the present, and tentatively suggested a date of 12,000–32,000 BP for the discoveries in Dang. However, there is no evidence to link these peoples to modern inhabitants of the hills. See Gudrun Corvinus, 'The Prehistory of Nepal: After Ten Years of Research' in Thapa and Baaden (eds) *Nepal: Myths and Realities*.
26. See Georg Miehe, Colin Pendry, et al., *Nepal: An Introduction to the Natural History, Ecology, and Human Impact of the Himalayas*,

pp. 325–9. The site is at Lake Rukche (3,500 metres). Rather than swidden agriculture, fire may have been used to promote pasture in some instances.

27. Rai mythology happens to be a close fit with Martin Heidegger's claim (in his essay 'Building, Dwelling, Thinking') that the essence of being human is to build, dwell in a certain place, cultivate, and be aware of mortality. 'Only man dies,' according to Heidegger, 'and indeed continually, as long as he remains on earth …'

28. *Himalayan Space: Cultural Horizons and Practices*, edited by Balthasar Bickel and Martin Gaenszle. Mark Turin gives a lengthy review in *Contributions to Nepalese Studies*, vol. 26, no. 2.

29. Christopher Evans, et al., *Grounding Knowledge/Walking Land: Archaeological Research and Ethno-Historical Identity in Central Nepal*. The village of Khola is supposed to be the last place where all the Gurung ancestors lived together as a single community. Carbon dating indicated it was occupied around 1000–1300 AD.

30. The modern word in Nepali for 'indigenous' (which was first coined in Hindi by activists in India in the 1930s) is 'adivasi', literally meaning 'first dwellers'. Prior to the increasing adoption of this term in Nepal, these communities were, and still are, often referred to as 'janajati' (meaning something like 'common folk', itself a neologism to translate the English word 'tribe'); or 'matwali' ('alcohol drinkers', now archaic and pejorative).

31. Michael Witzel, 'Nepalese Hydronomy: Towards a History of Settlement in the Himalayas', in Toffin (ed.), *Nepal Past and Present*. In more recent, documented, times there is also a trend of eastward movement, as Part 2 will show.

32. John Whelpton, *A History of Nepal*, p. 12.

33. Nicoletti, *The Ancestral Forest*, pp. 227–8.

34. Ben Campbell, *Living between Juniper and Palm: Nature, Culture and Power in the Himalaya*, p. 13.

35. A. W. Macdonald, 'Preliminary Notes on Some *Jhakri* of the Muglan' in Hitchcock and Jones (eds), *Spirit Possession in the Nepal Himalaya*, pp. 322–3. The Burheni command seven sok-pa, which are hairy giants that leave 18-inch footprints. 'The folkloric themes grouped around sok-pa are almost the same as those that surround the yeti.' p. 338, n. 67.

36. Tamer, domestic gods and spirits are present in the stones of the hearth and in the fields and village spring. Again, the details vary between communities throughout Nepal. Household rituals typically begin with a dedication to the protectors and ancestors present in the

hearth stones. Farmers worship Bhumi, the lord or lady of the soil, and offerings can be made at water sources, which are associated with a goddess and fertility. Priests deal with the orderly spirit world, the fertility of the land and so on; and shamans deal with the chaos and disorder inflicted by ghosts and witches upon individual households, with the ancestors, and with the spirits of the wild forest. See, for example, Tautscher, p. 41, 44. Allen, *Miyapma*, p. 10, Nicoletti, *The Ancestral Forest*, p. 200.
37. Nicoletti, *The Ancestral Forest*, p. 172.
38. Nicholas Allen, 'The Vertical Dimension in Thulung Classification', *Journal of the Anthropological Society of Oxford*, vol. 3, no. 2, 1972.
39. For a brief published version, different in some respects but clearer than some of the things I was told, see World Wildlife Fund, *Sacred Waters: Cultural Values of Himalayan Wetlands*, 2009, pp. 79–80.

Part 2: Agriculture
1. Sindhupalchowk district was the most traumatised of those surveyed. The rate of psychological trauma across all of the earthquake-affected districts surveyed was 19 per cent. Asia Foundation, 'Synthesis Report: Independent Impacts and Recovery Monitoring Phase 3: September 2016', p. 26.
2. The project began in 1998. In 2022 Kathmandu began to receive the Melamchi water.
3. Ben Campbell, 'From Remote Area to Thoroughfare of Globalization: Shifting Territorializations of Development and Boarder Peasantry in Nepal', in Smadja (ed.), *Territorial Changes and Territorial Restructurings in the Himalayas*, p. 275.
4. Gabriele Tautscher, *Himalayan Mountain Cults: Territorial Rituals and Tamang Histories*, pp. 142–3.
5. Jayayakshya Malla of Bhaktapur walked nine days to reach Gosainkund by the Trisuli Valley route and stayed for three nights.
6. In the Newari language of the Kathmandu Valley, Gosainkund is called Silu.
7. Pratapaditya Pal dates this painting to c. 1775 in *Himalayas: An Aesthetic Adventure*, pp. 88–9. However, it shows buildings that were only completed in the nineteenth century (private communication with Niels Gutschow).
8. See Thomas Bell, *Kathmandu*, especially Chapter 4.
9. See Diana Eck, *India: A Sacred Geography*, p. 4, 157.
10. Harka Gurung, *Vignettes of Nepal*, pp. 270–1.

11. Gosainkund is also said to be the destination of the Majhi ancestors. Corneille Jest, 'The Kushwar of Chaithali (Central Nepal)', *Contributions to Nepalese Studies*, vol. 4, no. 2, 1977.
12. It seems that the process of discovering a divine presence in a particular location is occurring at Lauribina today. According to Harka Gurung (*Vignettes*, p. 269) the place name relates to the fact that pilgrims used to leave their walking sticks here in a heap (as a kind of offering, akin to the heaps of stones more commonly left in other places). Presumably because the words sound similar, the name is taken by some to be Lauribinayak, Binayak being another name for Shiva's son, the god Ganesh.
13. For a literary account of the god whose body is the Himalaya, see for example the ancient poet Kalidasa, in a scene where Himavat brings gifts for his daughter and son-in-law.

    'From a distance The Mountain advanced to honor them, carrying his offerings while his footsteps made the earth bend under their massive weight.' *Kumarasambhavam: The Origin of the Young God*, translated by Hank Heifetz.
14. See Sondra Hausner, *Wandering with Sadhus: Ascetics in the Hindu Himalayas*.
15. Francis Khek Gee Lim, 'Zombie Slayers in a "Hidden Valley" (*Sbas Yul*): Sacred Geography and Political Organisation in the Nepal–Tibet Borderland', *European Bulletin of Himalayan Research*, vol. 27, 2004.
16. The first evidence of human occupation in Langtang is from the late fifteenth century. Miehe and Pendry (eds), *Nepal: An Introduction to the Natural History*, pp. 331–6.
17. Helmut Heuberger, Ludwig Masch, Ekkehard Preuss and Alfred Schröcker, 'Quaternary Landslides and Rock Fusion in Central Nepal and in the Tyrolean Alps', *Mountain Research and Development*, vol. 4, no. 4, 1984. See also Miehe, Pendry, et al., *Nepal*, pp. 106–9.
18. Miehe, Pendry, et al., *Nepal*, pp. 104–6.
19. Bus crashes are common. For example, thirty-one people were killed when a bus fell into the Trisuli in October 2017, about a year after our journey.
20. There is no trace of any kingdoms existing in the hills between Jumla and Kathmandu prior to the fourteenth century.
21. All the indications in the anthropological literature are that the indigenous peoples of the hills did not have wet rice agriculture, ploughing, irrigation, or terracing before the Khasa-Malla period in the west, and before the arrival (by a gradual eastward movement) of caste Hindus elsewhere in what's now Nepal. An isolated but

important exception was the Kathmandu Valley, where there was rice cultivation, Hinduism, kingship, and taxation. However, except in a couple of immediately neighbouring valleys, the agriculture of the Kathmandu Valley civilisation does not appear to have been adopted in the hills beyond. (Tellingly, in their study 'Un Araire Dans La Tête … Réflexions Sur La Répartition Géographique De L'outil En Himalaya', Pascale Dollfus, Marie Lecomte-Tilouine, and Olivia Aubriot show that the ancient plough design used in Kathmandu is different from that adopted throughout the neighbouring hills.) Due to the paucity of written evidence, the earlier absence of these agricultural technologies in the hills cannot be known for certain, although the lack of written evidence in this case may actually be a positive indication that these were not settled, cereal-growing communities. Anyway, it is not necessary for my argument – which is that wet rice cultivation was the basis of the creation of the Nepali state – that wet rice was completely unknown in the Nepal hills prior to the arrival of caste Hindus. At the least, it is necessary that indigenous groups outside Kathmandu cultivated little wet rice, whereas caste Hindus organised themselves around rice cultivation, and that this was the basis of their success.

22. The Karnali Mallas should not be confused with the unrelated dynasty of the same name that ruled the Kathmandu Valley for several centuries. The word means strongman or wrestler in Sanskrit.
23. Mahes Raj Pant, 'Towards a History of the Khasa Empire', in Lecomte-Tilouine (ed.), *Bards and Mediums: History, Culture and Politics in the Central Himalayan Kingdoms*.
24. Christopher Evans and David Gibson, 'The Sinja Valley Excavation in 2000', *Ancient Nepal*, vol. 153, 2003. A radio-carbon date of 1270–1420 AD was obtained.
25. Philippe Ramirez, 'From the Principality to the Nation State, Gulmi, Argha-Khanchi and the Gandaki Kingdoms', in Ramirez (ed.), *Resunga: Mountain of the Horned Sage*, pp. 111–14.
26. This situation is the opposite of that described by James Scott in highland South East Asia in *The Art of Not Being Governed*, in which the seemingly 'tribal' or indigenous people of the hills were once refugees from lowland state authority. Here it is the ruling castes who came to the hills as refugees and established state authority there.
27. Corneille Jest, et al., 'The Populations of Gulmi and Argha-Khanchi' in *Resunga*, pp. 53–5. In these places the caste Hindus became the *raithane* or original native people.
28. Pascale Dollfus, Marie Lecomte-Tilouine and Olivia Aubriot, 'Un Araire Dans La Tete … Reflexions Sur La Repartition Geographique

De L'outil En Himalaya,' *Techniques et Culture*, no. 37, 2001. The authors argue that the plough design in western Nepal relates to the Malla kingdom, while those in central and eastern Nepal relate to later waves of Hindu migration originally from the south, and especially to the migration of the Dalit craftsmen who made and used ploughs and whose migration history is little recorded by other sources. They argue that the uniformity of plough design among indigenous groups reflects late adoption under the influence of Hindu farmers. Their research shows that plough designs in the Himalaya have changed little for hundreds of years, and are culturally transmitted (that is, they are 'in the head') rather than being adapted to physical conditions such as soil type in the local area where they are used.

29. The use of the term 'feudalism' in Nepal reflects the Marxist idea of the stages of economic production and class formation. The detailed (and varied) aspects of how feudalism functioned in South Asia are not the same as in Europe.
30. James Scott, *Against the Grain*. His account, based on ancient Mesopotamia, has striking similarities to what happened in the central Himalaya, although the process reached here much later.
31. The agricultural state requires administration and writing, which is why the anthropologist Claude Lévi-Strauss, while pointing out that writing appears in history at the same time as kingship, claimed that writing seems to favour the exploitation rather than the enlightenment of mankind. Peasant rebels always attack and destroy state records, as they did in England in 1381, and as the Maoist rebels did in Nepal at the turn of the twenty-first century.
32. Gorkha, presumably significantly, has the benefit of not one but two large alluvial tablelands: Palungtar and Salyantar.
33. Even further east in the Himalaya, and in the plains of Bengal, rice farming was similarly extended by a process of imperial political and religious expansion – in that case of the Muslim Mughal empire. See Richard Eaton, *The Rise of Islam and the Bengal Frontier 1204–1760*.
34. Translated by Theodore Riccardi, 'The Royal Edicts of King Ram Shah of Gorkha', *Kailash*, vol. 5, no. 1, 1977. Other edicts mostly concern the status of certain priestly or noble families, or religious obligations such as performing sacrifices at the kingdom's forts and maintaining the caste system.
35. It might be expected that along with taxation and royal administration urban development would be part of the picture. Yet (although the Kathmandu Valley had developed urbanism through the growth and merger of villages since the first millennium AD) the rice states

of the hills had settlements only the size of villages, even as their capitals. Any kind of Gorkhali urbanism was slow to develop. In his purported deathbed testament, the *Dibya Upadesh*, Prithvi Narayan Shah derides the people or rulers of Kathmandu as city dwellers, without wisdom or courage, who drank water from cisterns (while he and his men presumably drank from springs and streams). He states that he intended to establish his capital elsewhere, away from the 'empty pomp and pleasure' of Kathmandu (Stiller, *Dibya Upadesh*, p. 43). Prithvi Narayan's court, and those of his early successors, did indeed spend much time at Nuwakot, where he died in 1775, but they never established an alternative capital to Kathmandu following their conquest of the city in 1768. Moreover, the Gorkhalis seem to have had relatively little impact on the Kathmandu Valley's urban character until the palace-building boom that began at the end of the nineteenth century. Towns (such as Birgunj, est. 1897) were first founded in the plains only at around the same time. Mid-nineteenth-century accounts, such as Henry Oldfield's, even suggest the Kathmandu Valley's urban fabric was decaying after decades of Shah rule.

36. An alternative version, told elsewhere, involves eating a hot bowl of rice porridge from the cooler edges.
37. Olivia Aubriot, 'Irrigation as a Mirror of Kinship. The Example of Aslewacaur', in Ramirez (ed.) *Resunga: Mountain of the Horned Sage*. Village irrigation has also been seen as an archive of social organisation in Tunisia and Morocco.
38. Kumar Pradhan, *The Gorkha Conquests*, pp. 124–5.
39. Francis Buchanan, *An Account of the Kingdom of Nepal*.
40. On Buchanan's work as a botanist see Mark Watson and Henry Noltie, 'Career, Collections, Reports and Publications of Dr Francis Buchanan (later Hamilton), 1762–1829: Natural History Studies in Nepal, Burma (Myanmar), Bangladesh and India. Part 1', *Annals of Science*, vol. 73, no. 4, 2016.
41. Cited by Marie Lecomte-Tilouine, 'On Francis Buchanan Hamilton's Account of the Kingdom of Nepal', *European Bulletin of Himalayan Research*, no. 14, 1998, p. 58.
42. Dhaulagiri, in western Nepal, is currently recorded at 8,167 metres (26,795 ft), the seventh-highest mountain in the world. Besides more accurate measurement, earthquakes must account for some fraction of the difference between these readings.
43. John Shipp, *Memoirs of the Extraordinary Military Career of John Shipp: Late a Lieutenant in His Majesty's 87th Regiment* (1829).

44. See Lionel Caplan, *Warrior Gentlemen: 'Gurkhas' in the Western Imagination*.
45. General Donald Macintyre in 1878, cited by Caplan, *Warrior Gentlemen*, p. 131.
46. General Sir Francis Tuker in 1957, cited by Caplan, *Warrior Gentlemen*, p. 141.
47. Tuker, cited by Caplan, *Warrior Gentlemen*, p. 131.
48. The qualities awarded to Gurkhas are similar to those that were earlier given to British bulldogs, when they were adopted as a national emblem. According to Keith Thomas, this animal united the twin preoccupations of the eighteenth-century ruling class: a concern for pedigree and a taste for aggressive war (*Man and the Natural World*, p. 109). Caplan actually raises the suggestion that the Gurkhas were regarded by the British as 'pets'.
49. Caplan, *Warrior Gentlemen*, pp. 189–90.
50. B. R. Mullaly in 1950, cited by Caplan, *Warrior Gentlemen*, p. 100.
51. John Masters, cited by Caplan, *Warrior Gentlemen*, p. 187. Caplan notes that the sentimental, imperial rhetoric concerning Gurkhas has continued in the British army (and British press) since Indian independence, yet Indian army officers (and the Indian public) do not entertain the same illusions concerning Gurkha regiments that remained in the Indian army.
52. In one case, some British people came to misunderstand that those doing a certain job (mercenary soldier) belonged to an ethnic group ('Gurkha') which in fact does not exist. In the other case, the name of an ethnic group (Sherpa) is mistreated as being interchangeable with a particular job (high-altitude guide or porter). In both cases people in these roles are mythologised as having extraordinary physical powers, simplicity, unflagging good humour, and self-sacrificing devotion to their employers.
53. Marie Lecomte-Tilouine, 'On Francis Buchanan Hamilton's Account of the Kingdom of Nepal', *European Bulletin of Himalayan Research*, no. 14, 1998.
54. *Regmi Research Series*, year 13, p. 99.
55. *Regmi Research Series*, year 14, pp. 79–80.
56. John Claude White, 'Nepal: A Little-Known Kingdom', *National Geographic*, October 1920.
57. The Hodgeson Collection, British Library, MSS EUR HODGESON/3, ff. 359–359b. See also MSS EUR HODGESON/2 ff. 99–111.
58. *Narratives of the Mission of George Bogle to Tibet*, p. xl.

59. Published in *Regmi Research Series*, year 17, pp. 97–103. The term Nepal still referred especially, or most specifically, to the Kathmandu Valley then.
60. Apparently the story of the Russian dancer, entrepreneur, and socialite Boris Lisanevich introducing strawberry cultivation to Nepal in the twentieth century is not accurate.
61. 'Confidential Report on Nepal Prepared in the Intelligence Branch of the Quarter Master General's Department in India By Brevet Major E.R. Elles. R.A.', *Regmi Research Series*, year 18, pp. 41–8.
62. Girish Giri relates his family history in his own book, *Birgunj*.
63. During the Tihar festival (which is also called Diwali, especially in India).
64. Gerard Toffin mentions a local tradition of a Ghale raja in the upper Ankhu Valley, but that area is rather more remote. 'The Peoples of the Upper Ankhu Khola Valley', *Contributions to Nepali Studies*, vol. 3, no. 1, 1976.

    In his brief purported memoir, the *Dibya Upadesh*, Prithvi Narayan says that in the course of his campaign he went to receive blessings from the goddess at Salyankot, because she was said to give inspiration. He does not mention a Ghale raja. 'Morning and evening [for several days] I sat at the [temple] gate, reading, worshipping and praying. One night I had a dream. A seven or eight year old maiden came to me, bearing a sword in either hand ... I asked her who her father was. She answered that she was the daughter of the Rana [Magar] priest of the temple. Saying this she placed the swords in my hands ... [and said] "whatever you wish for you will receive".' He awoke, and the temple priest as well as his own astrologers told him he had received the goddess's blessing. He immediately made an endowment to the temple and recommenced his campaign (Stiller, *Dibya Upadesh*, pp. 40–1). This story can be read to infer a similar significance to that of the old men's story of the Ghale raja – that it represents the transfer of authority from indigenous people (represented by the Magar priest and his goddess) to Prithvi Narayan Shah.
65. In fact the Budhi Gandaki hydropower project is subject to intense political controversy over whether the contract should be awarded to a Chinese or Indian company, which has caused delays.
66. To be honest, Girish flattered me with this assumption.
67. Sanyasis are the descendants of 'renouncers', or mendicant holy men. Damai, Kami, and Sarki are types among Dalits, whose traditional occupations are respectively tailors-cum-musicians, -blacksmiths, and -leatherworkers. Brahmins are the highest, priestly, caste.

68. Simon Schama, *Landscape and Memory*, p. 15.
69. At the beginning of the nineteenth century the Gorkhalis referred to their territory as Hinduany, in distinction to Muslim-ruled India, which was Mogulany.
70. On the system of forts/temples called kot see Marie Lecomte-Tilouine, *Hindu Kingship, Ethnic Revival and Maoist Rebellion in Nepal*, Chapter 2.

    The early Gorkhali state was sometimes referred to as the dhungo, meaning the stone, implying (as I understand it) both 'a permanent entity transcending the ruler', and also referring to a particular stone in Gorkha which was worshipped as a state deity. See Regmi, *Imperial Gorkha*, and Edict 26 in Riccardi, 'The Royal Edicts of King Ram Shah of Gorkha', *Kailash*, vol. 5, no. 1. On the coronation ritual see Michael Witzel, 'The coronation rituals of Nepal, with special reference to the coronation of King Birendra in 1975', in Niels Gutschow and Axel Michaels (eds), *Heritage of the Kathmandu Valley: Proceedings of an International Conference in Lübeck, June 1985*. On early concepts of the Nepali state see Richard Burghart, 'The Formation of the Concept of Nation-State in Nepal', *Journal of Asian Studies*, vol. 44, no. 1, 1984; and on the development of nationalism, John Whelpton, 'Political Identity in Nepal: State, Nation and Community', in Gellner, Pfaff-Czarnecka, and Whelpton (eds), *Nationalism and Ethnicity in Nepal*.
71. Mahesh Chandra Regmi, *Landownership in Nepal*, p. 20.
72. *Regmi Research Series*, year 7, pp. 217–18.
73. *Regmi Research Series*, year 2, p. 173.
74. Jean Jamrès, *Histoire Socialist de la Révolution Français*, vol. 1, pp. 76–7, cited by Eric Hezan, *A People's History of the French Revolution*, p. 18. Among the feudal rights Jamrès mentions are *arenne*, the right of only nobles to keep ferrets, and *colombier*, 'which gave the lord's pigeons the peasants' grain', as well as rights over wild animals that ate the peasants' crops, and 'over the wind that turned the mill'.
75. *Regmi Research Series*, year 16, p. 78. This is contrary to the common opinion in later and current times that Madhesi cultivators in the Terai are more recent or unauthorised arrivals. Another similar order of 1817 (*RRS*, year 16, p. 118) relates to attracting Indian ryots to cultivate Rautahat. At around the same time, Buchanan (p. 168) observed, 'The inhabitants of this part of the Tariyani [between the Koshi and Gandaki Rivers] which I had the opportunity of seeing, are quite the

same in their circumstances, language, dress, persons, and customs, with the Hindus of the northern part of Behar.'
76. *Regmi Research Series*, year 2, pp. 220–1.
77. Former terraces, which have now returned to forest, show that even quite marginal lands were cultivated, especially for dry upland crops, as the population swelled. T. B. S. Mahat, D. M. Griffin and K. R. Shepherd, 'Human Impact on Some Forests of the Middle Hills of Nepal, Part 4. A Detailed Study in Southeast Sindhu Palchok and Northeast Kabhre Palanchok', *Mountain Research and Development*, vol. 7, no. 2, 1987.
78. See *Regmi Research Series*, year 13, pp. 83–4, for a royal order of 1847. The law codes (Muluki Ain) of 1866 (*RRS*, year 13, p. 129) and 1918 (*RRS*, year 13, p. 130) contained similar forestry provisions.
79. Mahesh Chandra Regmi, *Imperial Gorkha*, p. 36.
80. In 1806 it took thirty-four days for mail to reach Kathmandu from Kangara in today's Himachal Pradesh, India. In 1834 it was thirty days from Kathmandu to Doti, now Far West Nepal. For a list of delivery times see *Regmi Research Series*, year 13, pp. 167–8.
81. Regmi, *Imperial Gorkha*, p. 27.
82. D. Holmberg, K. S. March, S. Tamang, and Tamang elders, 'Local Production/Local Knowledge: Forced Labor from Below', *Studies in Nepali History and Society*, vol. 4, no. 1, 1999.
83. *Regmi Research Series*, year 17, p. 129.
84. *Regmi Research Series*, year 6, pp. 1–4. The tendency to migrate to escape exploitation partly belies the idea of sedentary peasants as the opposite of mobile pastoralists or swidden cultivators. In the Himalaya, the peasants were potentially mobile too.
85. For example 'Padmagiri's Chronicle' translated in Bikrama Jit Hasrat, *History of Nepal: As Told by its Own and Contemporary Chroniclers*, p. 59, places such an incident in the reign of a Kathmandu Valley king, Trilokyamalla. 'Gunananda's Chronicle', translated by Manik Bajracharya and Axel Michaels as *History of Kings of Nepal: A Buddhist Chronicle*, p. 91, has an almost identical account in the reign of his son Jagajjyoti Malla.
86. See, for example, John Hitchcock, 'Ecologically Related Differences between a Transhumant and a Sedentary Himalayan Village', paper presented at the symposium in New Orleans, Louisiana, 1973.
87. Donald Messerschmidt, 'Ecological change and adaptation among the Gurungs of the Nepal Himalaya', *Human Ecology*, vol. 4, 1976.
88. See Lionel Caplan, *Land and Social Change in East Nepal*; Phillipe Sagant, *The Dozing Shaman*; Ian Fitzpatrick, *Cardamom and Class*.

89. For a description of the intricacies of changing land use on a single slope see Marie Lecomte-Tilouine and Catherine Michaud, 'From the Mine to the Fields: The History of the Exploitation of the Slope in Darling (Gulmi)', in Ramirez (ed.), *Resunga*.
90. Marie Lecomte-Tilouine, 'About Bhume: A Misunderstanding in the Himalaya', in Toffin (ed.) *Nepal Past and Present*; and 'Hindu Power in a Tribal Territory: The Cult of Bhume among the Magars', *Hindu Kingship, Ethnic Revival and Maoist Rebellion in Nepal*.
91. See *Regmi Research Series*, year 1, p. 14; and year 2, p. 148.
92. Marie Lecomte-Tilouine, 'Spirits, Shamans and Englishmen: Perceptions of the Others in *Vir Caritra*, a Nineteenth Century Nepalese Novel', *Hindu Kingship, Ethnic Revival and Maoist Rebellion in Nepal*.
93. Lecomte-Tilouine, 'Spirits, Shamans and Englishmen,' p. 36.
94. A tea plant was identified in Kathmandu by the British resident Gardiner, in 1817, but his discovery was ignored by botanical specialists. It had apparently been imported from China. Tea was discovered growing wild in Assam in 1823 by the brothers Robert and Charles Alexander Bruce, who were also ignored. Andrew Charlton's 1831 (re)discovery of wild tea in Assam was recognised in 1834 and led to tea cultivation in India in the subsequent decades. In Assam there was large-scale deforestation for tea in the 1840s, but repeated commercial setbacks. The first small tea gardens in Darjeeling were planted by Archibald Campbell in 1841. By the 1860s and 1870s tracts of the Darjeeling forest were being cleared for tea. See George van Driem, *The Tale of Tea*.
95. John McCosh, *Topography of Assam* (1837) cited in Jayeeta Sharma, 'Making Garden, Erasing Jungle: Tea Enterprise in Colonial Assam', in Kimar, Damodaran and D'Souza (eds), *The British Empire and the Natural World*.
96. Sharma, 'Making Garden, Erasing Jungle', in Kimar, et al. (eds), *The British Empire and the Natural World*, p.137.
97. D. G. Donovan, 'Forests at the Edge of Empire: The Case of Nepal', in Kimar, Damodaran and D'Souza (eds), *The British Empire and the Natural World*, p. 249.
98. J. V. Collier, who had previously visited Nepal in 1919 to arrange the extraction of sal railway sleepers, contributes an essay 'Forestry in Nepal' to Perceval Landon's *Nepal*, vol. 2, pp. 251–5.
99. Yogesh Raj, 'Remembering to Forget', *Kathmandu Post*, 9 June 2015.

Part 3: Architecture

1. Georg Miehe, et al., 'An Inventory of Forest Relicts in the Pastures of Southern Tibet', *Plant Ecology*, vol. 194, no. 2, 2008, pp. 157–77.
2. Chris Stevens, et al., 'Between China and South Asia: A Middle Asian corridor of Crop Dispersal and Agricultural Innovation in the Bronze Age', *Holocene*, vol. 26, issue 10, 2016.
3. Maharaj Pandit, *Life in the Himalaya*, pp. 136, 139, 140.
4. Perdita Pohle, 'Petroglyphs and Abandoned Sites in Mustang: A Unique Source for Research in Cultural History and Historical Geography', *Ancient Nepal*, vol. 153, June 2003.
5. Contractors hired by the local government to build a structure supposed to protect the site from flood waters poured concrete on the carved surface, which was also broken by heavy machinery. An anthropologist, Fidel Devkota, wrote that the 'site now lies in tatters'. Fidel Devkota, 'How Nepal Destroyed Kag Nyimba, a Pre-historic Site, in Mustang', onlinekhabar.com, 10 February 2024.
6. Angela Simons, Werner Schön, and Sukra Sagar Shrestha, 'Archaeological Research in Mustang: Report on the Fieldwork of the Years 1994 and 1995 by the Cologne University Team', *Ancient Nepal*, no. 140, 1998.
7. Karl-Heinz Knörzer, '3000 Years of Agriculture in a Valley of the High Himalayas', *Vegetation History and Archaeobotany*, vol. 9, 2000.
8. Charles Ramble, 'A Century of Trade and Tension: Stakeholders in the Kali Gandaki Salt Route, Mid-nineteenth to Mid-twentieth Centuries', in Jeannine Bischoff and Alice Travers (eds), *Commerce and Communities: Social and Political Status and the Exchange of Goods in Tibetan Societies*.
9. The southern border was disputed in the early nineteenth century before being established by the 1816 Sugauli Treaty. The northern border was established by the boundary treaties of 1961 and 1963 but not mapped in detail until 1979. From 1816 until 1951 the southern border was closed by Nepali policy, while the northern border was scarcely defined and open. That situation has been reversed since the 1950s, with the southern border being open and the northern border largely closed.
10. Christoph von Fürer-Haimendorf, *Exploratory Travels in Highland Nepal*, pp. 99–102.
11. See Charles Ramble, 'A Century of Trade and Tension'; and Carole McGranahan, 'Tibet's Cold War: The CIA and the Chushi Gangdrug Resistance, 1956–1974', *Journal of Cold War Studies*, vol. 8, no. 3.

12. Previously, a system of fraternal polyandry, in which several brothers married one woman and farmed the same family holding, kept scarce land intact through the generations. The 1964 land reform made the inheritance norms of the politically dominant caste Hindu population of Nepal the national law. See Perdita Pohle, 'Geographical Research on the History of the Cultural Landscape of Southern Mustang', *Ancient Nepal*, vol. 134, 1993.
13. Miehe, Pendry, et al., *Nepal*, p. 301.
14. *Republica*, 'Worst Flood in "3 Decades" Hits Mustang', 13 August 2018.
15. The flood of 13 August 2023. Sanot Adhikari and Sweccha Raut, 'Climate Risks in the Himalayas', *Kathmandu Post*, 23 August 2023.
16. The village was already abandoned when David Snellgrove came this way in 1956.
17. The term for a farming nomad is 'samadrok' in the language of Dolpo. See Kenneth Bauer, *High Frontiers*, p. 44.
18. According to David Snellgrove, this monastery was crumbling when he visited in 1956. It has been superseded by newer monasteries in the village.
19. Cited by Charles Ramble, *The Navel of the Demoness*, pp. 303–4.
20. Ramble, *The Navel of the Demoness* p. 38.
21. Ramble, *The Navel of the Demoness*, pp. 270–3. The annual performance of this oath fell into disuse after 1992.
22. Ramble, *The Navel of the Demoness*, p. 12.
23. Bauer, *High Frontiers*, pp. 53–5. To prevent large families collecting more dung from the common pastures, each household may only send one member for this activity.
24. Garrett Hardin, 1968, 'The Tragedy of the Commons', *Science*, vol. 162, pp. 1243–8. His larger, less well remembered argument is a Malthusian one, that a growing world population will inevitably degrade all of the world's common resources, such as water and air, and that poor people therefore shouldn't have an absolute right to reproduce.
25. Corneille Jest, 'Settlements in Dolpo', in Toffin (ed.), *Man and His House in the Himalaya*.
26. Sam van Schaik, *Tibet: A History*, p. 43.
27. van Schaik, *Tibet*, p. 48.
28. Palgyi Yonten's stuffed upper body was preserved in a temple associated with Atisha, near Nyetang Drolma Lhakhang, until the Cultural Revolution.

29. van Schaik, *Tibet*, p. 39. Many of these late Tantric, Indian Buddhist writings are known today only from their Tibetan translations.
30. *The Life of Milarepa* by Tsangnyön Heruka, translated by Andrew Quintman.
31. See Donald Lopez's introduction to Andrew Quintman's translation of Tsangnyön Heruka's *The Life of Milarepa*.
32. According to the biblical scholar Ernest Renan, 'The desert is monotheistic, sublime in its immense uniformity.'
33. *The Life of Milarepa*, p. 145.
34. *The Life of Milarepa*, p. 148.
35. Donald Messerschmidt, *Big Dogs of Tibet and the Himalayas*, p. 29.
36. *The Life of Milarepa*, p. 189.
37. *The Life of Milarepa*, p. 206.
38. Charles Ramble has called the nameless pre-Buddhist Tibetan religion Pagan, justifying the term by pointing out that it comes from the Latin word 'pagus', meaning a place or country district, and that early Tibetan religion seems to have been characterised by territorial divinities.

    Besides Buddhism, there is another Tibetan tradition called Bön, which is often thought of as a distinct religion, and is followed by many people in Dolpo. Bön is often identified with Tibet's pre-Buddhist religion. However, there is little to suggest that 'Bön' (as it is understood in the historical period) more closely resembles Tibet's early religion(s) than Tibetan Buddhism does. Since the history and characteristics of documented and contemporary Bön are essentially parallel and equivalent to Tibetan Buddhism, and because everything written here applies to both, and this chapter is hard enough already, I'm not going to complicate matters further by writing about Bön. For more on Bön see, for example: Per Kværne, *The Bon Religion of Tibet*; Marietta Kind, *The Bön Landscape of Dolpo: Pilgrimages, Monasteries, Biographies and the Emergence of Bön*; and Charles Ramble, 'Gaining Ground: Representations of Territory in Bon and Tibetan Popular Tradition', *Tibet Journal*, vol. 20, no. 1, 1995.
39. Klaus-Dieter Mathes, 'The Sacred Crystal Mountain in Dolpo: Beliefs and Pure Visions of Himalayan Pilgrims and Yogis', *Journal of the Nepal Research Centre*, vol. 11, 1999.
40. Adomnán of Iona, *Life of Saint Columba*, translated by Richard Sharpe. The devils were 'visible to his own bodily eyes'. Another interesting comparison is found in Yorkshire. Bede (672/3–735) describes the site at which St Cedd founded a monastery at Lastingham in the 650s, 'amid some steep and remote hills which seemed better

fitted for the haunts of robbers and the dens of wild beasts than for human habitation; so that, as Isaiah says, "In the habitations where once dragons lay, shall be grass with reeds and rushes." The man of God was anxious to cleanse the site for which he had received the monastery from the stain of former crimes by prayer and fasting, before laying the foundations.' Cited by Ian Wood, 'Lastingham in its Sacred Landscapes', The Fifth Lastingham Lecture, 2008, pp. 1–4.

41. David Snellgrove, *Four Lamas of Dolpo,* vol. 1. Snellgrove has rendered these men's names in literal translation, so Sonam Lodrö becomes Merit Intellect, Chyökyap Pelzang is Religious Protector, and Panden Lodrö is Glorious Intellect.

42. He saw the yul lha dressed in white robes and colourful silk turbans, galloping across the land with their warrior hoards, and subdued them in battles.

43. Charles Ramble, 'Patterns of places', in A.-M. Blondeau and E. Steinkellner (eds), *Reflections of the Mountain: Essays on the History and Social Meaning of the Mountain Cult in Tibet and the Himalaya.*

44. On the recent abandonment of blood sacrifice in a Mustang village, see Ramble, 'The Classification of Territorial Divinities in Pagan and Buddhist Rituals of South Mustang', in Anne- Marie Blondeau (ed.), *Tibetan Mountain Deities, Their Cults and Representations.* The same issue is explored in Stan Royal Mumford, *Himalayan Dialogue: Tibetan Lamas and Gurung Shamans in Nepal;* and Sherry B. Ortner, *High Religion: A Cultural and Political History of Sherpa Buddhism.*

45. On tertons and terma, see Janet Gyatso, 'The Logic of Legitimation in the Tibetan Treasure Tradition', *History of Religions,* vol. 33, no. 2, 1993.

46. On hidden lands, see Giacomella Orofino, 'The Tibetan Myth of the Hidden Valley in the Visionary Geography of Nepal', *East and West,* vol. 41, no. 1/4, 1991; Marietta Kind, ''Jag 'Dul – A Bon Mountain Pilgrimage In Dolpo, Nepal', in Amy Heller and Giacomella Orofino (eds), *Proceedings of the Tenth Seminar of the IATS, 2003.* Vol. 8, *Discoveries in Western Tibet and the Western Himalayas;* Francis Khek Gee Lim, 'Zombie Slayers in a "Hidden Valley" (*Sbas Yul*): Sacred Geography and Political Organisation in the Nepal-Tibet Borderland', *European Bulletin of Himalayan Research,* no. 27, 2004.

47. In fact, as Western scholars now understand, the physical appearance of these wrathful deities is described in the Indian Tantras.

48. There is a general resemblance between some Himalayan religious architecture, such as mani walls and the simple chortens built as heaps of stones, and works by Western sculptors in the land art movement

such as Robert Smithson or Richard Long, although the intention is quite different.
49. See Donald Messerschmidt, *Big Dogs of Tibet and the Himalayas*.
50. Messerschmidt, *Big Dogs*, pp. 28, 29.
51. The following passage is indebted to Peter Bishop's *The Myth of Shangri-la: Tibet, Travel Writing, and the Western Creation of a Sacred Landscape*.
52. Rousseau, *Confessions*, translated by Angela Scholar (end of book 4).
53. Bishop, *The Myth of Shangri-la*, p. 69.
54. This view continues to appear, for example, in Peter Matthiessen's 1978 book *The Snow Leopard*.
55. Ruskin, *Modern Painters*, vol. 4, p. 126.
56. Ruskin, *Modern Painters*, vol. 4, pp. 348–9.
57. Ruskin, *Modern Painters*, vol. 4, pp. 376–7.
58. Ruskin, *Modern Painters*, vol. 4, pp. 155–6.
59. Temple, *Travels in Nepal and Sikkim 1881–7*, cited Bishop, p. 127.
60. Cited Bishop, *The Myth of Shangri-la*, p. 128.
61. Cited Bishop, *The Myth of Shangri-la*, p. 161.
62. Cited Bishop, *The Myth of Shangri-la*, p. 162.
63. Cited Bishop, *The Myth of Shangri-la*, p. 224.
64. Cited Bishop, *The Myth of Shangri-la*, p. 229.
65. Donald Lopez, *Prisoners of Shangri-La: Tibetan Buddhism and the West*, pp. 103–04.
66. According to the anthropologist James Fisher (*Himalayan Traders*, p. 34) Nyingma Tsering 'wielded vast personal power and settled disputes at least as far away as Tichurong, although he held no official political or ecclesiastical status'. He died in 1963.
67. The cleric's original name was Namgyal, and he entered Saltser monastery. He 'was outstanding in the domains of both religion and also of worldly affairs ... He lived till the age of 80 ... He became very prominent as the Ordained Monk Döndrub. After his death, it is said, he remained [in meditation] for three full weeks – twenty-one days.'
68. In this generation the author identifies himself as Paldzon's brother, without giving his own name. He counts seven generations up to his own. The text says of this abbot (Trulku Karma Khamsu Wangdü), 'From the time of the Great Tenzin Repa [1646–1743], known as the Trulku of Shey, there had been many occupants of the abbatial seat up to the time of Trulku Karma Khamsu Wangdü.'
69. Cited Marietta Kind, *The Bön Landscape of Dolpo*, p. 53.
70. Or to visualise doing so, in some cases.
71. Corneille Jest, *Tales of the Turquoise: A Pilgrimage in Dolpo*.

72. Gustave Flaubert, *Flaubert in Egypt*, translated by Francis Steegmuller, p. 71.
73. The Cap of Hades is a more ancient comparison.
74. Allen, *Miyapma*, p. 93.
75. This is the assumption made by some landscape archaeologists (who call their approach phenomenological) – that remarkable- seeming locations would once have been sacred to people who worshipped the landscape.

Part 4: Conservation

1. Shamanism is widespread and important throughout the Nepal hills, nowhere more so than in the west. Due to the structure I've adopted for this book I won't discuss it again here, but to indicate something of the diversity of its forms I'd like to note the fascinating example from western Nepal of bajyu cults, described by Gregory C. Maskarinec. These spirits, which are controlled (for want of a better word) by shamans, belong to Brahmin women who committed suicide in protest against unbearable acts of injustice by royal rulers. They are appealed to by living people suffering injustice. According to Maskarinec, this tradition offers clues to a centuries-old class struggle. See 'Conflicting Powers: Struggles Between Rulers and Oracular Mediums in Jajarkot District, Nepal' in *Bards and Mediums*, ed. Marie Lecomte-Tilouine, pp. 55–61.
2. Although there was no mobile reception there, sometime that night a text message made it through with the news that in Norwich, England, my sister's daughter Miriam had been born. Welcome, Miriam!
3. Genesis I.28. For more on the themes of this passage see Donald Worster, *Nature's Economy*, and Keith Thomas, *Man and the Natural World: Changing Attitudes in England 1500–1800*.
4. John Donne, 'To Sir Edward Herbert at Julyers'. Donne goes on to claim that the man who has driven wild beasts from his personality can sow corn there instead.
5. Rousseau, *Reveries of a Solitary Walker*, 'The Fifth Walk', translated by Peter France. It would be more unusual in later generations to find someone who *doesn't* profess this taste.
6. Robert Wokler, *Rousseau, the Age of Enlightenment, and Their Legacies*, p. 74, citing *The Confessions*.
7. Wokler, *Rousseau, the Age of Enlightenment*, p. 73.
8. Rousseau, *Reveries of a Solitary Walker*, 'The Fifth Walk'.
9. Rousseau, *Reveries of a Solitary Walker*, 'The Seventh Walk'.

10. See, for example, Wilhelm Halbfass, *India and Europe: An Essay in Understanding*; Jean W. Sedlar, *India in the Mind of Germany: Schelling, Schopenhauer, and Their Times*; Alan D. Hodder, '"Ex Oriente Lux": Thoreau's Ecstasies and the Hindu Texts', *Harvard Theological Review*, 86, 4; David Scott, 'Rewalking Thoreau and Asia: "Light from the East" for "a Very Yankee Sort of Oriental"', *Philosophy East & West*, 57, 1.
11. William Jones, *Sacontala, or the Fatal Ring: An Indian Drama by Calidas*. Arthur Ryder's 1912 translation of the same lines is easier to appreciate:
    Eight forms has Shiva, lord of all and king;
    And these are water, first created thing;
    And fire, which speeds the sacrifice begun;
    The priest, and time's dividers, moon and sun;
    The all embracing ether, path of sound;
    The earth, wherein all seeds of life are found;
    And air, the breath of life, may he draw near,
    Revealed in these, and bless those gathered here.
12. Cited by T. S. Rukmani, 'Literary Foundations for an Ecological Aesthetic: Dharma, Ayurveda, the Arts, and Abhijnanasakuntalam', in Chapple and Tucker (eds), *Hinduism and Ecology*.
13. 'Alexander von Humboldt strove, in successive books, to promulgate a new ecological concept of relations between man and the natural world which was drawn almost entirely from the characteristically holist and unitary thinking of Hindu philosophers ... [and] formed the basis for a universalist and scientifically reasoned interpretation of the ecological threat posed by the unrestrained activities of man.' Richard Grove, *Green Imperialism*, p. 11.
14. Although I love this quotation I can no longer find the reference.
15. Evolution seemed to match socialist goals of sweeping away aristocracy and questioning the authority of the church, by toppling the creationist natural history written by country parsons. In 1848, when the Chartists took to British streets embracing evolutionary theory (among other principles) the scientific gentry and Tory clergy literally took up arms against them.
16. Cited by Andrew Desmond and James Moore, *Darwin*, p. 485. In our own times understandings of nature as a networked system are inevitably attractive, such as the fungal networks connecting forest trees ('the wood-wide web'), and (the recognition of queen bees notwithstanding) the idea of a monarchy is replaced by the hive mind.
17. NRs 100 was worth about $1.

18. Cited Alan D. Hodder, '"Ex Oriente Lux": Thoreau's Ecstasies and the Hindu Texts', *Harvard Theological Review*, 86, 4, 1993.
19. As Marx and Engels noted approvingly in the *Communist Manifesto*, 'The bourgeoisie, during its rule of scarce one hundred years, has created more massive and more colossal productive forces than have all preceding generations together. Subjection of Nature's forces to man, machinery, application of chemistry to industry and agriculture, steam-navigation, railways, electric telegraphs, clearing of whole continents for cultivation, canalisation of rivers, whole populations conjured out of the ground – what earlier century had even a presentiment that such productive forces slumbered in the lap of social labour?'
20. Since Thoreau is the only person cited by name in this passage, and as an early advocate of preserving wild areas he became a progenitor of the national parks that were established in the decades after his death, I should note he had a keen appreciation that the land had previously been occupied by indigenous peoples – a fact his successors dispensed with.
21. William Cronon, 'The Trouble with Wilderness', in Cronon (ed.), *Uncommon Ground: Rethinking the Human Place in Nature*.
22. William Cronon, 'The Uses of Environmental History', *Environmental History Review*, vol. 17, no. 3, 1993, p. 19.
23. This includes twelve national parks, as well as six conservation areas, the Koshi Tappu wildlife reserve, and the Dhorpatan hunting reserve.
24. Throughout Nepal there is a taboo against women ploughing.
25. Joanne McLean, 'Conservation and the Impact of Relocation on the Tharus of Chitwan, Nepal', *Himalaya*, vol. 19, no. 2, 1999.
26. Meenakshi Ganguly, 'Nepal Park Guards Accused of Persecuting Indigenous People', *Human Rights Watch*, 28 July 2020.
27. Joel Heinen and Bijaya Kattel, 'A Review of Conservation Legislation in Nepal: Past Progress and Future Needs', *Environmental Management*, vol. 16, no. 6, 1992.
28. A report published by the World Wildlife Fund (WWF), which examined allegations that the WWF took insufficient steps to address rights violations where it worked in Chitwan National Park, details ten serious allegations including murder, torture, and arbitrary detention against the army or national park authorities in the Chitwan and Bardia national parks between 2005–16. It found that the WWF did not always raise rights concerns when it was aware of alleged abuses, and that it showed very poor judgement or failed to exercise due diligence in some instances. However, it did not find evidence of wrongdoing by the WWF. (Independent Panel of Experts report, *Embedding Human*

Rights in Nature Conservation: From Intent to Action, November 2020.)

Six extrajudicial killings allegedly committed by the army in national parks in southern Nepal (the victims including a twelve-year-old child) were documented in a 2010 United Nations report, *Investigating Allegations of Extra-Judicial Killings in the Terai*. In 2020, army park guards in Chitwan were again accused of killing a man, who had apparently entered the park to collect snails. Meenakshi Ganguly, 'Nepal Park Guards Accused of Persecuting Indigenous People', Human Rights Watch, 28 July 2020.

29. Nina Bhatt, 'Kings as Wardens and Wardens as Kings: Post-Rana Ties between Nepali Royalty and National Park Staff', *Conservation and Society*, vol. 1, no. 2, 2003.
30. Melvin Bolton, *Rara Lake Nation Park Management Plan 1976–81*, 1976, UN Food and Agriculture Organization, FAO Library AN:251367.
31. Bolton, *Rara Lake*, p. 29.
32. Joel T. Heinen, 'Parks, People, and Conservation: A Review of Management Issues in Nepal's Protected Areas', *Population and Environment*, vol. 14, no. 1, 1992.
33. Christoph von Fürer-Haimendorf, *Exploratory Travels in Highland Nepal*, p. 131.
34. 'The land to the north of Rara has been largely deforested to support the villages of Rara and Chapra. When these villages have been removed the forest should be allowed to regenerate naturally, this it will do quite quickly, with pine colonising the cleared ground.' Bolton, *Rara Lake*, p. 29.
35. Two steles stand near it. I was told that ten years ago there were five steles standing here. The ground was covered in snow, so I couldn't see if the other three are still lying nearby.
36. Apparently there were no doctors present at Mugu district hospital at the time of the incident.
37. Cited by M. R. Pant, 'Towards a History of the Khasa Empire', in Marie Lecomte-Tilouine (ed.), *Bards and Mediums: History, Culture and Politics in the Central Himalayan Kingdoms*. Presumably this is a conventional literary description, reminiscent of the imaginative description of legendary Himalayan palaces in Kalidasa's *Cloud Messenger*, written a thousand years earlier. (Following Prawin Adhikari's advice I have changed 'king goose' in the original translation to 'swan' [raajhansa = swan].)

38. Christopher Evans and David Gibson with U. Acharya, T. Harward, and R. Kunwar, 'The Sinja Valley Excavation in 2000 A.D.' *Ancient Nepal*, vol. 153, 2003.
39. Perhaps it is no coincidence that Nepal's great antiquarian, Yogi Naraharinath (who, along with but separately from Giuseppe Tucci, is credited with the 'discovery' of the Khasa-Malla kingdom in the mid-twentieth century), is from the neighbouring district of Kalikot. He must have been as inspired by the traces of the past all around him as Deependra Upadhyaya is.
40. John Ruskin, *The Storm-Cloud of the Nineteenth Century*, a lecture delivered on 4 February 1884.
41. See Richard Grove, *Green Imperialism: Colonial Expansion, Tropical Island Edens and the Origins of Environmentalism, 1600–1860* (1996), pp. 408–9, p. 413.
42. Cited Grove, *Green Imperialism*, p. 437. By the 1840s a growing body of data appeared to support the connection between deforestation, drought, and famine. Grove, *Green Imperialism*, pp. 441, 449, 468.
43. Grove, *Green Imperialism*, p. 468.
44. Sunil Amrith, *Unruly Waters: How Mountain Rivers and Monsoons Have Shaped South Asia's History*, 2020, p. 76.
45. See Ramchandra Guha, *The Unquiet Woods: Ecological Change and Peasant Resistance in the Himalaya*; and Vasant Saberwal, *Pastoral Politics: Shepherds, Bureaucrats and Conservation in the Western Himalaya*, 1990.
46. On the role of the Indian colonial administration and Indian scientists in the development of meteorology, see Amrith, *Unruly Waters*.
47. The share of Nepal government revenue from timber exports in the nineteenth century has been estimated in the region of 40 per cent according to D. G. Donovan, 'Forests at the Edge of Empire: the case of Nepal', in Deepak Kumar, Vinita Damodaran, and Robert D'Souza (eds), *The British Empire and the Natural World: Environmental Encounters in South Asia*, 2011. A British adviser to the Nepal government was appointed from the Indian Forest Service in 1923. He increased extraction by establishing a cross-border railway.
48. Guha, *The Unquiet Woods*.
49. Elvira Graner, *The Political Ecology of Community Forestry in Nepal*.
50. George Schaller, *Stones of Silence: Journeys in the Himalaya*, 1980, pp. 206–7.
51. For an account of the theory and its shortcomings see Thompson, et al., *Uncertainty on a Himalayan Scale*, and Jack Ives and Bruno

Messerli, *The Himalayan Dilemma: Reconciling Development and Conservation*.
52. The population of Nepal was growing fast enough to double in twenty-seven years.
53. This claim and prediction was made in a widely cited World Bank Report of 1979.
54. Ives and Messerli, *The Himalayan Dilemma*, pp. 5–6.
55. In 1985 forest cover was estimated at about 40 per cent of the country, with shrubland covering a further 9 per cent. In general, the density of tree cover was being degraded rather than the extent. See D. A. Gilmour, 'Not Seeing the Trees for the Forest: A Re-Appraisal of the Deforestation Crisis in Two Hill Districts of Nepal', *Mountain Research and Development*, vol. 8, no. 4, 1988. However, in some places forest cover had been reduced. Alan Macfarlane's *Resources and Population: A Study of the Gurungs of Nepal*, a study of one village, showed that the forest there had retreated within people's living memory and that the village diet had been adversely impacted.
56. A comparison of aerial photographs taken in 1964 and 1977 found no statistically significant change in forest cover. See D. M. Griffin, K. R. Shepherd, and T. B. S. Mahat, 'Human Impacts on Some Forests of the Middle Hills of Nepal, Part 3. Forests in the Subsistence Economy of Sindhu Palchok and Kabhre Palanchok', *Mountain Research and Development*, vol. 7, no. 1, 1987; 'Human Impact on Some Forests of the Middle Hills of Nepal, Part 4. A Detailed Study in Southeast Sindhu Palchok and Northeast Kabhre Palanchok', *Mountain Research and Development*, vol. 7, no. 2, 1987; 'Human Impact on Some Forests of the Middle Hills of Nepal, Part 5. Comparisons, Concepts, and Some Policy Implications', *Mountain Research and Development*, vol. 8, no. 1, 1988.
57. Ives and Messerli, *The Himalayan Dilemma*.
58. The Nepali government is widely said to have financed its victory in the 1980 referendum (on whether to continue party-less royal government) through illegal timber sales, and the forest department has long been a notorious centre of corruption. In these contexts hardwood forests in the Terai plains were exploited. More recent allegations of corrupt timber extraction focus on the Chure range. The illegal cutting, transport, or export of timber would be impossible without official connivance.
59. On the history of community forestry in Nepal see Hemant Ojha and Andy Hall, 'Transformation as System Innovation: Insights

from Nepal's Five Decades of Community Forestry Development', *Innovation and Development*, 2021.
60. Arjun Poudel, 'Downpour Affects Life Across Country', *Kathmandu Post*, 14 August 2023; Arjun Poudel, 'Rainfall Data Remains Scarce Due to Fewer Gauging Stations', *Kathmandu Post*, 25 July 2023. On 13 August 2023, for example, half the annual average rainfall fell on a single day near Kagbeni in Mustang, causing a flood that destroyed thirty houses in the village. See Sanot Adhikari and Sweccha Raut, 'Climate Risks in the Himalayas', *Kathmandu Post*, 23 August 2023.
61. Arjun Poudel, 'Most of Tarai Is Reeling under Unusual Mid-Monsoon Drought', *Kathmandu Post*, 1 August 2023.
62. For a discussion of these issues, see for example Mohan Poudel, et al., 'Social Equity and Livelihood Implications of REDD+ in Rural Communities: A Case Study from Nepal', *International Journal of the Commons*, vol. 9, no. 1, 2015. The study concludes that poorer and low-caste households, and women in particular, suffered the greatest cost from increased restrictions on forest use, which was not matched by the share of the benefits they received. It found that REDD+ policies were a 'mismatch' for local contexts and deepened existing inequalities.

    In February 2021 the Nepali government signed an agreement with the World Bank's Forest Carbon Partnership Facility. 'Nepal's Emission Reductions Program Builds On More than Three Decades of Successful Community Forestry,' said Faris Hadad-Zervos, the World Bank's Nepal Country Director. 'The emissions reduction purchase is one pillar of a strategic program on forest landscapes and climate action in Nepal. This innovative financing agreement will address the drivers of deforestation and forest degradation, helping incentivise further community action across the country.' Nepal would reportedly be able to earn $5 per ton of carbon dioxide stored, up to $45 million by 2025. See Chandan Kumar Mandal, 'Everything You Need to Know about Nepal's Carbon Trade Deal', *Kathmandu Post*, 27 February 2021.
63. To my knowledge they are the last in the central Himalaya, at least.
64. For more on the Raute see the work of Jane Fortier, especially *Kings of the Forest: The Cultural Resilience of Himalayan Hunter Gatherers*. Fortier points out that while 'subjects of trees' (bot praja) and 'kings of the forest' (banko raja) seem contradictory, both formulations imply that the Raute are outside the structure of the Nepali state. She describes Raute religion as a 'sentient ecology' in which plants, rocks, the Raute themselves, and the monkeys they hunt, which they call their

'little brothers', are part of a 'great family' descended from the sun and moon. She describes Raute society as egalitarian (they have no property except what they move from one camp to another). Besides eating monkey and plants such as yams which they collect in the forest, they make wooden bowls which they trade with neighbouring settled people for foodstuffs and useful items.

65. In 1979–80 the Nepali government forcibly settled a band of Raute in Dadeldhura district. Within twenty years most had apparently been swindled by neighbouring farmers out of the land the government had given them and returned to their life in the forest. Fortier, *Kings of the Forest*, p. 27.

66. Marie Lecomte-Tilouine, 'The Panchakoshi of Dullu, the Fire Frame of the Malla Imperial Capital', in Marie Lecomte-Tilouine (ed.), *Bards and Mediums: History, Culture and Politics in the Central Himalayan Kingdoms*. In 2025 it was reported that 'enough methene to meet Nepal's demand for 50 years' had been discovered beneath the district. 'Over 1.12 billion cubic metres of natural gas found in Dailekh, preliminary report shows', *The Kathmandu Post*, 19 June 2025.

Select Bibliography

Adomnán of Iona, *Life of Saint Columba*, translated by Richard Sharpe (1995).
Aira, Cesar (2000) *An Episode in the Life of a Landscape Painter*, translated by Chris Andrews.
Allen, N. J. (1972) 'The Vertical Dimension in Thulung Classification', *Journal of the Anthropological Society of Oxford*, no. 3.
———— (1997) '"And the Lake Drained Away": An Essay in Himalayan Comparative Mythology', in A. W. MacDonald, ed., *Mandala and Landscape*.
———— (2013) *Miyapma: Traditional Narratives of the Thulung Rai*.
Amrith, Sunil (2018) *Unruly Waters: How Mountain Rivers and Monsoons Have Shaped South Asia's History*.
Barton, John (2019) *A History of the Bible: The Book and its Faiths*.
Bauer, Kenneth (2004) *High Frontiers: Himalayan Pastoralists in a Changing World*.
Bell, Thomas (2014) *Kathmandu*.
Bhatt, Nina (2003) 'Kings as Wardens and Wardens as Kings: Post-Rana Ties between Nepali Royalty and National Park Staff', *Conservation and Society*, vol. 1, no. 2.
Bickel, Balthasar and Martin Gaenszle (eds) (1999) *Himalayan Space: Cultural Horizons and Practices*.
Bishop, Peter (1989) *The Myth of Shangri-la: Tibet, Travel Writing, and the Western Creation of a Sacred Landscape*.
Bolton, Melvin (1976) UN Food and Agriculture Organization, *Rara Lake Nation Park Management Plan 1976–81*.
Braudel, Fernand (1949) *The Mediterranean and the Mediterranean World in the Age of Philip II*, translated by Siân Reynolds.
Burghart, Richard (1984) 'The Formation of the Concept of Nation-State in Nepal', *Journal of Asian Studies*, vol. 44, no. 1. Campbell, Ben (2013)

Living Between Juniper and Palm: Nature, Culture and Power in the Himalaya.

———— (2013) 'From Remote Area to Thoroughfare of Globalization: Shifting Territorializations of Development and Boarder Peasantry in Nepal', in Smadja (ed.), *Territorial Changes and Territorial Restructurings in the Himalayas.*

Caplan, Lionel (1970) *Land and Social Change in East Nepal: A Study of Hindu–Tribal Relations.*

———— (1995) *Warrior Gentlemen: Gurkhas in the Western Imagination.*

Chhetri, Lil Bahadur (1957) *Basain*, translated by Michael Hutt as *Mountains Painted with Turmeric.*

Corvinus, Gudrun (2000) 'The Prehistory of Nepal: After Ten Years of Research' in Thapa and Baaden (eds) *Nepal: Myths and Realities.*

Cowan, Sam (2019) *Essays on Nepal: Past and Present.*

Cronon, William (1983) *Changes in the Land: Indians, Colonists and the Ecology of New England.*

———— (1995) 'The Trouble with Wilderness', in Cronon (ed.) *Uncommon Ground: Rethinking the Human Place in Nature.*

———— (1993) 'The Uses of Environmental History', *Environmental History Review*, vol. 17, no. 3.

Darwin, Charles (1839) *The Voyage of the Beagle.*

Desmond, Andrew and James Moore (1991) *Darwin.*

Dollfus, Pascale, Marie Lecomte-Tilouine and Olivia Aubriot (2001) 'Un Araire Dans La Tete … Reflexions Sur La Repartition Geographique De L'outil En Himalaya', *Techniques et Culture*, no. 37.

Donovan, D. G. (2011) 'Forests at the Edge of Empire: The Case of Nepal', in Kumar, Damodaran and D'Souza (eds) *The British Empire and the Natural World: Environmental Encounters in South Asia.*

Eaton, Richard (1993) *The Rise of Islam and the Bengal Frontier 1204–1760.*

Eck, Diana (2012) *India: A Sacred Geography.*

Evans, Christopher and David Gibson with Acharya, T. Harward, and R. Kunwar (2003) 'The Sinja Valley Excavation in 2000 A.D.' *Ancient Nepal*, vol. 153.

Evans, Christopher, Judith Pettigrew, Yarjung Kromcha Tamu, and Mark Turin (2009) *Grounding Knowledge/Walking Land: Archaeological Research and Ethno-Historical Identity in Central Nepal.*

Fisher, James F. (1987) *Trans-Himalayan Traders: Economy, Society and Culture in Northwest Nepal.*

Fitzpatrick, Ian (2011) *Cardamom and Class.*

Fortier, Jane (2009) *Kings of the Forest: The Cultural Resilience of Himalayan Hunter Gatherers.*
Gilmour, D. A. (1988) 'Not Seeing the Trees for the Forest: A Re-Appraisal of the Deforestation Crisis in Two Hill Districts of Nepal', *Mountain Research and Development*, vol. 8, no. 4.
Guha, Ramchandra (1990) *The Unquiet Woods: Ecological Change and Peasant Resistance in the Himalaya.*
Graner, Elvira (1997) *The Political Ecology of Community Forestry in Nepal.*
Griffin, D. M., K. R. Shepherd, and T. B. S. Mahat (1987) 'Human Impacts on Some Forests of the Middle Hills of Nepal Part 3. Forests in the Subsistence Economy of Sindhu Palchok and Kabhre Palanchok', *Mountain Research and Development*, vol. 7, no. 1.
Grimmett, Richard, Carol Inskipp, Tim Inskipp, and Hem Sagar Baral (2016) *Birds of Nepal.*
Grove, Richard (1995) *Green Imperialism: Colonial Expansion, Tropical Island Edens and the Origins of Environmentalism, 1600–1860.*
Gurung, Harka (1980) *Vignettes of Nepal.*
——— (1983) *Maps of Nepal.*
Gyatso, Janet (1993) 'The Logic of Legitimation in the Tibetan Treasure Tradition', *History of Religions*, vol. 33, no. 2.
Halbfass, Wilhelm (1988) *India and Europe: An Essay in Understanding.*
Hagen, Toni (1961) *Nepal: The Kingdom in the Himalaya.*
Hamilton, Francis Buchanan (1819) *An Account of the Kingdom of Nepal.*
Hardin, Garrett (1968) 'The Tragedy of the Commons', *Science*, vol. 162.
Harris, Clare E. (2012) *The Museum on the Roof of the World: Art, Politics and the Representation of Tibet.*
Hausner, Sondra (2007) *Wandering with sadhus: Ascetics in the Hindu Himalayas.*
Heinen, Joel and Bijaya Kattel (1992) 'A Review of Conservation Legislation in Nepal: Past Progress and Future Needs', *Environmental Management*, vol. 16, no. 6.
Heuberger, Helmut, Ludwig Masch, Ekkehard Preuss, and Alfred Schröcker (1984) 'Quaternary Landslides and Rock Fusion in Central Nepal and in the Tyrolean Alps', *Mountain Research and Development*, vol. 4, no. 4.
Hilton, James (1933) *Lost Horizon.*
Hitchcock, John (1973) 'Ecologically Related Differences between a Transhumant and a Sedentary Himalayan Village', paper presented at the symposium in New Orleans, Louisiana.
Hobsbawm, Eric (1969) *Bandits.*

Hodder, Alan D. (1993) '"Ex Oriente Lux": Thoreau's Ecstasies and the Hindu Texts', *Harvard Theological Review*, 86, 4.

Hogan, Erin (2008) *Spiral Jetta: A Road Trip Through the Land Art of the American West*.

Holmberg, D., K. S. March, S. Tamang, and Tamang elders (1999) 'Local Production/Local Knowledge: Forced Labor from Below', *Studies in Nepali History and Society*, vol. 4, no. 1.

Hooker, Joseph (1854) *Himalayan Journals*.

Hughes, Ted (1970) *Crow*.

——— (1998) *Birthday Letters*.

Ives, Jack and Bruno Messerli (1989) *The Himalayan Dilemma: Reconciling Development and Conservation*.

Jest, Corneille (1977) 'The Kushwar of Chaithali (central Nepal)', *Contributions to Nepalese Studies*, vol. 4, no. 2.

——— (1991) 'Settlements in Dolpo', in Toffin (ed.) *Man and his House in the Himalaya*.

——— (1998) *Tales of the Turquoise: A Pilgrimage in Dolpo*.

Kalidasa (1796) *Sacontala, or the Fatal Ring: An Indian Drama by Calidas*, translated by William Jones.

——— (1912) *Shakuntala*, translated by Arthur Ryder.

——— (1990) *Kumarasambhavam: The Origin of the Young God*, translated by Hank Heifetz.

——— (2017) *Meghadutam: The Cloud Messenger*, translated by Srinivas Reddy.

Kaul, Shonaleeka (2018) *The Making of Early Kashmir: Landscape and Identity in the Rajatarangini*.

Kawaguchi, Ekai (1909) *Three Years in Tibet*.

Kind, Marietta (2002) 'Jag 'Dul—A Bön Mountain Pilgrimage in Dolpo, Nepal', in Amy Heller and Giacomella Orofino (eds) *Proceedings of the Tenth Seminar of the IATS*, vol. 8, *Discoveries in Western Tibet and the Western Himalayas*.

——— (2012) *The Bön Landscape of Dolpo: Pilgrimages, Monasteries, Biographies and the Emergence of Bön*.

Knörzer, Karl-Heinz (2000) '3000 Years of Agriculture in a Valley of the High Himalayas', *Vegetation History and Archaeobotany*, vol. 9.

Koirala, Shankar (1961) *Khaireni Ghat*, translated by Larry Hartsell.

——— (1968) 'Koshi Pradesh Ka Majhi Jati', *Ancient Nepal*, no. 3. Translated as "The Majhi Community of the Koshi Region" in *Regmi Research Series*, year 12.

Klatzel, Francis (2001) *Natural History Handbook for the Wild Side of Everest: The Eastern Himalaya and Makalu-Barun Area*.

Kværne, Per (1995) *The Bön Religion of Tibet*.
Landon, Perceval (1928) *Nepal*.
Lecomte-Tilouine, Marie (1990) 'About Bhume: A Misunderstanding in the Himalaya', in Toffin (ed.) *Nepal Past and Present*
———(1998) 'On Francis Buchanan Hamilton's Account of the Kingdom of Nepal', *European Bulletin of Himalayan Research*, no. 14.
———(2009) 'The Panchakoshi of Dullu, the Fire Frame of the Malla Imperial Capital', in Marie Lecomte-Tilouine (ed.) *Bards and Mediums: History, Culture and Politics in the Central Himalayan Kingdoms*.
———(2011) *Hindu Kingship, Ethnic Revival and Maoist Rebellion in Nepal*.
Lecomte-Tilouine, Marie (ed.) (2009) *Bards and Mediums: History, Culture and Politics in the Central Himalayan Kingdoms*.
Lim, Francis Khek Gee (2004) 'Zombie Slayers in a "Hidden Valley" (*sbas yul*): Sacred Geography and Political Organisation in the Nepal–Tibet Borderland', *European Bulletin of Himalayan Research*, vol. 27.
Lopez, Donald (1998) *Prisoners of Shangri-La: Tibetan Buddhism and the West*.
Lyell, Charles (1830–3) *Principles of Geology: Being an Attempt to Explain the Former Changes of the Earth's Surface, by Reference to Causes Now in Operation*.
Macdonald, A. St J. (1942) *Circumventing the Mahseer and Other Sporting Fish in India and Burma*.
Macdonald, A. W. (1976) 'Preliminary Notes on Some *Jhakri* of the Muglan' in Hitchcock and Jones (eds) *Spirit Possession in the Nepal Himalaya*.
McLean, Joanne (1999) 'Conservation and the Impact of Relocation on the Tharus of Chitwan, Nepal', *Himalaya*, vol. 19, no. 2.
Mahat, T. B. S., D. M. Griffin, and K. R. Shepherd (1987) 'Human Impact on Some Forests of the Middle Hills of Nepal Part 4. A Detailed Study in Southeast Sindhu Palchok and Northeast Kabhre Palanchok', *Mountain Research and Development*, vol. 7, no. 2.
———(1988) 'Human Impact on Some Forests of the Middle Hills of Nepal. Part 5. Comparisons, Concepts, and Some Policy Implications', *Mountain Research and Development*, vol. 8, no. 1. Mathes, Klaus-Dieter (1999) 'The Sacred Crystal Mountain in Dolpo: Beliefs and Pure Visions of Himalayan Pilgrims and Yogis', *Journal of the Nepal Research Centre*, vol. 11.
McGranahan, Carole (2006) 'Tibet's Cold War: The CIA and the Chushi Gangdrug Resistance, 1956–1974', *Journal of Cold War Studies*, vol. 8, no. 3.

Messerschmidt, Donald (1976) 'Ecological Change and Adaptation among the Gurungs of the Nepal Himalaya', *Human Ecology*, vol. 4.
————(2010) *Big Dogs of Tibet and the Himalayas*.
Miehe, Georg et al. (2008) 'An Inventory of Forest Relicts in the Pastures of Southern Tibet', *Plant Ecology*, vol. 194, no. 2.
Miehe, Georg, Colin Pendry et al. (2015) *Nepal: An Introduction to the Natural History, Ecology, and Human Impact of the Himalayas*.
Nicoletti, Martino (2004) *Riddum: The Voice of the Ancestors*.
————(2007) *The Ancestral Forest: Memory, Space and Ritual among the Kulunge Rai of Eastern Nepal*.
Ojha, Hemant and Andy Hall (2021) 'Transformation as System Innovation: Insights from Nepal's Five Decades of Community Forestry Development', *Innovation and Development*.
Orofino, Giacomella (1991) 'The Tibetan Myth of the Hidden Valley in the Visionary Geography of Nepal', *East and West*, vol. 41, no. 1.
Pandit, Maharaj (2017) *Life in the Himalaya: An Ecosystem at Risk*.
Pant, M. R. (2009) 'Towards a History of the Khasa Empire', in Marie Lecomte-Tilouine (ed.), *Bards and Mediums: History, Culture and Politics in the Central Himalayan Kingdoms*.
Pradhan, Kumar (1991) *The Gorkha Conquests: The Process and Consequences of the Unification of Nepal, with Particular Reference to Eastern Nepal*.
Pohle, Perdita (1993) 'Geographical Research on the History of the Cultural Landscape of Southern Mustang', *Ancient Nepal*, vol. 134.
————(2003) 'Petroglyphs and Abandoned sites in Mustang a Unique Source for Research in Cultural History and Historical Geography', *Ancient Nepal*, vol. 153.
Rai, Indra Bahadur (2018) *Long Nights of Storm*, translated by Prawin Adhikari.
Ramble, Charles (1995) 'Gaining Ground: Representations of Territory in Bön and Tibetan Popular Tradition', *Tibet Journal*, vol. 20, no. 1.
————(1996) 'Patterns of Places', in A.-M. Blondeau and E. Steinkellner (eds), *Reflections of the Mountain: Essays on the History and Social Meaning of the Mountain Cult in Tibet and the Himalaya*.
————(1997) 'The Creation of the Bön Mountain of Kongpo', in A. W. Macdonald (ed.), *Mandala and Landscape*.
————(1998) 'The Classification of Territorial Divinities in Pagan and Buddhist Rituals of South Mustang', in Anne-Marie Blondeau (ed.), *Tibetan Mountain Deities: Their Cults and Representations*.
————(2007) *The Navel of the Demoness*.

——— (2018) 'A Century of Trade and Tension: Stakeholders in the Kali Gandaki Salt Route, Mid-19th to Mid-20th Centuries', in Jeannine Bischoff and Alice Travers (eds), *Commerce and Communities: Social and Political Status and the Exchange of Goods in Tibetan Societies*.
Ramirez, Philippe (ed.) (2000) *Resunga: Mountain of the Horned Sage*, translated by Susan Keyes.
Regmi, Mahesh Chandra (ed.) (1969–89) *Regmi Research Series*, 21 vols.
Regmi, Mahesh Chandra (1996) *Landownership in Nepal*.
——— (1999) *Imperial Gorkha: An Account of Gorkhali Rule in Kumaun 1791–1815*.
Riccardi, Theodore (1977) 'The Royal Edicts of King Ram Shah of Gorkha', *Kailash*, vol. 5, no. 1.
Rousseau, Jean-Jacques (1755) *A Discourse on Inequality*, translated by Maurice Cranston.
——— (1782) *Confessions*, translated by Angela Scholar.
——— (1782) *Reveries of the Solitary Walker*, translated by Peter France
Ruskin, John (1856) *Modern Painters*, vol.4.
——— (1884) 'The Storm Cloud of the Nineteenth Century'.
Sagant, Philippe (1996) *The Dozing Shaman: The Limbus of Eastern Nepal*, translated by Nora B. Scott.
Schaller, George (1980) *Stones of Silence: Journeys in the Himalaya*.
Scott, David (2007) 'Rewalking Thoreau and Asia: "Light from the East" for "a Very Yankee Sort of Oriental"', *Philosophy East & West*, 57, 1.
Scott, James C. (2009) *The Art of Not Being Governed: An Anarchist History of Upland Southeast Asia*.
——— (2017) *Against the Grain: A Deep History of the Earliest States*.
Schama, Simon (1995) *Landscape and Memory*.
Scurr, Ruth (2006) *Fatal Purity: Robespierre and the French Revolution*.
Searle, Mike (2013) *Colliding Continents: A Geological Exploration of the Himalaya, Karakoram, & Tibet*.
Sedlar, Jean W. (1982) *India in the Mind of Germany: Schelling, Schopenhauer, and Their Times*.
Sharma, Jayeeta (2011) 'Making Garden, Erasing Jungle: Tea Enterprise in Colonial Assam', in Kumar, Damodaran, and D'Souza (eds) *The British Empire and the Natural World: Environmental Encounters in South Asia*.
Shipp, John (1829) *Memoirs of the Extraordinary Military Career of John Shipp: Late a Lieutenant in His Majesty's 87th Regiment*.
Shrestha, Tej Kumar (1997) *The Mahseer: In the Rivers of Nepal Disrupted by Dams and Ranching Strategies*.
Simons, Angela, Werner Schön, and Sukra Sagar Shrestha (1988) 'Archaeological Research in Mustang: Report on the Fieldwork of the

Years 1994 and 1995 by the Cologne University Team', *Ancient Nepal*, no. 140.
Smadja, Joëlle (ed.) (2009) *Reading Himalayan Landscapes Over Times: Environmental Perception, Knowledge and Practice in Nepal and Ladakh*, translated by Bernadette Sellers.
Snellgrove, David (1957) *Buddhist Himālaya: Travels and Studies in Quest of the Origins and Nature of Tibetan Religion*.
——— (1967) *Four Lamas of Dolpo*.
Stevens, Chris et al. (2016) 'Between China and South Asia: A Middle Asian Corridor of Crop Dispersal and Agricultural Innovation in the Bronze Age', *Holocene*, vol. 26, issue 10.
Stiller, L. F. (1968) *Prithvi Narayan Shah in the Light of the Dibya Upadesh*.
Tautscher, Gabriele (2007) *Himalayan Mountain Cults: Territorial Rituals and Tamang Histories*.
Thapar, Romila (2003) *Early India: From the Origins to AD 1300*.
Thomas, Keith (1983) *Man and the Natural World: Changing Attitudes in England 1500–1800*.
Thompson, Michael, Michael Warburton, and Tom Hatley (1986) *Uncertainty on a Himalayan Scale: An Institutional Theory of Environmental Perception and a Strategic Framework for the Sustainable Development of the Himalaya*.
Thoreau, Henry (1854) *Walden, or, Life in the Woods*.
Toffin, Gerard (1976) 'The Peoples of the Upper Ankhu Khola Valley', *Contributions to Nepali Studies*, vol. 3, no. 1.
Tsangnyön Heruka (2010) *The Life of Milarepa*, translated by Andrew Quintman.
van Driem, George (2019) *The Tale of Tea: A Comprehensive History of Tea from Prehistoric Times to the Present Day*.
van Schaik, Sam (2011) *Tibet: A History*.
von Fürer-Haimendorf, Christoph (1975) *Himalayan Traders*.
——— (1989) *Exploratory Travels in Highland Nepal*.
von Humboldt, Alexander (1814–29) *Personal Narrative of a Journey to the Equinoctial Regions of the New Continent*, abridged and translated by Jason Wilson.
Watson, Mark and Henry Noltie (2016) 'Career, Collections, Reports and Publications of Dr Francis Buchanan (later Hamilton), 1762–1829: Natural History Studies in Nepal, Burma (Myanmar), Bangladesh and India. Part 1', *Annals of Science*, vol. 73, no. 4.
Whelpton, John (1997) 'Political Identity in Nepal: State, Nation and Community', in Gellner, Pfaff-Czarnecka and Whelpton (eds), *Nationalism and Ethnicity in Nepal*.

——— (2005) *A History of Nepal*.
Witzel, Michael (1985) 'The Coronation Rituals of Nepal, with Special Reference to the Coronation of King Birendra in 1975', in Niels Gutschow and Axel Michaels (eds) *Heritage of the Kathmandu Valley: Proceedings of an International Conference in Lübeck*.
——— (1990) 'Nepalese Hydronomy: Towards a History of Settlement in the Himalayas', in Toffin (ed.), *Nepal Past and Present*.
Wokler, Robert (2012) *Rousseau, the Age of Enlightenment, and Their Legacies*.
Wordsworth, William (1805) *The Prelude*.
Worster, Donald (1977) *Nature's Economy: A History of Ecological Ideas*.
Wulf, Andrea (2015) *The Invention of Nature: The Adventures of Alexander von Humboldt, the Lost Hero of Science*.
WWF Independent Panel of Experts report (2020) *Embedding Human Rights in Nature Conservation: From Intent to Action*.